Praise for
The Distance Between Us

2012 National Book Critics Circle Awards Finalist

"I've been waiting for this book for decades. The American story of the new millennium is the story of the Latino immigrant, yet how often has the story been told by the immigrant herself? What makes Grande's beautiful memoir all the more extraordinary is that, through this hero's journey, she speaks for millions of immigrants whose voices have gone unheard."
—Sandra Cisneros, author of *The House on Mango Street*

"Reyna Grande is a fierce, smart, shimmering light of a writer with an important story to tell."
—Cheryl Strayed, author of *Wild: From Lost to Found on the Pacific Crest Trail*

"Through her brutally honest firsthand account of growing up in Mexico without her parents, Grande sheds light on the often overlooked consequence of immigration—the disintegration of a family."
—Sonia Nazario, Pulitzer Prize winner and author of *Enrique's Journey*

"Reyna Grande's extraordinary journey toward the American dream will be an inspiration to anyone who has ever dreamed of a better life."
—Ligiah Villalobos, writer and executive producer of *La misma luna* (*Under the Same Moon*)

"Grande captivates and inspires."
—*Publishers Weekly* (starred review)

"Heartwarming. . . . Even with the challenges of learning English, earning good grades, and fighting her way through turbulent adolescence, Grande emerged as a successful writer whose prose has the potential to touch the generation of youth whose story is so reminiscent of her own."

—*NBC Latino*

"The sadness at the heart of Grande's story is unrelenting; this is the opposite of a light summer read. But that's okay, because . . . this book should have a long shelf life."

—*Slate*

"A timely and a vivid example of how poverty and immigration can destroy a family."

—*The Daily Beast*

"Grande grabs your heart and strums music on it."

—*The Dallas Morning News*

"Makes palpable a human dilemma and dares us to dismiss it."

—*The California Report*

"A visceral experience of poverty."

—*The Christian Science Monitor*

The Distance Between Us

A MEMOIR

TENTH ANNIVERSARY EDITION

Reyna Grande

WASHINGTON
SQUARE PRESS

ATRIA

NEW YORK   LONDON   TORONTO   SYDNEY   NEW DELHI

**WASHINGTON
SQUARE PRESS**

ATRIA

An Imprint of Simon & Schuster, Inc.
1230 Avenue of the Americas
New York, NY 10020

First Washington Square Press trade paperback edition March 2013
Washington Square Press trade paperback tenth anniversary edition September 2022

WASHINGTON SQUARE PRESS / **ATRIA** PAPERBACK and colophon are trademarks of Simon & Schuster, Inc.

For information about special discounts for bulk purchases, please contact Simon & Schuster Special Sales at 1-866-506-1949 or business@simonandschuster.com.

The Simon & Schuster Speakers Bureau can bring authors to your live event. For more information or to book an event contact the Simon & Schuster Speakers Bureau at 1-866-248-3049 or visit our website at www.simonspeakers.com.

Designed by Kyoko Watanabe

Manufactured in the United States of America

33   35   36   34

Library of Congress Cataloging-in-Publication Data

Grande, Reyna.
The distance between us : a memoir / Reyna Grande.—1st Atria Books hardcover ed.
p.   cm.
1. Grande, Reyna—Childhood and youth.   2. Mexican Americans—Biography.
3. Immigrants—United States—Biography.   4. Abused children—United States—Biography.   5. Mexico—Emigration and immigration—Social aspects.   6. United States—Emigration and immigration—Social aspects.   7. Mexican Americans—California—Los Angeles—Biography.   8. Los Angeles (Calif.)—Biography.
9. Mexican American women authors—Biography.   I. Title.
E184.M5G665 2012
973'.046872—dc23 2012001634

ISBN 978-1-4516-6177-4
ISBN 978-1-4516-6178-1 (pbk)
ISBN 978-1-4516-6180-4 (ebook)

To my father, Natalio Grande

1947–2011

And to all DREAMers

"Nothing happens unless first we dream."

—CARL SANDBURG

The Distance Between Us
TENTH ANNIVERSARY EDITION

"But when you're poor, no matter how close things are,
everything is far away."

ONCE THERE WAS a girl named Reyna whose parents abandoned her. They didn't realize they were abandoning her. They believed they were building the house of their future, a dream sweeter than an orange Fanta soda. All they wanted was to save enough to build their own home. To do this meant they had to leave their children behind and work in another country. How close that dream seemed, and yet it always scurried further ahead of them.

Reyna and her siblings were left in the care of an awful grandmother. This grandmother wasn't always awful. Life had damaged her so severely she had to transform herself into a dragon. In time, Reyna's mother was also transformed by life. Drowning in a tsunami of fear, she panicked because she didn't know how to swim and seized anyone who might rescue her. Finally, Reyna's father was transformed, too, when a monster called grief sat down on his heart. He could only brave battling this beast by numbing himself with drink. Everyone was guilty of trying to survive.

And so, our protagonist Reyna had a real heroine's journey ahead of her. She may not have realized it herself, but she had to face more obstacles than simply crossing a border. Her true story reads like the trials in myth or fairy tales because, as Joseph Campbell has pointed out, we are all heroines and heroes in our life journey.

How do you survive your own life journey when you are poor?

1. You take refuge at the library to fortify yourself (if you're lucky enough to have a public library). And/or you stay home (if you're lucky enough to have a home) in order to stay alive. Especially after sundown.

2. Someone, maybe a mother/father/teacher, instills the importance of an education, and this knowledge is a magical weapon against defeat. You may lose material objects, but once you have knowledge, no one can take that away from you. Ever.

3. Someone, maybe a mother/father/teacher, instills in you that failing is NOT an option. This is the most powerful magic of all. Failure is inevitable in life, but success is how you pick yourself up from failure and continue forward on your journey.

4. You realize on your long trek towards your goal that tenacity is more important than talent and *ganas* is more important than tenacity.

5. If you are lucky, a mentor will recognize your gifts and illuminate your path. (WARNING: Beware of false mentors. True mentors help you, not help themselves to you.)

Reyna meandered, made mistakes, was often afraid, depressed, and lonely. But she transformed her rage to will, continued resolutely on her path, and ultimately became the storyteller she was meant to be.

Tales and mythologies serve as a way of making sense out of

crisis and guiding one through it. Reyna cites many fairy tales when interpreting her life. I remember novelist Leslie Marmon Silko once stating that when a community has no sacred mythology at hand, it grasps for flimsy ones. The current popularity of Spider-Man and other comic book heroes flooding film, television, novels, and games tells me a lot about us as a nation and our intense need for a superhero to rescue us from our super fears, a prescription for our times. Stories, after all, are medicine.

Our contemporary fairy tales are the *telenovelas,* the soap operas where, as Reyna says, "beautiful girls are saved from their miserable poverty by handsome rich men who fall desperately in love with them." How dangerous these tales are for countless women around the globe. I shudder when I see girls and young women learning how to be women from these destructive models.

Reyna, however, is not rescued by a handsome prince. She is blessed from birth with a name she will grow into, a gift from her mother, one she didn't appreciate as a child. She's a queen, and in this tale called her life, she learns to ascend to her throne and save herself.

Just as in fairy tales, enchanted beings appear to assist our protagonist during the darkest gloom. The fairy godmother of this book is educator Dr. Diana Savas, who generously shared her own home with Reyna when Reyna found herself without one. Every young woman needs a safe home to become herself. Dr. Savas gave Reyna the gift to become Reyna Grande.

My favorite part of Reyna's book was when the child Reyna had to have her hair cut off because of lice. She writes about this shameful experience with exquisite precision: "The scissors hissed near my ear. I squirmed even more at watching my curls land on the ground and on my lap, falling one by one like the petals of a flower. Then my grandmother's chickens came clucking to see what was happening, and they picked up my curls and shook them around, and when they realized they weren't food, they stepped all over them and dragged them with their feet across the dirt." This tale was so magically told, I expected the chickens to come to Reyna's rescue. They would've if this was fiction.

When I met Reyna, she was already Reyna Grande the author. Am I right in remembering we met at the Miami Book Fair ten years ago? I remember a green room filled with rowdy authors and a table littered with lunch. "Take out a piece of paper," I said to Reyna, "I'm going to dictate your book blurb." And I did, right then and there, at that messy table cluttered with Cuban sandwiches and pasta salad.

Years later at a writers' conference in Tepoztlán, I was on a panel with Reyna Grande. Someone in the audience asked Reyna if she had not left Mexico what would she have become. She said without hesitation, "A maid." It shocked the audience, but not this writer. I knew the distance between us Mexican-American writers and Mexican-Mexican writers is economic class and color, because it's tough for a poor woman in Mexico to get an education. Though education in Mexico is purportedly free, the exorbitant costs of books, uniforms, and supplies make it impossible for humble families to educate their children beyond the sixth grade.

This tenth anniversary edition of *The Distance Between Us* is cause for a celebration. When I first read it, I sighed with relief because readers had often begged me to write the immigrant's story. Believe me, I wanted to, but I didn't have the information to write a story I didn't know firsthand. I was waiting for someone who had *lived* the story to write it.

I wish I could say Reyna's memoir is history, that this is not happening now and will never happen again. But the truth is there are too many stories like Reyna's emerging on our border and on borders across the globe.

"Papi said we had broken the law by coming to the United States, but back then I didn't understand much about laws. All I could think of was why there would be a law that would prevent children from being with their father. That was the only reason I'd come to this country, after all."

After the Twin Towers fell on 9/11, Buddhist monk Thich Nhat Hanh said we lost an opportunity for global compassion. The key question we should have asked our neighbors, he added, is "How can I make you feel safe?" It seems to me as human beings, we should be capable of imagining beyond fences and cages.

Thankfully since the appearance of Reyna's book, other testimonies have been published, including Alberto Ledesma's graphic novel *Diary of a Reluctant Dreamer*; *Children of the Land* by Marcelo Hernández Castillo; *Solito, Solita: Crossing Borders with Youth Refugees from Central America,* edited by Steven Mayers and Jonathan Freedman; Dan-el Padilla Peralta's *Undocumented*; Javier Zamora's poetry collection, *Unaccompanied,* and his recent memoir, *Solito.*

But Reyna's story stands out because it was written from a girl's perspective.

The Distance Between Us, and the testimonies that followed, affirm there is no *one* immigrant story. There are as many stories as there are human beings. Every human being has their own extraordinary story to tell and their own extraordinary journey. Knowing *how* to tell the story is a gift, and that's the gift Reyna Grande shares with us, her readers.

Sandra Cisneros
February 1, 2022
Casa Coatlicue, San Miguel de Allende

Introduction

IN FEBRUARY 2020, I was invited to be a guest speaker on a television special for Oprah's Book Club. While on the show, I said something that had taken me a long time to claim:

"Now, I realize that being a border crosser is my superpower."

It took me years of writing and self-reflection to get to the place where I could see my immigrant journey, including my immigrant trauma, as my greatest source of strength.

Before I wrote *The Distance Between Us*, I hadn't gotten to that place of discovery yet. I didn't know it, but I felt it—that I *needed* to write this book. After so many years of enduring discrimination and microaggressions in the United States, I'd grown ashamed of my border crossing, my immigrant identity, and my Mexican roots. To hide this part of me and remain silent was an option. But it was one that, in the end, would have led to even more shame and trauma. So instead, I made a different choice. I decided to confront my past and reframe it. Writing my immigrant story was an act of rebellion. It was a way of pushing back against a society that forces its immigrants—especially immigrants of color—to hide or deny who they are.

Writing my own story on my *own* terms was liberating. Empowering.

I didn't know that this act of self-empowerment would lead to others' empowerment, too. But the emails and letters I have received from readers through the years—especially those from immigrants and children of immigrants—tell a different story. When readers tell me they see themselves reflected in *The Distance Between Us*, I know that by finding the courage to tell my story, I've inspired others to celebrate theirs, too. It makes me excited to observe that in the past decade, the literature written by the undocumented has grown. But, as I expressed to Oprah, the opportunities to publish such stories are still limited, and immigrant writers continue to be underpublished, underrepresented, and underpaid.

I also wrote *The Distance Between Us* as a call for change. I'd grown tired of how our political leaders have failed the immigrant community again and again. I hoped that writing about my experiences being separated from my parents, crossing the border, and coming of age in the U.S. as an undocumented immigrant would contribute to the conversation on immigration in a way that centered our humanity. Instead of statistics, I offered a deeply personal story of a young Mexican immigrant trying to find her place in the U.S. while striving to reach her full potential.

While I was writing this book, the DREAM Act (Development, Relief, and Education Act for Minors) failed to pass again. People like me, who came to this country as children, were denied the opportunity to legalize their status and make a permanent home here. Then, in 2012, two months before the publication of *The Distance Between Us*, Barack Obama, who was up for reelection, introduced DACA (Deferred Action for Childhood Arrivals), a temporary, two-year program that offers relief from deportation and a work permit to DREAMers at a hefty fee. But a two-year program can never offer its recipients what comprehensive immigration reform and a pathway to citizenship could give—a chance to build a life, a future, on something permanent and long term.

The quarantines and lockdowns we've all experienced in the era of Covid-19 provide insight into the chronic anxiety undocumented immigrants suffer when attempting to plan their lives. We all know, firsthand, what it's like to try to make plans for the next month or holiday and suffer through the anxiety of *not knowing* if any of it would even be possible. Undocumented immigrants live with this uncertainty every day of their lives.

Soon after the young readers version of *The Distance Between*

Us came out in the fall of 2016, Donald Trump became president, and anti-immigrant sentiment reached an all-time high. Family separations also reached new heights. It had never been so clear to me how different my story is from the immigrants of today. And even now, I can't forget that when I was writing *The Distance Between Us* and then its sequel, *A Dream Called Home*, I was doing so from a place of privilege. I am now a U.S. citizen. I live an upper-middle-class life as a college graduate and a professional writer. In short, I had nothing to lose in telling my own story.

The American Dream that I am now enjoying could easily have turned into the American Nightmare that others are enduring today. Though migration to the United States has always had its perils, I know that if I were to have crossed the border today instead of in the 1980s, this book probably wouldn't even exist. The truth is that I might have faced a completely different fate than the undocumented success story I wrote in my memoirs.

And yet, I've also come to understand that had I not immigrated to the U.S. and taken advantage of every opportunity life afforded me, I wouldn't be the writer I am today. And the thought that, had circumstances been different, I might have never had books and writing in my life gives me tremendous grief. Despite the trauma I've endured before, during, and after my migration journey, despite the hoops I've had to jump through to finally be allowed to make a home here, despite the fact that I will have to keep "earning" my right to remain and work hard so that others see me as someone who "deserves" to be here—the sacrifices have been worth it.

I was reminded of this when *The Distance Between Us* was published in Mexico in 2017. I traveled to Oaxaca to participate as a featured speaker as part of the city's annual book fair. Over the years, I've returned to Mexico every so often to visit my relatives. But this was my first time visiting my native country to participate in a book festival. This event meant so much to me. My journey since I'd emigrated had been long and arduous, and now I had returned to the land of my birth, feeling proud of what I had accomplished. I had transformed myself from an undocumented immigrant to a university graduate and bestselling author.

It didn't take long for my visit to turn from sweet to bitter. I discovered that in Mexico, my book sells for 220 pesos, or $16, about the same price as it costs here in the United States. But the minimum *daily* wage in Mexico—especially in poor rural areas like the city where I was born—is around 100 pesos. In other words, if Mexicans want to buy my book, it will cost them *two days'* worth of wages. For poor families like mine, reading is a luxury. You either eat or you read.

It is no wonder that, although I had about two hundred people in the audience at my event, most of them handed me a piece of paper to autograph instead of a book at the signing.

After the day's events, the book fair organizers hosted the authors for dinner at a fancy restaurant in downtown Oaxaca. We were inside, eating mole negro and drinking mezcal, talking about our writing careers, the book fair panels, our current projects. Outside of the restaurant, I could see children looking through the windows and glass doors, trying to get our attention. They had trays of gum and candy they wanted to sell to us. If any of them tried to get in, the restaurant staff would quickly usher them out.

That used to be me, I thought as I watched them shaking their trays. I remembered myself as a little girl back in my hometown, Iguala, carrying boxes of candy, gum, and cigarettes, hoping to sell enough to have something to eat that day. I was suddenly split in half. Half of me—the bestselling author Reyna Grande—was in that restaurant drinking and rubbing elbows with distinguished writers. The other half of me—little Reyna—was outside, hungry and helpless, looking at that other me through the glass doors.

That visit to my native country reminded me of this irrefutable fact—I wouldn't be a writer today if I had never come to the United States. As I looked around the restaurant, at the writers with whom I had shared the stage and celebrated our publishing accomplishments, the thought that kept going through my head was that if things had been different, instead of their peer, I could have been their maid.

In California, I found opportunities that I didn't have in my hometown. But one small, basic thing would have a tremendous impact on my life: access to a public library.

In neighborhoods like the one where I was born, public libraries don't exist. With little or no access to books, there were no readers in my family, let alone writers. My maternal grandfather was illiterate.

My father only made it to third grade and my mother didn't get past sixth grade. They never developed the habit of reading or came to love books. They literally couldn't afford to.

Not all readers are writers, but all writers are readers. And that was true in my case. But in my native country, I would have been neither. Luckily for me, by immigrating, books were suddenly within my reach.

I was in junior high school the first time I set foot in the Arroyo Seco Public Library in northeast Los Angeles, near my school. I quickly came to love it. I was desperate to learn English so I could get out of the ESL program I had been placed in and rid myself of the stigma of being an English-language learner. Reading books, especially books on tape (now called audiobooks), is how I learned the language. Every week, I stopped by the public library to check out ten books, the maximum I was allowed to borrow. I devoured them and came back for more. Soon, I wasn't reading to learn English. I was reading because I fell in love with stories. And then, I began to write my own.

As a low-income, formerly undocumented immigrant, English-language learner, and first-generation college student, I had a long fight to become a professional writer. After all, I was trying to make a career in an industry where not many people like me exist. I had to write my way into existence. I knocked down barriers with my pen, built bridges with my words.

The dream I am living now is woven with the stories I write.

But the one thing I'll never forget is that my story could have been a tragedy instead of a fairy tale. Through the years, I am often confronted with the realization of how close I came to not living the life I have now. If my family and I had crossed the border in today's America instead of in 1985, I would have been separated from my father when we got caught by border patrol, and he would have been blamed for our separation. I would have been one of the thousands of children thrown into a cage. Or worse, I could have died in the crossing, which—due to the border wall that was approved by the first Bush administration, then constructed in the 1990s under Clinton, and then expanded incrementally in the decades that followed—is so much more dangerous now than it was in the '80s. When I read the horror stories in the news, of migrant children being found dead in the desert or washing up on the banks of the Río Grande (RIP Valeria Martínez)—I think, *That could have been me*.

"That could be you," I hear teachers tell their immigrant students whenever I speak at high schools and colleges around the country. I am an "undocumented success story" now. I am the candy girl who escaped her poverty, who didn't get locked up, who didn't get deported. I'm the girl living the dream.

But I never forget about those who are still on the outside looking in.

Thank you for reading *The Distance Between Us*. Now my dream is to see more immigrant stories being read and celebrated. I want to see immigrant writers being given the opportunity to write their own stories on their own terms and being recognized for their contributions to American literature. But above all, I want *all* immigrants to be treated with respect and with the dignity they deserve.

Maybe one day, we as a country can finally be proud to claim that our superpower is our immigrant community.

Reyna Grande
Woodland, California

Book One

MI MAMÁ ME AMA

Prologue

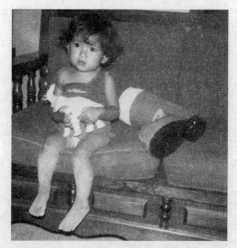

Reyna, at age two

My FATHER'S MOTHER, Abuela Evila, liked to scare us with stories of La Llorona, the weeping woman who roams the canal and steals children away. She would say that if we didn't behave, La Llorona would take us far away where we would never see our parents again.

My other grandmother, Abuelita Chinta, would tell us not to be afraid of La Llorona; that if we prayed, God, La Virgen, and the saints would protect us from her.

Neither of my grandmothers told us that there is something more powerful than La Llorona—a power that takes away parents, not children.

It is called The United States.

In 1980, when I was four years old, I didn't know yet where the

3

United States was or why everyone in my hometown of Iguala, Guerrero, referred to it as El Otro Lado, the Other Side.

What I knew back then was that El Otro Lado had already taken my father away.

What I knew was that prayers didn't work, because if they did, El Otro Lado wouldn't be taking my mother away, too.

1

Carlos, Reyna, and Mago with Mami

I T WAS JANUARY. The following month, my mother would be turning thirty. But she wouldn't be celebrating her birthday with us. I clutched at my mother's dress and asked, "How long will you be gone?"

"Not too long," was her response. She closed the latch on the small suitcase she had bought secondhand for her trip to El Otro Lado, and I knew the hour had come for her to leave.

Sometimes, if I promised to be good, my mother would take me along with her as she went out into the neighborhood to sell Avon products. Other times she would leave me at Abuelita Chinta's house. "I won't be gone for long," she would promise as she pried my fingers from hers. But this time, when my mother said she wouldn't be gone long, I knew it would be different. Yet I never imagined that "not too long" would turn out to be never, because, if truth be told, I never really got my mother back.

"It's time to go," Mami said as she picked up her suitcase.

My sister Mago, my brother Carlos, and I grabbed the plastic bags filled with our clothes. We stood at the threshold of the little house we had been renting from a man named Don Rubén and looked around us one last time. Mami's brothers were packing our belongings to be stored at Abuelita Chinta's house: a refrigerator that didn't work but that Mami hoped to fix one day, the bed Mago and I had shared with Mami ever since Papi left, the wardrobe we'd decorated with *El Chavo del Ocho* stickers to hide the places where the paint had peeled off. The house was almost empty now. Later that day, Mami would be handing the key back to Don Rubén, and this would no longer be our home, but someone else's.

As we were about to step into the sunlight, I caught a glimpse of Papi. Tío Gary was putting a photo of him into a box. I ran to take the photo from my uncle.

"Why are you taking that?" Mami said as we headed down the dirt road to Papi's mother's house, where we would be living from then on.

"He's my papi," I said, and I clutched the frame tight against my chest.

"I know that," Mami said. "Your grandmother has pictures of your father at her house. You don't need to take it with you."

"But *this* is my papi," I told her again. She didn't understand that this paper face behind a wall of glass was the only father I'd ever known.

I was two years old when my father left. The year before, the peso was devalued 45 percent to the US dollar. It was the beginning of the worst recession Mexico had seen in fifty years. My father left to pursue a dream—to build us a house. Although he was a bricklayer and had built many houses, with Mexico's unstable economy he would never earn the money he needed to make his dream a reality.

Like most immigrants, my father had left his native country with high expectations of what life in El Otro Lado would be like. Once reality set in, and he realized that dollars weren't as easy to make as the stories people told made it seem, he had been faced with two choices: return to Mexico empty-handed and with his head held low, or send for my mother. He decided on the latter, hoping that between the two of them, they could earn the money needed to build the house he dreamed of. Then he would finally be able to return to the country of his birth with his head held high, proud of what he had accomplished.

In the meantime, he was leaving us without a mother.

Mago, whose real name is Magloria, though no one called her that, took my bag of clothes from me so that I could hold Papi's photo with both hands. It was hard to keep my balance on a dirt road littered with rocks just waiting to trip me and make me fall, but that January morning I was extra careful because I carried my papi in my arms, and he could break easily, like the bottle of Coca-Cola Mago was carrying the day she tripped. The bottle broke into pieces, the sweet brown liquid washing away the blood oozing from the cut on her wrist. She had to have three stitches. But that wasn't her first scar, and it wouldn't be her last.

"¿Juana, ya te vas?" Doña María said. She was one of Mami's Avon clients. She ran down the dirt road with an empty shopping bag on her way to el mercado. Her lips were painted hot pink with the Avon lipstick she had bought on credit from Mami.

"Ya me voy, amiga," Mami said. "My husband needs me at his side." I'd lost track of how many times Mami had said that since my father's telephone call three weeks before. It hadn't taken long for the whole colonia of La Guadalupe to learn that Mami was going to El Otro Lado. It made me angry to hear her say those words: *My husband needs me.* As if my father were not a grown man. As if her children didn't need her as well.

"My mother will be collecting the money you owe me," Mami told Doña María. "I hope you don't mind."

Doña María didn't look at her. She nodded and wished my mother a safe trip. "I'll pray for a successful crossing for you, Juana," she said.

"Don't worry, Doña María, I won't be running across the border. My husband has paid someone to drive me across with borrowed papers. It was expensive, but he didn't want to put me in any danger."

"Of course, how could he do otherwise?" Doña María murmured as she walked away.

Back then, I was too young to realize that unlike me, Mami didn't walk with her eyes to the ground because she was afraid of the rocks tripping her. I was too young to know about the men who leave for El Otro Lado and never return. Some of them find new wives, start a new family. Others disappear completely, reinventing themselves as soon as they arrive, forgetting about those they've left behind.

It was a worry that kept my mother up at night, although I didn't know it back then. But in the weeks since my father's phone call, she walked differently. She didn't look down at the ground anymore. *My husband has sent for me. He needs me,* she said to everyone, and the women, like Doña María, whose husband left long ago, would lower their eyes.

We didn't live far from my grandmother's adobe house, and as soon as we rounded the corner, it came into view. Abuela Evila's house sat at the bottom of the hill. It was shaped like a box, and it had once been painted white, but by the time we came to live there the adobe peeked through where the plaster had cracked like the shell of a hard-boiled egg. It had a terra-cotta tile roof, and bougainvillea climbed up one side. The bougainvillea was in full bloom, and the vine, thick with red flowers, looked like a spreading bloodstain over the white wall of the house.

My grandmother's property was the length of four houses and was surrounded by a corral. To the east of the house was an unpaved street that led to the church, the school, and the tortilla mill. To the west was a dirt road that led past Don Rubén's house and curved east to the dairy farm, the canal, the highway, the cemetery, the train station, and el centro. Her house sat on the north side of the lot, my aunt's brick house sat on the south side, and the rest of the property was a big yard with several fruit trees.

Aside from being one of the poorest states in Mexico, Guerrero is also one of the most mountainous. My hometown of Iguala de la Independencia is located in a valley. My grandmother lived on the edge of the city, and that morning, as we walked to her house, I kept my eyes on the closest mountain. It was big and smooth, and it looked as if it were covered with a green velvety cloth. Because during the rainy season it had a ring of clouds on its peak and looked as if it had tied a white handkerchief around its head, the locals named it the Mountain That Has a Headache. Back then, I didn't know what was on the other side of the mountain, and when I had asked Mami she said she didn't know either. "Another town, I suppose," she said. She pointed in one direction and said Acapulco was somewhere over there, about three hours away by bus. She pointed in the opposite direction and said Mexico City was over there—again, a three-hour bus ride.

But when you're poor, no matter how close things are, everything is far away. And so, until that day, my twenty-nine-year-old mother had never been on the other side of the mountains.

"Listen to your grandmother," Mami said, startling me. I hadn't noticed how quiet we'd all been during our walk. I took my eyes off the Mountain That Has a Headache and looked at Mami as she stood before us. "Behave yourselves. Don't give her any reason to get angry."

"She was born angry," Mago said under her breath.

Carlos and I giggled. Mami giggled, too, but she caught herself. "Hush, Mago. Don't talk like that. Your abuela is doing your father and me a favor by taking you in. Listen to her and always do as she says."

"But why do we have to stay with her?" Carlos asked. He was about to turn seven years old. Mago, at eight and a half, was four years older than me. Both of them had to miss school that day, but of course they didn't mind. How could they think of numbers and letters when our mother was leaving us and going to a place most parents never return from?

"Why can't we stay with Abuelita Chinta?" Mago asked.

I thought about Mami's mother. I loved my grandmother's gap-toothed smile and the way she smelled of almond oil. Her voice was soft like the cooing of the doves she had in cages around her shack. But even as much as I loved Abuelita Chinta, I didn't want to stay with her or with anyone else. I wanted my mother.

Mami sighed. "Your father wants you to stay with your abuela Evila. He thinks you will be better off there—"

"But why do you have to leave, Mami?" I asked again.

"I already told you why, mija. I'm doing this for you. For all of you."

"But why can't I go with you?" I insisted, tears burning my eyes. "I'll be good, I promise."

"I can't take you with me, Reyna. Not this time."

"But—"

"Basta. Your father has made a decision, and we must do as he says."

Mago, Carlos, and I slowed down our pace, and soon Mami was walking by herself while we trailed behind her. I looked at the photo in my arms and took in Papi's black wavy hair, full lips, wide nose, and slanted eyes shifted slightly to the left. I wished, as I always did back then—as I still do now—that he were looking *at* me, and not past me. But his eyes were frozen in that position, and there was nothing I could do about it. "Why are you taking her away?" I asked the Man Behind the Glass. As always, there was no answer.

"¡Señora, ya llegamos!" Mami shouted from the gate. From across the street, the neighbor's dog barked at us. I knew Abuela Evila was home because my eyes burned from the pungent scent of roasting guajillo chiles drifting from the kitchen.

"¡Señora, ya llegamos!" Mami called again. She put a hand on the latch of the gate but didn't pull it open. From the start, my grandmother hadn't liked my mother, and ten years—and three grandchildren—later, she still disapproved of my father's choice for a wife, a woman who came from a family poorer than his own. So Mami didn't feel comfortable walking into my grandmother's house without permission. Instead, we waited at the gate under the scorching heat of the noon sun.

"¡Señora, soy yo, Juana!" Mami yelled, much louder this time. My grandmother was born in 1911, during the Mexican Revolution. When we came to her house, she was about to turn sixty-nine. Her long hair was silver, and she often wore it in a tight bun. She had a small hump on her back that made her body bend to the ground. As a child, she had suffered from a severe case of measles, and what remained of her illness was a left arm that hung at an angle and a limp that made her walk as if she were drunk.

Finally, she came out of the house through the kitchen door. As she headed to the gate, she dried her hands on her apron, which was streaked with fresh red sauce.

"Ya llegamos," Mami said.

"Ya veo," my grandmother replied. She didn't open the gate, and she didn't ask us to come inside to cool ourselves under the shade of the lemon tree in the patio. The bright sun burned my scalp. I got closer to Mami and hid in the shadow of her dress.

"Thank you for letting me leave my children here under your care, señora," Mami said. "Every week my husband and I will be sending you money for their upkeep."

My grandmother looked at the three of us. I couldn't tell if she was angry. Her face was in a constant frown, no matter what kind of mood she was in. "And how long will they be staying?" she asked. I waited for Mami's answer, hoping to hear something more definite than "not too long."

"I don't know, señora," Mami said. I pressed Papi's photo against my chest because that answer was worse. "For as long as necessary," Mami continued. "God only knows how long it's going to take Natalio and me to earn the money for the house he wants."

"*He* wants?" Abuela Evila asked, leaning against the gate. "Don't you want it, too?"

Mami put her arms around us. We leaned against her. Fresh tears came out of my eyes, and I felt as if I'd swallowed one of Carlos's marbles. I clutched at the thin material of Mami's flowery dress and wished I could stay there forever, tucked into its folds, wrapped in the safety of my mother's shadow.

"Of course, señora. What woman wouldn't want a nice brick house? But the price will be great," Mami said.

"American dollars go a long way here," Abuela Evila said, pointing at the brick house built on the opposite side of her property. "Look at my daughter María Félix. She's built herself a very nice house with the money she's made in El Otro Lado."

My aunt's house was one of the biggest on the block. But she didn't live in it. She hadn't returned from El Otro Lado even though she went there long before Papi did. She had left her six-year-old daughter behind, my cousin Élida, who—when we came to Abuela Evila's house—was already going on fourteen and had been living with our grandmother ever since El Otro Lado had taken her mother away.

"I wasn't referring to the money," Mami said. She got choked up and wiped the moisture from her eyes. Abuela Evila looked away, as if embarrassed by Mami's tears. Perhaps because she lived through the Revolution, when over a million people died and the ones who lived had to toughen up to survive, my grandmother was not prone to being emotional.

Mami turned to us and bent down to be at eye level with us. She said, "I'll work as hard as I can. Every dollar that we earn will go to you and the house. Your father and I will both be back before you know it."

"Why did he only send for you and not me?" Mago asked Mami, as she'd done several times already. "I want to see Papi, too."

As the oldest, Mago was the one who remembered my father most clearly. When Mami gave us the news that she was leaving to join him in El Otro Lado, Mago had cried because Papi hadn't sent for her as well.

"Your father couldn't afford to send for us all. I'm only going there to help him earn money for the house," Mami said again.

"We don't need a house. We need Papi," Mago said.

"We need you," Carlos said.

Mami ran her fingers through Mago's hair. "Your father says a man must have his own house, his own land to pass down to his children," she said. "I'll be gone a year. I promise that by the end of the year, I will bring your father back with me whether we have enough money for a house or not. Do you promise to take care of your hermanos for me, be their little mother?"

Mago looked at Carlos, then at me. I don't know what my sister saw in my eyes that made her face soften. Had she realized then how much I would need her? Had she known that without her strength and unwavering love, I would not have survived what was to come? Her face was full of determination when she looked at Mami and said, "Sí, Mami. I promise. But you'll keep your promise, right? You will come back."

"Of course," Mami said. She opened her arms to us, and we fell into them.

"Don't go, Mami. Stay with us. Stay with *me*," I said as I held on to her.

She kissed the top of my head and pushed me toward the closed gate. "You need to get out of the sun before it gives you a headache," she said.

Abuela Evila finally opened the gate, and we were allowed inside, but we didn't move. We stood there holding our bags, and I suddenly wanted to throw Papi's photo against the ground so that it shattered into pieces because I hated him for taking my mother from me just because he wanted a house and a piece of land to call his own.

"Don't leave me, Mami. Please!" I begged.

Mami gave us each a hug and kissed us goodbye. When she kissed me, I pressed my cheek against her lips painted red with Avon lipstick.

Mago held me tightly while we watched Mami walk away, pebbles dancing in and out of her sandals, her hair burning black under the sun. When I saw her blurry figure disappear where the road curved, I escaped Mago's grip on my hand and took off running, yelling for my mother.

Through my tears, I watched a taxicab take her away, leaving a cloud of dust in its wake. I felt a hand on my shoulder and turned to see Mago standing behind me. "Come on, Nena," she said. There were no tears in her eyes, and as we walked back to my grandmother's house, I wondered if, when Mami asked Mago to be our little mother, it had also meant she was not allowed to cry.

Carlos was still standing by the gate, waiting for us so that we could go in together. I looked at the empty dirt road once more, realizing that there was nothing left of my mother. As we walked into my grandmother's house, I touched my cheek and told myself there was something I still had left. The feel of her red lips.

2

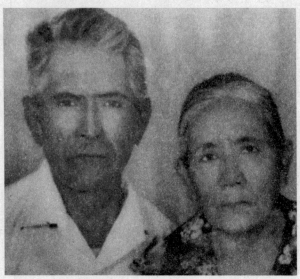

Abuelo Augurio and Abuela Evila

MAGO, CARLOS, AND I were given a corner of my grandfather's bedroom. Abuelo Augurio and Abuela Evila didn't sleep in the same room because when my cousin Élida came to live at their house my grandmother kicked him out of her bed to make space for her favorite grandchild. My grandfather's room smelled of sweat, beer, and cigarette smoke. His bed was in the farthest corner, next to some boxes, an old wardrobe, and his gardening tools. The light that streamed through the only window was too weak to make the room less somber.

Close to the door was a twin-size box spring raised on bricks and covered with a straw mat. The "bed" was pushed up against the wall, underneath the tiny window that looked out onto an alley.

This is where Mago, Carlos, and I slept. I was in the middle, so I wouldn't fall off. Mago slept against the wall because if a scorpion crawled down and stung her, she would be okay. Scorpions couldn't do anything to my hot-blooded Scorpio sister. Carlos slept on the edge because a week after Mami left he began to wet the bed. We hoped that sleeping on the edge would make it easier for him to get up in the middle of the night to use the bucket by the door.

My grandfather's room was next to the alley. Since the window above our heads didn't have any glass to muffle the outside noises, we could hear everything that went on in that alley. Sometimes, we heard grunting noises coming from there. Mago and Carlos got up to look, and they giggled about what they saw, but they never picked me up so that I could see for myself. Other times we heard drunken men coming from the cantina down the road. They yelled obscenities that echoed against the brick walls of the nearby houses. Sometimes we could hear them urinating on the rock fence that surrounded Abuela Evila's property while singing borracho songs. *¡No vale nada la vida, la vida no vale nadaaaa!* I hated that song those drunks liked to sing. Life isn't worth anything?

One night, the noises we heard were a horse's hooves hitting the rocks on the ground. My skin prickled with goose bumps. I wondered who could be in the alley so late.

"What is that?" Carlos asked.

"I don't know," Mago said. "Get up and look." Just then, dogs started to bark.

"Nah," Carlos said.

"You're such a sissy," Mago said. She got up from the bed and stood over us as she looked out the window. With all the noise we were making, you would think Abuelo Augurio would wake up, but he didn't. I wished he would wake up. I wished he would be the one to look out the window and reassure us that everything was all right. I looked at the opposite side of the room and knew he was asleep. When he was awake, he would lie in bed for hours smoking cigarettes in the darkness, the red tip of the cigarette winking at me like an evil eye. His silence always made me uncomfortable. I didn't like my grandmother constantly yelling at us, but my grandfather acted as if we weren't even there. Somehow, I felt that was worse. He made me feel invisible.

Mago gasped and quickly fell on top of us, crossing herself over and over again.

"What did you see?" I asked her. "Who was that in the alley?"

"It was a man, a man on a horse," Mago whispered. The clop-clopping of the hooves grew fainter and fainter.

"So?" Carlos said.

"But he was dragging something behind him in a sack!"

"You're lying," Carlos said.

"I'm not, I swear I'm not," Mago insisted. "I swear I saw him drag a person away."

"We don't believe you," Carlos said again. "Right, Reyna?"

I nodded, but none of us could fall back to sleep.

"That's the devil making his rounds," Abuela Evila said the next morning when we told her what Mago had seen. "He's looking for all the naughty children to take back to Hell with him. So you three better behave, or the devil is going to take you away."

Mago told us not to believe anything Abuela Evila said. But at night, we huddled together even closer when we heard a horse pass by our window, the sound of its hooves sending chills up our spines. *Who would protect us if the devil came to steal us and take us far away where we would never see our parents again?* I wondered. Every night, I would bury my face in my pillow and hold on tight to my sister.

My mother had asked Mago to be our little mother, and she and my father would have been proud to see how bravely their older daughter had taken on that role. Sometimes she took it a little too far for my taste, but Mago was there when my father and my mother were not.

One day, about a month after Mami left, Mago and I were passing by the baker's house on our way to the tortilla mill when he came out wearing a big basket that looked like a giant straw hat filled with sweet bread. My mouth watered at the thought of sinking my teeth into a sweet, fluffy concha de chocolate.

The baker's wife looked at us and said to her husband, "Mirálas, pobrecitas huerfanitas."

"We aren't orphans!" I yelled at her, forgetting all about the sweet bread. I grabbed a rock to throw at her, but I knew Mami would be disappointed in me if I threw it. So I let it fall to the ground.

Still, the baker's wife had seen the look in my eyes. She knew what I was about to do. "Shame on you, girl!" she scolded.

"Oh, don't be too harsh on her," the baker said. "It's a sad thing not to have any parents." He got on his bicycle to deliver his bread. I watched him until he turned the corner, amazed at how he weaved his bike through the rocks scattered throughout the dirt road without losing his balance and spilling all the bread he carried on that giant hat basket.

"If your mother ever comes back, I will be sure to tell her of your behavior," the baker's wife said, pointing a finger at me. Then she went into her house and slammed the door shut.

"I can't believe you," Mago said angrily. She hit me hard with the straw tortilla basket.

"But we aren't orphans!" I said to Mago. She was too angry to speak to me, so she held me tightly by the wrist and hurried me along to the mill to buy tortillas for the midday meal. I stumbled on a rock, and I would have fallen if Mago hadn't been holding me. She slowed her pace and loosened her hold on my wrist.

"I don't want people feeling sorry for me," I told her.

She stopped walking then. She touched her cheek and ran her finger over the scar she had there. When she was three, she had almost lost her eye while playing hide-and-seek. She'd hidden underneath an old bed that had metal springs sticking from it like spiky fingers. One of them dug into Mago's eyelid, another into her cheek, another on the bridge of her nose. The scars the stitches left on her eyelid looked like miniature train tracks. Ever since then, whenever anyone noticed her scars, they would look at her with pity.

After a brief silence she said, "I'm sorry I hit you, Nena." Then she took my hand, and we continued our walk.

When we got back from the tortilla mill, Élida was waiting by the gate asking why we took so long with the tortillas, and couldn't we see she was hungry? Élida had a round chubby face and big puffy eyes that Mago teased her about, calling them frog eyes. At first, we had tried to be friends with Élida. We thought that since we were in the same situation—having been left behind by our parents—we would be friends. Élida wasn't interested in being our friend, and, like the neighbors, called us the little orphans. Technically, she was a little orphan, too. But the fashionable clothes Abuela Evila made for her on her sewing machine and the many gifts her mother sent her from El Otro Lado helped Élida transform herself from the little orphan to a privileged granddaughter. She was everything we were not.

Seeing her, I was angry again at being called an orphan, at being hit by Mago, at my mother leaving, at my father for taking her away. I wanted to yank Élida's braid, but at the sight of Abuela Evila hovering nearby, I knew it wise not to. Instead I said, "Your hair looks like a horse's tail."

"¡Pinche huérfana!" she said, and yanked my pigtail. Abuelita Evila took the tortillas from Mago but didn't say anything to Élida for pulling my hair.

My grandfather and my aunt, Tía Emperatriz, were sitting at

Mago, before the scars

the table in the kitchen. My grandfather worked in the fields nearby and was only there for lunch. My aunt worked at a photo studio. She was twenty-five years old and was still single. The youngest of my grandmother's five living children, she had yet to find someone who my grandmother felt was good enough to marry her prettiest daughter. Any man that came knocking would be scared off by my grandmother.

Carlos, Mago, and I sat on the two concrete steps leading from the kitchen to my grandmother's room since the table was only big enough for four people, and those seats were already taken. Abuela Evila gave a pork chop to Abuelo Augurio, another to Élida, the third went to Tía Emperatriz, and the last pork chop she took for herself. By the time the frying pan came our way, there was nothing left. Abuela Evila scooped up spoonfuls of oil in which she had fried the meat and mixed it in with our beans. "For flavor," she said.

If Papi were here, if Mami were here, we wouldn't be eating oil, I thought.

"Isn't there any meat left?" Tía Emperatriz asked.

Abuela Evila shook her head. "The money you left me this morning didn't go very far at el mercado," she said. "And the money their parents sent is gone."

Tía Emperatriz looked at our oily beans and then got up and grabbed her purse. She gave Mago a coin and sent her to buy a soda for us. Mago came back with a Fanta. We thanked our aunt for the soda and took turns sipping from the bottle, but the sweet, orangey taste didn't wash away the oil in our mouths.

"What's the point of our parents being in El Otro Lado, if we're going to be eating like beggars?" Mago said after our meal, once we were out of earshot. I had no answer to give my sister, so I said nothing. Tía Emperatriz and Abuelo Augurio went back to work. Élida went to watch TV. Carlos took the trash can out to the backyard to burn the pile of garbage, and I helped Mago take all the dirty dishes out to the stone lavadero. Then we cleaned the table and swept the dirt floor.

"¡Regina!" Abuela Evila called out from her bedroom, where she was mending her dresses. "¡Regina, ven acá!" It took me a moment to realize she was calling *me*, since Regina isn't my name. My grandmother thought it should have been because I was born on September 7, the day of Santa Regina. When my mother went to city hall to obtain my birth certificate, she had been angry at my grandmother for constantly criticizing her cooking or the way she cleaned, so in an act of small defiance, my mother registered me as Reyna. My grandmother never called me by my given name.

"¡Regina!" Abuela Evila called again.

"¿Sí, Abuelita?" I said as I stood at the threshold of her room.

"Go buy me a needle," she said, handing me the money she took out of the coin bag she kept in her brassiere. "And hurry back," she said. I glanced at the living room where Élida was watching *El Chavo del Ocho* while eating a bag of chicharrones sprinkled with red sauce.

Don Bartolo's two daughters were playing hopscotch outside his store. When they saw me walking past them, they pointed at me and said, "Look, there goes the little orphan." This time, I didn't think twice about it. This time, I didn't care if the whole colonia thought I was wild and a disgrace to my family. I threw the coin as hard as I could. It hit one of the girls above her right eye. She screamed and called to her father. I ran home, forgetting to pick up the coin on the ground. When Abuela Evila asked me for her needle, I had no choice but to tell her the truth.

She called Mago over and said, "Take your sister to apologize to Don Bartolo, and don't come back without my needle."

Mago grabbed my hand and pulled me along. "Now you've done it," she said.

"She shouldn't have called me an orphan!" I yanked my hand from Mago's and stopped walking. Mago looked at me for a long time. I thought she was going to hit me. Instead she took my hand again but pulled me in the opposite direction of Don Bartolo's store.

"Where are we going?" I asked. She didn't tell me where she was taking me, but as soon as we turned the corner, our little house came into view. We stopped in front of it. The window was open, and I could smell beans cooking. I heard a woman singing along to the radio. Mago said she didn't know who Don Rubén's new tenants were, but that this house would always be where we had lived with our parents. "No one can take that away," she said. "I know you don't remember Papi at all, but whatever you remember about Mami and this house is yours to keep forever."

I followed her down to the canal on the opposite side of the hill from Abuela Evila's house. Mami would come to do the washing here when we lived in Don Rubén's house. Mago said, "This is where Mami saved your life, Nena. Remember?"

When I was three, I had almost drowned in that canal. The rainy season had turned it into a gushing river, and the current was swift and strong. Mami told me to sit on the washing stones and stay by her side, but she let Mago and Carlos get in the water and play with the other kids. I wanted to get in, and when Mami was busy rinsing our clothes and looking the other way, I jumped in. The current pulled me down the canal. My feet couldn't touch the bottom, and I got pulled under. Mami got to me just in time.

We went back to Abuela Evila's house, not knowing what we were going to tell her. But before we went into the house itself, Mago took me into the shack made of bamboo sticks and cardboard near the patio. Inside were large clay pots, a griddle, and other things my grandmother didn't have space for in her kitchen. This is where Mami and Papi had first lived when they were married.

Mago and I sat on the dirt floor, and she told me about the day I was born exactly the way Mami used to tell it. She pointed to the circle of rocks and a pile of ash and told me that during my birth, a fire had been on while Mami had squatted on the ground, over a straw mat, grabbing the rope hanging from the ceiling. When I was born, the midwife put me into my mother's arms. She turned to face the fire so that the heat would keep me warm. As I listened to Mago, I closed my eyes and felt the heat of the flames, and I heard Mami's heart beating against my ear.

Mago pointed to a spot on the dirt floor and reminded me that my umbilical cord was buried there. *That way,* Mami told the midwife, *no matter where life takes her, she won't ever forget where she came from.*

But then Mago touched my belly button and added something to the story my mother had never told me. She said that my umbilical cord was like a ribbon that connected me to Mami. She said, "It doesn't matter that there's a distance between us now. That cord is there forever." I touched my belly button and thought about what my sister had said. I had Papi's photo to keep me connected to him. I had no photo of my mother, but now my sister had given me something to remember her by.

"We still have a mother and a father," Mago said. "We aren't orphans, Nena. Just because they aren't with us doesn't mean we don't have parents anymore. Now come on, let's go tell our grandmother we have no needle for her."

I took Mago's hand and together we left the shack. "She's going to beat me," I told her as we headed to the house. "And she's going to beat you, too, even though you didn't do anything."

"I know," she said.

"Wait," I said. I ran out of the gate before I lost my nerve. I ran down the street as fast as I could. Outside the store, Don Bartolo's daughters were playing again. They glared at me the moment they saw me. Suddenly, my feet didn't want to keep walking. I put a finger on my belly button, and I thought about Mami, and about everything my sister had just said. It gave me courage.

"I'm sorry I hit you with the coin," I told the older girl.

She turned to look at her father, who had just come out of the store to stand by the door. She said, "My papi says that we're lucky he has the store because if he didn't, he would have to leave for El Otro Lado. I wouldn't want him to go."

"I didn't want Mami to go, either," I said. "But I know she'll be back soon. And so will my papi."

Don Bartolo took my grandmother's coin from his pocket and handed it to me. "Don't ever think that your parents don't love you," he said. "It is because they love you very much that they have left."

As I walked home with the needle for my grandmother, I told myself that maybe Don Bartolo was right. I had to keep on believing my parents left me because they loved me too much and not because they didn't love me enough.

3

Carlos, Reyna, Mago

ÉLIDA'S HAIR WAS so long, it tumbled down her back like a sparkling black waterfall. Every few days, Abuela Evila washed Élida's hair with lemon water because, according to her, lemon juice cleans the impurities of the hair and makes it shiny and healthy. In the afternoons, she would fill up a bucket from the water tank, pick a few lemons from the tree, and squeeze the juice into the water.

Mago, Carlos, and I would hide behind a pink oleander bush and watch their ritual through the narrow leaves. Abuela Evila washed Élida's hair as if she were washing an expensive silk rebozo. Afterwards, Élida would sit under the sun to dry her hair. My grandmother would come out to brush it in small strokes, beginning with the tips and working her way up. She spent half an hour running the comb through Élida's long hair while we watched.

Our hair was louse-ridden, our abdomens swelled with round-worms, but my grandmother didn't care. "I can be sure that my daughters' children are really my grandchildren," Abuela Evila often said to us. "But one can't trust a daughter-in-law. Who knows what your mother did when no one was looking."

It was my mother's bad luck to have been the only daughter-in-law. My father had a brother who died at seven years old. His name was Carlos, and my brother inherited his name. My grandfather would take Tío Carlos to the fields to work, and since they left very early in the morning, Tío Carlos would be too sleepy to stay awake during the ride to the fields. My grandfather would tie him to the horse to keep him from falling. One day, the horse lost its footing and fell, crushing my uncle beneath it.

But my uncle's death didn't save my father from the fields. When he was in third grade, he left school to harvest crops alongside my grandfather. If only Tío Carlos had lived and married, my mother would have had an ally, and we would have had cousins to share the burden of my grandmother's mistrust.

"Your mother is not coming back for you," Élida said to us one afternoon while lying in the sun to let her hair dry after Abuela Evila's lemon treatment. Mago and I were scrubbing our dirty clothes on the washing stone. "Now that she's got a job and is making dollars, she won't want to come back, believe me."

Three weeks before, Mami told us she got a job at a garment factory where she worked all day trimming loose threads off clothes. She said she was finally going to help Papi save money for the house and promised to send us money for Abuela Evila to buy us shoes and clothes. We couldn't tell Mami not to bother, that the money they sent disappeared by the time my grandmother made it home from the bank. My grandmother hovered above us while we talked on the phone, and if we said anything bad about her, she would spank us afterward.

"She'll be back. I know she will," Mago told Élida. In the two and a half months we'd been there, my parents had called us every other weekend, but Mami had yet to send us the letters she promised she would write. But every time she called, Mago would be sure to remind her of her promise—that she would return within the year.

"Don't lie to yourself," Élida said. "They're going to forget all about you, you'll see. You and your brother and sister are always going to be Los Huerfanitos."

"Speak for yourself. It's your mother who's not coming back," Mago said. "Doesn't she have another child, over there in El Otro Lado?"

At being reminded of her American brother, Élida looked away. Abuela Evila came out of the house carrying a large plastic comb. She sat behind Élida and combed into shiny black silk her long hair that smelled of lemonade. Élida was quiet, and she didn't answer Abuela Evila when she asked her what was wrong.

An hour later, Élida was back in the patio. She lay down on the hammock and watched us do our chores. Mago swept the ground, and I watered Abuela Evila's pots of vinca and geranium on the edges of the water tank. Carlos was in the backyard clearing the brush, a chore my grandfather had given him. As always, Élida didn't have to do any work.

She rocked herself on the hammock eating a mango on a stick she had bought at Don Bartolo's store. It was a beautiful mango cut to look like a flower. Its yellow flesh was sprinkled with red chili powder. My mouth watered at seeing her take a big bite. Élida was always eating goodies she would buy with the money our grandmother gave her, and she never shared them with us. But when our other grandmother, Abuelita Chinta, would visit, bringing us oranges, cajeta, or lollipops, we had to share them with Élida or Abuela Evila would take them away.

"My mother loves me," Élida said. "That's why she sends me everything I ask her for. That's why she writes to me."

"¡Ya cállate, marrana!" Mago said. She turned the broom to face Élida and started to sweep toward her.

"¡Pinche huérfana!" Élida yelled, scrambling to get away from the cloud of dust Mago had just sent her way. "¡Pinche piojosa!"

"So what if I have lice?" Mago said. "And if you aren't careful, I'll give them to you, and we'll see what happens to all that hair of yours." Mago pulled me to her and started parting my hair. "¡Mira, mira, un piojo!" she said, holding an imaginary louse toward Élida.

"¡Abuelita! ¡Abuelita!" Élida yelled, her eyes opened wide with fear. She ran into the house clutching her thick long braid. Mago and I looked at each other.

"Look what you've done. We're really going to get it now," I said to Mago.

I thought we were going to get a beating with my grandmother's wooden spoon, or a branch or a sandal, the usual choices. I would have preferred a beating to what we got.

In the evening, when Tía Emperatriz came home from work, Abuela Evila told her to take care of our lice problem.

"Can't it wait for the weekend?" Tía Emperatriz asked. "It's been a long day for me."

"They're going to pass their lice on to me, Abuelita," Élida said, still clutching her braid. "Please, Abuelita."

"Do as I say," Abuela Evila said to my aunt.

Tía Emperatriz glanced at Élida, who was smirking behind Abuela Evila's hunched figure, and I caught a glimpse of anger, a hint of jealousy in my aunt's eyes. She gave Mago some pesos and sent her down to Don Bartolo's store to buy lice shampoo and a fine-tooth comb.

"That's not going to work," Abuela Evila said. "Get kerosene."

"But Amá, that's dangerous," Tía Emperatriz said.

"Nonsense," Abuela Evila said. "In my day, there was no better remedy than kerosene."

The last rays of the sun were gone, and the world became wrapped in darkness. My grandmother turned on the light in the patio, but it didn't work. There was no electricity that night, so she brought out her candles and set them on the water tank.

When Mago came back with the kerosene, my aunt had us sit down one by one.

"What if that doesn't work?" Élida asked.

"If the kerosene doesn't work, I'm shaving off their hair!" Abuela Evila said.

At hearing my grandmother's words, I stopped squirming. I sat so still I could hear the mosquitoes buzzing around. They bit my legs and arms, but the thought of getting my head shaved kept me from moving. My aunt gently tilted my head all the way back and in the dim candlelight combed my hair with the fine-tooth comb for five minutes. The comb kept getting caught in my curls, and I felt as if needles were digging into my scalp. Tía Emperatriz soaked a towel in kerosene and then wrapped it around my head, making sure every strand of hair was tucked in before tying a plastic bag over my head to keep the towel in place. The smell was overpowering, and I had to struggle not to scratch my scalp, which was throbbing from the sting of the kerosene.

"Now off to bed," Tía Emperatriz said when she was done, "and stay away from the lit candles in the house."

That night was long and restless. I wanted to scratch, scratch, scratch. But could not. The overwhelming smell of the kerosene made it almost impossible to breathe. I reached for my towel and pulled on it, not able to bear the pain and the dizziness any longer.

"Leave it alone," Mago said.

"It hurts so much," I said. "I need to scratch. I really need to."

"My scalp feels as if it's on fire!" Carlos said. "I can't take it anymore."

"Don't do it," Mago said. "We'll get our hair chopped off if you ruin it now."

"I don't care!" With one swoop of his hand, Carlos pulled off the towel.

Shortly thereafter, when I reached my limit, I did the same.

Abuela Evila was true to her word. The next afternoon, when my grandfather came home from work, she had him take out his razor blade and scissors. Carlos didn't put up much of a fuss because he was always trying to please my grandfather. His hair was completely shaved off. We ran our hands over his bald head, feeling the stubble tickle our palms. When she saw him, Élida said, "You look like a skeleton." She was always making fun of him because Carlos was really skinny, except for his bloated abdomen, and now with his head completely bald, he did look like a skeleton. Élida started to sing a song, "La calaca, tilica y flaca. La calaca, tilica y flaca." I laughed because it was a funny song, and I could picture a skeleton dancing along to it.

"Regina, it's your turn," Abuela Evila said.

"Please, Abuelita, no!" I yelled as my grandmother dragged me to the chair. My grandfather hit me on the head with his hand and ordered me to sit still.

"Allá tú si te quieres mover," he said when I wouldn't stop. I jerked around, crying and yelling for Mami to come. I hated myself for being so weak the night before when I tore the towel off. My scalp still burned and my head hurt, but it had all been for nothing. I cried for my hair. It was the only beautiful thing I had. Curls so thick, women in the street would stop and touch it and tell Mami, "Qué bonito pelo tiene su hija. She looks like a doll." Mami would smile with pride.

"Don't move, Nena, he's doing a really bad job!" Mago said. But I didn't listen, and the scissors hissed near my ear. I squirmed even more at watching my curls land on the ground and on my lap, falling one by one like the petals of a flower. Then my grandmother's chickens came clucking to see what was happening, and they picked up my curls and shook them around, and when they realized they weren't food, they stepped all over them and dragged them with their feet across the dirt.

In the end, when Abuelo Augurio was done, I ran to my aunt's dresser mirror and gasped. My hair was as short as a boy's, and it was so uneven it looked as if one of the cows from the dairy farm down the road had nibbled on it. I looked at Papi's photo hanging on the wall, right below the small window. I'd seen myself in the mirror enough times to know that his slanted eyes were just like mine. We both had small foreheads, wide cheeks, and a wide nose. And now, we both had short black hair.

"When are you coming back?" I asked the Man Behind the Glass.

I wished we had a picture of Mami. I wanted to tell her that I missed being with her. I missed watching her getting the dirty clothes ready, putting them inside a blanket and tying the corners to make a sack, then throwing the sack on her head. "Vámonos," she would say, and I walked alongside her to the canal. There I would sit on the washing stone while she scrubbed the clothes and told me stories. If the water was low, she would let me get in. I would chase after the soap bubbles as she dunked the clothes into the water to rinse.

I missed watching her go through her pretty Avon merchandise—smelling the perfumes, trying on the lotions that smelled of spring-time—and seeing her face glow with pride after each sale.

I missed going with her to visit Abuelita Chinta, and taking a nap on Abuelita's bed while they talked. I would fall asleep listening to Mami's voice and the cooing of Abuelita Chinta's doves. And at night, I missed snuggling with her on the bed she had slept in with Papi before he left. Mago and I had tried to keep Mami warm so she wouldn't miss him so much.

Mago came in to tell me it was dinnertime, and I looked at her and hated her because she didn't get her hair chopped off. She dealt with the stupid itching all night long. Even though her scalp was irritated and blistered, the lice were all dead. She washed her hair twenty times with Tía Emperatriz's shampoo that smelled of roses, but it still reeked of kerosene. But at least she didn't look like a boy.

"Leave me alone," I said.

"Come on, Nena, come and eat."

My stomach didn't care that my hair got butchered. It groaned with hunger, and I had no choice but to go out into the kitchen where everyone could see me. Tía Emperatriz, who was at work when the hair cutting took place, gasped at seeing me and said, "Ay, Amá, what did you do to this poor girl?"

Élida said, "What girl? Isn't that Carlos?" When I glared at her, she laughed and said, "Oops, I thought you were your brother."

That night, I had a dream about Mami. In my dream she was washing my hair with lemon water and scrubbing it so gently my body shuddered with pleasure. I awoke with such longing that I felt like weeping. And then I realized that Carlos had wet the bed.

4

La Guadalupe

B y June, we had been at Abuela Evila's house for six months.
During the time Carlos, Mago, and I lived there with her, we
were never taken anywhere, like to el zócalo downtown, the plaza
with a monument to the Mexican flag and stone tablets explaining
the role Iguala played in Mexico's War of Independence; the beautiful San Francisco church built in the nineteenth century and surrounded by thirty-two tamarind trees; the bus station, el mercado, or
the city's popular train station that connected Iguala to Cuernavaca
and Mexico City to the north, and the state capital, Chilpancingo, to
the south.

The city of Iguala de la Independencia is actually the third-largest
city in the state of Guerrero, the two others being Chilpancingo and
Acapulco. My grandmother's house was in a neighborhood known
as La Guadalupe, on the outskirts of the city, although no one would
call it the outskirts anymore. Whenever I can't resist the pull of my

birthplace, I visit Iguala, and I have seen it grow to more than 110,000 inhabitants. The neighborhood where I grew up is no longer the undeveloped part of the city. It's the new neighborhoods encroaching upon the foothills where the poorest people now live. Most of the streets of La Guadalupe have been paved and electricity is fairly stable, although running water is still not readily available.

Back then, Carlos, Mago, and I had mostly stayed on my grandmother's property. We only ventured outside when my grandmother and Élida left for el centro on Saturday mornings. We would rush to the huge vacant lot near her house. There was an abandoned car there and we liked to play in it, but first we had to check for snakes. The car was rusty and the seats were full of holes. It had no tires, but the steering wheel worked just fine. I didn't know how long that rusty car had been there, but I liked to believe Papi had played in it as a child. But since he stared working when he was nine, I don't think he really had much of a childhood.

"Where are we off to today?" Carlos asked, taking his turn at the wheel. He made noises like the revving of an engine and turned the wheel to the left and to the right.

"To El Otro Lado," I said.

"Here we go," Carlos said.

The noises got louder. The car went faster. Carlos said, "Hold on tight for the jump!" He was a big fan of *The Dukes of Hazzard*, and his favorite character was the blond guy named Bo. In the evenings, Carlos would sneak out of the house and run to the baker's to watch TV with his kids. He would get a piece of sweet bread because he didn't mind being called a little orphan as long as he got a treat. While he was gone, Mago and I had to keep Abuela Evila from finding out where he was, although usually we didn't need to say anything. Abuela Evila, Élida, and Tía Emperatriz would be sitting in the living room watching a telenovela and wouldn't pay much attention to our whereabouts.

"Yeee-haa!" Carlos said. As he drove, I looked at the Mountain That Has a Headache and was sure El Otro Lado was over there. Mago said El Otro Lado was really far away, and back then nothing seemed farther away than an unknown town on the other side of the mountain.

"Head that way," I told him. "That's where Mami and Papi are."

Carlos at four

Carlos started the noises again. The engine revved and soon we were off. "Yeee-haa!"

Because I'd decided that my parents must be on the other side of the Mountain That Has a Headache, I got in the habit of looking at it each night and wishing my parents a buenas noches. In the morning, I wished them a buenos días. Carlos and Mago would do it as well, even though Élida would laugh and tell us we were a bunch of pendejos to believe our parents were that close.

"We aren't idiots," I would say to Élida. "My mami and papi are as close as I want them to be."

At first, I hadn't really known where to find Papi. All I had was his photo and the rich brown color of Mago's skin, which was the color of rain-soaked earth, like his. But one day, as we were walking to the store, Mago stopped outside a house to listen to "Escuché las Golondrinas," which was playing on the radio, and said, "Papi loved that song." That is how I learned I could find him in the voice of Vicente Fernández. Another time, as we were walking to the tortilla mill, a man passed by us on his bicycle and we caught a whiff of something spicy, like cinnamon, and Mago said, "That's how Papi smelled!" So

I would find him in the empty bottle of Old Spice we were lucky enough to discover in a trash heap.

It was easier to find Mami. She was in the smell of the apple-scented shampoo we asked Tía Emperatriz to buy for us. I found her in the scent of her favorite Avon perfumes I smelled on her old clients when Mago and I stood in line with them at the tortilla mill. I found the color of her lips in the flowers of the bougainvillea climbing up Abuela Evila's house. I heard her in the lyrics of her favorite songs from Los Dandys: *"Eres la gema que Dios convirtiera en mujer para bien de mi vida . . ."* And when Abuelita Chinta came to visit us every other week, I saw Mami in her eyes.

Whenever I would go into the little shack where I was born, I'd trace a circle around the spot where my umbilical cord was buried and think about the special cord that connected me to Mami.

Every two weeks, when they called, I would find my parents in my grandmother's phone. But always, those precious two minutes Abuela Evila allowed us on the phone went by too quickly. Two minutes to tell them everything we felt. So many things to say to them, but one night in August we said nothing at all. It was Mami who talked, who gave Mago the worst news of all.

She was going to have a baby.

"They're replacing us," Mago said after handing the phone back to Abuela Evila. Élida smirked at hearing the news. We went to our room, and since only a thin curtain separated the room from the rest of the house, I could hear my grandmother telling my parents how tough things were and could they please send more money. "Your children need shoes and clothes . . ." Abuelita Evila said.

"They'll leave us here and forget all about us," Mago said as she lay on the bed. We had been at my grandmother's for eight long months. What had sustained us through that time was the belief that our mother would be back within the year. Now, with this new baby on the way, Mami's plans had changed. Why would she come back to Mexico to have her baby, when she could stay on that side of the border and give birth to an American citizen?

"She promised," Mago said. Carlos and I tried to make her feel better, yet no matter what we said, Mago was inconsolable. Almost every night, I heard her crying, and all I could do was wrap my arms around my sister and cry with her. I felt so angry at my parents. I couldn't understand why they asked God for another child as if we three weren't enough. I put a finger on my belly button and reminded myself about the cord that tied me to Mami. I told myself that as long as that cord existed, she wouldn't forget me, no matter how many other children she had. But Papi, what connected me to him? What would keep him from forgetting me? In his sleep Carlos couldn't hide his sadness, and some times in the middle of the night I'd feel something warm seeping into my dress.

The day after the telephone call, Mago refused to go to school, and Carlos had to walk there by himself. Mago spent all day in the room we shared with my grandfather. She grabbed one of Élida's old history books and flipped through the pages until she found a map. She kept tracing a line between two dots, and because I couldn't read yet, I couldn't make out what the letters said. When I asked her what she was doing, she showed me the map. "This is Iguala. And this is Los Angeles, and this," she said as she made her finger go from one dot to the other, "this is the distance between us and our parents."

I touched my belly button and said, "But we're connected."

She shrugged and said there was no such bond. "I just made that up to make you feel better."

"You're lying!" I said. I kicked her on the calf and ran out of the room with a finger on my belly button. I hid in the shack where I was born and traced a circle around the spot on the dirt floor where my umbilical cord was buried.

Someone shouted my grandmother's name from the gate, and I went out and saw Doña Paula had arrived. We didn't have running water, so Doña Paula would come every three days to deliver water to Abuela Evila from the community well. Her donkey carried two large containers on either side. Her two little boys would ride on the donkey while she walked alongside it, pulling on the reins. The older was my age and the younger was three.

"Buenas tardes," she said to Abuela Evila as she led the donkey through the gate.

As always, she pecked each of her sons on the mouth as she helped them get off the donkey one by one. I tried not to look, but my eyes were glued to Doña Paula, to the way her lips pressed against the soft flesh of her sons' cheeks, the mark they left. I thought of my mother, of the kiss she had given me the day she left, of the fact that her lipstick had rubbed off all too quickly. I tried to recall what my mother's kiss had felt like, but I could not.

"Look at those little jotos," Mago said from behind me. "Being kissed by their mami." She went back into the house, murmuring something about them being a bunch of sissies and mama's boys.

I stood there watching Doña Paula's sons, thinking that there had once been a time when my own mother had kissed me, but now she would soon be leaving the imprint of her lips on another child.

"Jotos," I whispered under my breath. And making sure that their mother wasn't looking, I stuck my tongue out at them.

"Regina, tell your sister to go buy Doña Paula a Fanta," Abuela Evila told me as I stood there by the patio. I nodded and did as she said.

"Why doesn't she go get her the soda?" Mago said. "It's not like we get any of that water." The water Doña Paula brought was dumped into the tank and used for washing dishes and for Élida, my grandmother, my aunt, and my grandfather to bathe with. If we wanted to bathe, we had to go to the community well to get our own water and bring it back in buckets. One time Mago slipped and almost fell into the well, but while she held desperately onto the rope and dangled in the air, Carlos and I grabbed her feet to get her back to the edge. We only bathed once or twice a week because it was a hassle getting the water, and since no one told us to bathe, we only did it when we felt like it. That meant we were nearly always covered in dirt and our clothes looked as if we had mopped the floor with them. You wouldn't have known by looking at us that we had two parents working in El Otro Lado. If our grandmother hadn't kept the money my parents sent for us, perhaps we would have been like Élida, who was always flaunting all the pretty clothes and shoes she bought with the money her mother sent from El Otro Lado, and no one would have dared to call us orphans.

We ran to the store with an empty bottle to exchange for a new soda. When we got back, Mago handed Doña Paula the Fanta, then we watched her drink it. She had the strangest way of drinking soda

I've ever seen. She would raise the bottle two inches from her lips and would tilt it just enough for the liquid to cascade down into her mouth. She never touched her lips to the brim of the bottle, saying that since the bottles were used again and again by the soda company, other mouths had touched the glass. She would drink half of it and then hand the bottle to her boys, who'd finish it off while she unloaded the containers and dumped the water into the tank.

After drinking the soda, Doña Paula told her sons to go play with us while she visited with my grandmother. We loved playing in the backyard, but Mago didn't want to play with Doña Paula's sons that day, and I didn't either. So they went off on their own to the backyard, and we went to the north side of the house where the alley was, and there, right by the rock corral encircling Abuela Evila's property, was a big pile of caca. We could tell whoever had pooped there had recently eaten black beans because we could see little pieces of bean skin peeking out from the caca.

Mago yanked my arm and said, "Nena, go get me two tortillas."

"What for?"

"Just do it, and heat them up."

I sneaked into the kitchen, being careful not to get caught. I didn't know what Mago was up to. I ran back to Mago and gave her the hot tortillas. She jumped over the corral and scooped up some caca with a stick and buttered the tortillas with it. Then she rolled them up and went to find Doña Paula's boys. Realizing what she was about to do, I pulled on her arm and begged her not to. She pushed me away so hard, I fell to the ground. She looked at me, and for a second, my little mother was there, worried that she had hurt me. But then the anger came back into her eyes, and she walked away and left me there on the ground. I got up and ran after her. It was one thing to call them names, but a completely different thing to feed them poop.

"You boys hungry?" she asked. The boys said they weren't, but Mago forced them to take the tacos.

"We don't want any," they said, eyeing the tacos with distrust, as if they knew Mago was up to no good.

She held her hand up and curled it into a fist. "If you don't eat them, I'm going to beat you up," she said. "I mean it."

"Mago, cut it out," I said, but Mago pushed me away again. I watched in horror as she bullied those boys into taking a bite out of the tacos.

Their eyes widened with disgust as they chewed. "What's in them?"

"They're just bean tacos," Mago said.

"We don't want them," they said, tossing the tacos before running back to their mother.

We watched Doña Paula do her usual routine—first she picked up the older boy, kissed him on the mouth, and put him on the donkey, then she bent down and picked up the other one. But this time when she kissed him, she made a face. She sniffed and sniffed and then wiped something off the corner of his mouth.

"You smell like caca, mijo," she said. She sniffed the finger she used to wipe his mouth and then said, "It *is* caca. Why do you have it on your mouth?" The little boy pointed at us and told her we had given them bean tacos. "You stupid brats, why did you feed caca to my sons?"

We didn't wait to hear what Abuela Evila said to her. We raced to the backyard and climbed up the guamúchil tree and didn't come down when our grandmother called us. She stood below us waving a branch. "Malditas chamacas, you better get down right now!" But we didn't come down. She finally tired of yelling and went back into the house. "You'll come down soon enough when you're hungry," she said.

We were there for so long Élida and Carlos came home from school. Carlos couldn't get us to come down either. So instead, he climbed up the tree and sat with us. "Élida was right all along," Mago said. "Mami won't be coming back. Neither is Papi. They're going to have new children over there and leave us here for good."

"No, they won't, Mago," I said.

"They'll come back," Carlos said.

"Why would they want us now, when they're going to have American children?"

Even though I was little then, I knew what she'd meant. Every time someone mentioned El Otro Lado, there was a reverence in their voice, as if they were talking about something holy, like God. Anything that came from over there was coveted, whether it was a toy, or a pair of shoes, or a Walkman, like the one Élida had gotten the month before from her mother. She was the envy of the whole colonia. Wouldn't it be the same for my mother then, if she had a baby who was made in that special place?

Carlos tried to make Mago laugh by telling us his favorite jokes about a boy named Pepito. He said, "One day, Pepito's brother, Jesús, took Pepito's leather sandals. When Pepito woke up, he didn't have any shoes to wear to school. Pepito went from street to street trying to find his brother Jesús and get his huaraches back. As he was passing by a church, he heard the priest chant, 'Jesús is ascending to Heaven.' Then Pepito burst into the church, screaming, 'Stop him! Stop him! He's stealing my sandals!'"

Carlos and I laughed. Mago cracked a hint of a smile, but when Carlos started on his next joke, Mago told him to shut up. The sun went down and soon the fireflies were out and about. Mosquitoes buzzed around and bit us, but it was too hard to see them and scare them off. Our bottoms were numb from sitting on the hard branch of the guamúchil tree. From up there, we saw Tía Emperatriz come home. We called out her name.

"Ay, Dios mio, niños. What are you doing up there in that tree at this hour?" We told her what we did, and even though she tried to stop Abuela Evila from giving us a beating, she didn't succeed.

Abuela Evila made us each cut a branch from the guamúchil tree. She hit us one by one, beginning with Mago because she was the instigator. Mago bit her lips and didn't cry when the branch whistled through the air and hit her on the legs, back, and arms. Carlos did cry—first, because he didn't do anything and, second, out of humiliation because Abuela Evila made him pull down his pants, saying that if she hit him with pants on, he wouldn't learn his lesson. As the branch whipped my legs and butt, I wailed like La Llorona herself and called out for my missing mother.

5

*Mago cutting her and
Reyna's birthday cake*

A MONTH LATER on September 7, just as the rainy season was coming to an end, I turned five, but my birthday came and went without notice. Since Mago's birthday is in late October, Abuela Evila said our birthdays would be celebrated together. That meant I had to wait a month and two weeks. That whole time I was angry at Mago because it was easier to take it out on her than to rebel against my grandmother's decision. Why did Mago have to be a hot-blooded Scorpio and not an easygoing Virgo, like me? Why couldn't it be she who celebrated her birthday early, instead of me celebrating mine late?

Finally, one Saturday morning, my grandmother reluctantly handed Tía Emperatriz the money my parents had sent to buy us a cake. My aunt did more than that. She came home with a roasted chicken, two cans of peas and carrots, which she used for a salad, and small presents for me and Mago: shiny ties and barrettes for our hair. This was the third birthday I celebrated without Papi being there. The first without Mami.

The cake was beautiful. It was white and had pink sugar flowers all around. My grandmother's oldest daughter brought her children to the house, not because she cared about our birthdays, but who could resist getting a free meal and a slice of cake? Even Élida put her pride aside and asked for seconds. Not once did she try to ruin our special moment with one of her usual remarks about us being orphans. That's what a fancy store-bought cake does to people.

Tía Emperatriz took pictures of us cutting the cake to send to my parents. We rarely had our photographs taken, and the thought of these pictures making their way to El Otro Lado—to Papi and Mami—was exciting. I thought those pictures would remind them of us, and that way they wouldn't forget they still had three children waiting for them back home. I smiled the biggest smile I could manage because I wanted them to know I appreciated the money they'd sent for the cake. Carlos smiled halfway. He was very self-conscious about his teeth. Back then, not only were his teeth crooked, but there was also a tiny little tooth wedged between his two front teeth. Since he didn't want anyone to see them, he would purse his lips and smile without showing any teeth. He looked as if he were constipated.

Mago didn't smile. She said that if she looked sad, then maybe our parents would see how much she truly missed them, and they would come back. From that point on, she continued to look sad in almost every picture we took.

Her tactic didn't work. The pictures were sent, the months went by, and still our parents did not return.

The one who did come back, however, was Élida's mother.

We had been at Abuela Evila's house for over a year when Élida turned fifteen. She officially became a señorita, and Tía María Félix came to Iguala to throw a big quinceañera for Élida. She arrived loaded with so many suitcases she hired two taxis to take her from the bus station to Abuela Evila's house. While everyone greeted her and made a big fuss about her arrival, we eyed the suitcases, wondering if our parents had sent us something.

Élida's little brother, Javier, was six years old. He held on to Tía María Félix and when Élida tried to hug my aunt, Javier pushed Élida away and said, "No, she's my mommy." Tía María Félix laughed and said it was cute. Abuela Evila scolded him and said that Élida was his sister, and Tía María Félix was Élida's mother, too. But he wouldn't let go of his mom.

Mago would have taken advantage of this opportunity to say something mean to Élida. But the news Tía María Félix gave us sent us to our room, where we spent the night crying. "Your mother just had a little girl," she said. "Elizabeth, I think, is what your mom named her."

We lay on our bed, huddled so close together our limbs were entangled. At night, barking dogs serenaded la colonia as they wandered through the dark streets. We listened to them, watching their shadows streaming in through the small window. *What's her name?* I wondered. Elisabé? I'd never heard this name before.

"A baby girl," Mago said, breaking the silence. And it suddenly hit me: I was no longer the youngest. Some other girl I did not know had replaced me.

The next day all my cousins showed up to see what Tía María Félix had brought for them from El Otro Lado. We didn't see our cousins often, but now they were all there, having come as soon as they heard Tía María Félix had arrived. We watched as she gave our cousins presents—a shirt, a pair of shoes, a toy. We waited our turn, and when the suitcases were empty, Tía María Félix turned to us with a sad look on her face and said, "Your parents sent you something, but unfortunately I lost that suitcase at the airport."

"That's a lie," Mago said softly.

"What did you say?" Tía María Félix asked.

"Those toys that you gave away were for us!" Mago yelled. "I know it. I just know it." I wanted to believe that Mago was right. The

Papi and Elizabeth in El Otro Lado

thought that our parents had neglected to send us gifts really hurt. What if they had been too busy tending to their new baby to think about us?

"You insolent child," Abuela Evila said. "I'm going to teach you to respect your elders." She looked around for something to hit Mago with, and when she couldn't find anything, she took off her sandal. By the time she unbuckled the strap, the three of us were already bolting out the door and heading to the backyard to climb up the trees.

"She could have given us something from the stuff she brought. It's not our fault she lost the suitcase," Carlos said.

"No seas pendejo," Mago said, punching him on the arm. She jumped off the branch, climbed over the corral, and disappeared down the dirt road that led to Don Rubén's house.

The preparations for Élida's quinceañera were completed quickly because Tía María Félix had to return to her job in El Otro Lado. Tía Emperatriz spent hours making decorations for the hall, and Mago and I had to help. The times we refused, Tía María Félix spanked us under Élida's mocking gaze. We made garlands using paper flowers and straws. Abuela Evila spent all day making dresses on her sewing machine. Élida's dress was made in the U.S. because Tía María Félix said she had to have the best for her daughter. But when Élida tried it on, the dress wouldn't zip up. She was put on a crash diet, and Tía

María Félix bought her a girdle. Even then the dress wouldn't fit, so it had to be altered.

By the end of the week everyone had a new dress except for Mago and me. It wasn't until the day before the party that Abuela Evila was finally done with everyone else and was able to start on our dresses. She bought a few yards of a silver material, shiny like a brand-new peso. She made Mago's dress first. In the evening, she made my dress. By then she was so tired she made a mistake. The shiny part was on the inside. The dull part was on the outside.

"But, Abuelita, I can't wear the dress like that, it looks like I'm wearing it inside out! Please fix it."

"I'm too tired," she said as she stood up and stretched her back. "You're going to have to wear your dress just as it is."

The next day we watched while everyone fussed over Élida. A hairstylist came and did her hair up in tiny braids held together by pink and white bows. Then her mother, our grandmother, and Tía Emperatriz helped her put on the crinoline, the girdle, and the beautiful pink dress made with layers of satin and tulle. I hated seeing Tía Emperatriz fussing over Élida so much. Usually she didn't pay much attention to her, but she was always nice to us.

While everyone was at church for the ceremony, we spent the whole morning plucking chickens. Tía María Félix hired a woman to help with the cooking, and she showed up with huacales of live chickens clucking and shedding feathers that floated in the air like white flower petals.

She killed the chickens by grabbing them by the head and spinning them around like a matraca until the necks broke. She told Carlos to help her, but he was too gentle on the chicken, and when he put it down, the poor chicken had a broken neck but still ran around and around, its head hanging to one side.

The cook told him he was no good at killing chickens and made him help Mago and me pluck feathers. Our job was to hold the dead chickens by their feet and dunk them into boiling water to soften the skin. Then we put a chicken on our lap and pulled out the feathers. We complained about having to do it. "Why should we be helping out for Élida's party?" we wanted to know. I'd never plucked a chicken and couldn't pull hard enough for the big feathers to come out. The small downy feathers would stick to my fingers, and I couldn't scratch my legs when mosquitoes bit me. Carlos kept complaining that this was a girl's job, and why should he be plucking chickens?

"Because you aren't man enough to kill them," the cook said.

Mago loved plucking chickens. She threw herself into it with a frenzy, and she plucked, plucked away, plucking so hard sometimes the chicken skin would come off along with the feathers, and I wondered what the poor chickens had done to her to deserve such fury.

By the time we were finished, the whole patio was covered in feathers. Flies buzzed around, settling on the chicken guts spilled on the ground as the cook chopped the meat to pieces on the washing stone before boiling it.

Afterward, even though we took a bath and scrubbed ourselves hard with the apple-scented shampoo we liked, we still smelled like wet chicken feathers, and once in a while throughout the evening we pulled out feathers buried in our hair. I pretended I was turning into a dove. I imagined flying in search of my parents.

The quinceañera was held at a beautiful hall near la colonia called Las Acacias. Élida looked like a princess wearing her puffy pink dress and matching slippers. Mago spent the whole time sitting in a corner of the hall, feeling sorry for herself, her jealousy consuming her to the point where she couldn't even talk without saying a bad word in every sentence. "That stupid frog-eyes doesn't deserve this stupid party."

Carlos, who didn't get any new clothes, took advantage of the fact that everyone was too busy to see him sneaking into the kitchen to grab some sodas and a plate piled high with chicken mole and rice. I spent the whole time hiding from people, ashamed about wearing a dress that had the shiny part on the inside and the dull part on the outside. *It's a new dress,* I told myself again and again, *I should be happy because it's a new dress.* But I crawled under a table and cried about the dress, and about the fact that my parents had replaced me.

I only came out to see the waltz, which is the highlight of any quinceañera party. Élida danced with her chambelán, and when that waltz was over, she danced with her godparents. The last waltz was meant to be danced with her father, as is tradition, but since she had no father, she danced that waltz with my aunt's cousin, Tío Wenceslao, who was a butcher. He raised and killed pigs and had a restaurant in La Guadalupe where he sold pozole, chorizo, chicharrón, and everything else that comes from pigs. "Look at her, dancing with the pig man," Mago said. "How appropriate."

My eyes got watery as I watched Élida dance with the butcher whom we called uncle even though he wasn't an uncle but a distant cousin. But since the only male she could have danced with—our grandfather—was passed out on a chair from too much drinking, and the other male—my father—was away, what choice did Élida have but to dance with this man, this distant cousin of ours?

I prayed and hoped for Papi to come back soon. When I turned fifteen, I didn't want to dance El Vals de las Mariposas with anyone but him.

Carlos had been following Élida's American brother around to ask him to say things in English. When little Javier did, Carlos would burst out laughing so hard, he didn't care that everyone could see his crooked teeth. He thought Javier sounded so funny speaking English. "Do you really think it's English he's speaking, or is he just making up words?" Carlos asked us.

Mago said, "He could be speaking Chinese for all we know." Back then, I could never have imagined that one day, I would speak English better than I spoke my native tongue.

As Tía María Félix was packing her suitcases and getting ready to leave, Carlos went up to ask her what El Otro Lado looked like. He said he wanted to know more about the place where our parents lived. My aunt looked at him and didn't say anything, and we thought that maybe she wouldn't answer, but then she smiled and said:

"El Otro Lado is a beautiful place. Every street is paved with concrete. You don't see any dirt roads there. No mosquitoes sucking the blood out of you," she said, as she slapped a mosquito dead on her leg. "There's no trash in the streets like here in Mexico. Trucks there pick up the trash every week. And you know what the best thing is? The trees there are special—they grow money. They have dollar bills for leaves."

"Really?" Carlos asked.

"Really." She took some green bills out of her purse and showed them to us. "These are dollars," she said. We had never seen dollars, but they were as green as the leaves on the trees we liked to climb. "Now, picture a tree covered in dollar bills!"

She left in the afternoon with little Javier. She promised Élida that one day soon she would send for her, and although she did eventually keep her promise, Élida had to stay behind for now and watch a taxicab take her mother away. Abuela Evila put her arm around Élida and held her while she cried. Élida buried her face in Abuela Evila's arms. It was so strange to see her crying. The ever-present mocking gaze was gone. The Élida that made fun of us, that laughed at us, that called us Los Huerfanitos, had been replaced by a weeping, lonely, heartbroken girl.

Mago grabbed our hands and took us to the backyard to give Élida privacy. "Los quiero mucho," she said, pulling us close to her. Then I realized how lucky Mago, Carlos, and I were. We at least had each other. Élida was on her own.

We climbed up the ciruelo and talked about those special dollar trees in El Otro Lado. Even though we knew that what Tía María Félix had said couldn't be true, we fantasized about them anyway.

"If we had trees like that here, Papi wouldn't have had to leave," Mago said. "He could have bought the brick and cement and built us a house with his own hands."

"And Mami would still be with us," I said.

"And the new baby would have been born here, like us," Carlos said.

We talked about the day our parents would return. Carlos's fantasy was that Papi and Mami would fly to us in their own private helicopter. "I can just picture it," he said. "It would land here, in the middle of the yard." We giggled at the image of Papi emerging from the helicopter, his hair blowing in the wind, his face framed by aviator sunglasses as handsome as Pedro Infante, then Mami coming to stand next to him, looking just as glamorous. We pictured the whole colonia rushing over to see them come home. And we would be so proud.

6

Reyna, Carlos, and Mago

I T WAS 8:00 AM sharp, and Carlos, Mago, and I lined up with the rest of the students around the school's courtyard to salute the flag.

"Who are they?" I asked Mago. I tugged on her dress and asked again, as I pointed to a group of six students wearing white uniforms and not the navy blue ones everyone else was wearing.

"That's la escolta," Mago said.

"And what do they do?" I asked.

"Just wait and see, and stop bugging me with all your questions. You'll soon learn your way around here."

I couldn't help being excited to be there. It was my first day of first grade. I'd been waiting for this day for a long time. Abuela Evila didn't send me to kindergarten because she said it was too expensive to have all four grandkids in school, as if my parents hadn't been sending money to pay for uniforms, school supplies, and the monthly school tuition. Even though we went to public school, there was nothing free about it. She held me back a year, but finally I was there, and I would get my own books, like the ones Mago and Carlos brought home. Books full of beautiful poetry and fun stories with colorful pictures of clouds, stars, people, and animals like foxes and birds. I liked it when Mago read to me from her books, but I wanted to learn to read them myself.

Tía Emperatriz spent the weekend at my grandmother's sewing machine making our school uniforms. On Mondays, when we honored the flag, we had to wear a uniform in navy blue with a white sailor shirt. The uniform for the rest of the week was made of a checkered print in white and green. We also got new patent leather shoes and a few pairs of knee-high socks with the extra money our parents sent.

The color guard began its march around the courtyard. The student in the middle carried the flag on a pole, another shouted out directions: "¡A la izquierdaaa, ya! ¡A la derechaaa, ya!" The green, white, and red colors of the flag blurred in my mind like salsa.

"I'm going to be a flag bearer when I'm in sixth grade," Mago said as she stared longingly at the escolta members, looking great in their crisp, white uniforms. I believed Mago would be a flag bearer one day. She was really smart and always brought home good grades, mostly tens and nines, not like Carlos who, with fives and sixes, almost flunked first grade. How shameful.

"I'm going to be a flag bearer, too," I told Mago. She laughed and said that it was my first day of first grade, and sixth grade was ages away. And I said it didn't hurt to plan for the future.

As the flag passed by me, I stood straighter and maintained my hand firmly pressed again my chest in salutation as I sang the Mexican anthem as loud as I could.

Mexicanos, al grito de guerra
el acero aprestad y el bridón.

¡Y retiemble en sus centros la Tierra,
al sonoro rugir del cañón!

Mago told me that we should be proud to have been born in Iguala because it was in our city that the treaty which ended the Mexican War of Independence was drafted. It was in Iguala that the first Mexican flag was made by a man named José Magdaleno Ocampo on February 24, 1821. This is why Iguala is called "Cuna de la Bandera Nacional," Birthplace of the National Flag. The first time the national anthem was sung, it was sung in Iguala.

I looked at the flag with new eyes, a newfound admiration, and as I sang el himno nacional on my first day of school, I puffed up my chest, feeling especially proud about being born in Iguala de la Independencia!

My school was small. It was laid out in a square, with all the class-rooms facing the courtyard. It had two bathrooms, one for boys and one for girls, but no running water. We had to fill up a bucket from the water tank inside and dump it in the toilet. But still, at least there was a toilet, although it was hard for me to get used to it after having to squat on the ground my whole life.

When the morning activities were over, we lined up, and our teachers led us into our classrooms. We took our seats and after a brief introduction, el maestro started the lesson by teaching us the alphabet. He said we should have learned it in kindergarten, but half the students in the class hadn't gone to kindergarten. We repeated after him, and I felt proud that I knew my letters already because Mago had taught them to me. When he told us to write our names down, I didn't have to look at the board to spell my name: *R-E-Y-N*—I felt a stinging on my hand, and it took me a second to realize that el maestro had hit me with his ruler.

"What are you doing?" el maestro asked. He held his ruler in his right hand and tapped it over and over on the palm of his left hand.

"I'm writing my name," I told him. "See?" I raised my brand-new notebook to show him.

"You are not to write with that hand," he said to me. He took the pencil from my left hand and made me grab it with my right. "If I see you using your left hand, I will have to hit you again, ¿entiendes?"

My eyes welled up with tears because everyone was looking at me. I took a deep breath and nodded. He walked away, and I looked down at my notebook. I wrote and erased, wrote and erased, and no matter how hard I tried, the letters didn't come out right. It was like trying to write with my feet.

Abuela Evila and Élida always teased me for being left-handed. My mother's father, Abuelito Gertrudis, had also been left-handed. Because he died a week before I was born, Mami said he had given this gift to me. And that is how I had always seen it, as a gift, until we came to Abuela Evila's house. She didn't agree. She said that the left hand was the hand of the devil and I was evil for using it. Sometimes during meals, she would hit my hand with a wooden spoon and tell me to eat with my right hand.

"Don't you know that the right side is the side of God?" she asked. "The left side is the side of evil. You don't want to be evil, do you?" Since I didn't want anything to do with the devil, I would pick up my spoon with my right hand and try to eat with it. But I could only manage a few bites before my spoon found its way back to my left hand.

Measles crippled my grandmother's left arm when the open sores got so infected they were crawling with maggots, but she would tell me that if I kept using my left hand it would shrivel up, just like hers. Even though it was a disease that crippled her, I lived with the constant fear of waking up one day with a shriveled left hand. It was ironic that it was Abuela Evila who ended up shriveling when osteoporosis set in several years later. And it would be Tía Emperatriz who had to change her diapers, who continued to tend to her because nobody else would.

"Don't listen to her, Nena," Mago would sometimes tell me. "There's nothing wrong with being left-handed." But just as Mago couldn't ignore Élida's taunts about her scars, I couldn't ignore Abuela Evila's or my teacher's. He didn't understand that my pencil obeyed my left hand, but not the right one. I tried once again to write my name, but the letters came out all twisted and ugly. When Mago taught me to write my name, she wrote it with beautiful letters and made the tail of the Y long and curly. It looked so pretty it made me finally start liking my name. I used to hate my name because some-times when Mami and I were on our way to el mercado, men would whistle at Mami from across the street and yell "¡Mi reina!"—my queen—and the way they said "mi reina" made me want to throw a rock at them and make them bleed. Then I would ask Mami why she gave me a name that sounds so foul in a man's mouth. I asked why she couldn't have just named me Regina, as Abuela Evila had wanted. I wished she had chosen another time to rebel against my grandmother's bossy ways. "Reyna is a very nice name," Mami would say. "Those men are just not saying it the right way. And it wasn't your grandmother's place to name you. You aren't her daughter!"

I looked at my name on the notebook. I had never hated it as much as I did at that moment. And I didn't stop hating my name until many years later, when I realized that it wasn't a name to be ashamed of, but one to live up to.

I met Mago and Carlos during recess by the jacaranda tree in the courtyard. By the entrance of the school, women were selling food. They had brought baskets filled with enchiladas, taquitos, and potato picaditas. The smell of the chile guajillo sauce, fresh cheese, and onion wafted toward us, and I asked my brother and sister why we weren't getting in line to buy food.

Mago laughed.

"Our grandmother never gives us money," Carlos said. "You better get used to it."

We watched the women put the food on paper plates and hand it to the students who did bring lunch money. We weren't the only ones drooling over the enchiladas. At least half of the children in the school were leaning against classroom walls, grabbing their empty bellies while looking at the food stands.

For the second time that day, I felt my eyes stinging with tears. "I hate school," I said.

"Why, because you're hungry?" Carlos asked. "I like it. At least it gets us out of our grandmother's house. Imagine if we had to be there all day long?"

"I've been there all day long all this time," I said. "Until today."

"Then you should be happy to be here," Mago said, but she didn't look at me. She was looking at a boy in my class who was heading toward us eating a mango on a stick.

"The teacher hit me because I was writing with my left hand," I said. "I think I'd rather stay home and clean Abuela Evila's house from top to bottom than to go to school."

"So you would rather stay home with our grandmother?" Mago asked. "I don't believe it."

I looked at the glass containers of agua fresca at the food stands: agua de melón, sandía, piña. From here, I could see the large cubes of ice swimming inside the glass containers. My throat was so dry I imagined that this was how the earth felt after months and months of waiting for rain. Mami used to say that the clouds go down under the mountains to drink water from the rivers, and once they're full they come up to the sky, ready to bathe the earth. Sometimes the clouds take too long to drink water and that's when the grass withers, the flowers die, the water in the canal narrows to a trickle and almost disappears. But sometimes the clouds drink too much water, and that's when the floods happen. Days and days of never-ending rains that turn the gentle river waters into aguas broncas, tearing down trees and dragging everything in their path, then spilling over the banks and bursting into people's homes.

Mago gasped, and I turned to see what she was looking at. The boy in my class had dropped his mango on the ground. He began to reach for it, but then stood up and walked away from it looking really sad. I looked at Mago and knew what she was thinking.

Every time we went out to run errands, she was always looking around to see if she could find a half-eaten fruit or a lollipop some unlucky kid had dropped. Sometimes she got lucky. Sometimes she didn't.

Mago looked at the mango, and I knew she couldn't resist picking it up. "Go get it," she told Carlos as she pointed to the mango.

"You go," Carlos said.

"Some of my classmates are over there. They'll see me. Ándale, you get it, Nena."

"No," I said. Mago looked at me, and I knew that sooner or later she would make me do it. "Mago, you shouldn't eat things from the ground. They're bad. They've been kissed by the devil," I said.

Mago waved my words away. "Those are just tales Abuela Evila likes to scare us with," she said. Abuela Evila used to say that when food falls to the ground, the devil, who lives right below us, kisses it and taints it with evil. "Look, I don't know if the devil exists or not, and I don't care. I'm hungry. So go get it!"

Mago pushed me toward the mango, but I shook my head. Tales or no tales, I wasn't going to risk it. But my mouth watered at the thought of sinking my teeth into the mango's crunchy flesh.

The bell rang, and the kids rushed back to their classrooms. Mago and Carlos waved and disappeared from sight. I stood there under the jacaranda tree, and my feet didn't want to move. I didn't want to go back to the classroom. I didn't want to go back and struggle to hold my pencil with my useless right hand. I didn't want to see el maestro looking at me and making me feel ashamed, making me feel as if I were evil. I didn't want him to hit me again and have my classmates jeer and laugh. But if I didn't go back, I knew I wouldn't learn to read and write. How could I ever write a letter to my parents and ask them to please, please, come back?

As I made my way to the classroom, I noticed the mango again. It lay on its side, its flesh yellow like the feathers of a canary. It was covered with red chili powder and dirt. *And what if Mago is right?* I asked myself. *What if the devil doesn't exist? If he doesn't exist, that means the left side isn't the side of the devil. And that would mean I am not evil for being left-handed.*

I looked around, and the courtyard was now empty. I bent down and picked up the mango, flicked the dirt off, and sank my teeth into it. The chili powder burned my tongue. The burning sensation made me feel warm all over. I stood there waiting for something to happen. I waited to see if the devil was going to burst out of the earth on his horse and drag me to hell with him. The jacaranda waved in the breeze, looking beautiful with its bright purple flowers. From above the brick fence, I could see the colorful papel picado hanging in rows over the cobblestone street. The church bells started ringing, and I turned to look at the two towers at the top of the hill, the metal cross glistening under the bright noon sun.

I returned to class, and el maestro looked disapprovingly at me. I sat at my desk and looked at my pencil. From the corner of my eye, I saw el maestro making his way toward me, his ruler going up and down, up and down. I reached for my pencil and clutched it tightly in my left hand.

7

Tía Emperatriz and Mago

M AGO AND ÉLIDA were in the habit of standing by the gate every afternoon to wait for el cartero, the mail carrier who came by on his bicycle. If he had mail for you, he would ring his little bell, a soft tinkling sound that could be the most beautiful sound in the world if only the mail were for you.

Instead, the sound of the bell was a little needle that pricked my heart because he never rang the bell for us. Always, the tinkling was for Élida or the neighbors.

One day, we watched him riding clumsily down the dirt road because he wasn't as good a rider as the baker. He had a box tied to the rack on the back of his bike, and as he neared the house, the tinkling of the bell began. But my heart was already breaking because I knew the sound wasn't for me. Élida pushed us out of the way and smiled at el cartero, her arms ready to receive the box. Christmas was in two days. Even though in Mexico children don't get presents on Christmas but rather on January 6, the Day of the Three Wise Men, Élida said her mother had sent her a Christmas present because that is what they do in El Otro Lado, and her mother knew all about American culture.

But the box was not for Élida! El cartero handed Mago the box and then was off to the next house.

"He made a mistake, that stupid man," Élida said as she tried to yank the box from Mago.

"There's no mistake," Mago said. Carlos and I held on to the box, too, in case Élida tried to snatch it away. When she saw Mago's name on the box, Élida stomped away and went into the house, calling out for Abuela Evila.

We quickly opened the box to see what was inside. Papi and Mami had sent Mago and me two identical dresses. The top was white and the bottom was the color of purple jacaranda flowers. The collar was trimmed with lace and in the center of it was a beautiful silk orchid. We also got shiny patent leather shoes. Carlos got a pair of jeans and a shirt.

We rushed to my grandfather's room to put on our pretty clothes. But it was as if our parents had not realized that while they'd been gone we had grown, as if somehow in El Otro Lado time stood still and over there I hadn't yet turned six, Mago ten, and Carlos almost nine. The shoes they sent were a size too small, and so were the dresses. The sleeves of Carlos's shirt were two inches above his wrists. The skirt of my dress didn't even graze my knees.

"What do we do now?" Carlos asked, unbuttoning his new shirt. "Maybe they should have sent us some toys."

Mago hit him on the head.

"Ouch, what did you do that for?" Carlos asked, massaging his head.

Mago sat down on the bed. "I don't know," she said. She looked down at the dirt floor, and I wondered what she was thinking. Part of me was desperate to wear those shoes. They were new. They had been sent to us by our parents. They were from El Otro Lado! But then I thought about my parents, and the fact that they didn't even know what size shoe I wore made me want to throw them in the trash.

If they don't even know something as basic as the size of our shoes and clothes, what else don't they know about us? And what don't we know about them?

The question was there, but neither Carlos, Mago, nor I was courageous enough to ponder on it for long. As the oldest, it was clearer to Mago, more than to Carlos and me, that the distance between us and our parents was destroying our relationship more than any of us could have imagined. And the consequences would be great. But back then, as our little mother, Mago's job was to take care of us and to shelter us from the reality that only she could fully grasp. I had her as a buffer, but she had no one but herself.

"Come on, Nena, let's wash our feet," she said. So we washed away the dirt caked on our feet and we put on the beautiful shiny shoes. "Curl your toes inward," Mago said to me. I curled my toes and that way the shoes didn't hurt as much.

Mago, Carlos, and I held hands and we started spinning around in a circle, turning and turning, blending into a blur of purple, pink, white, and blue. Then, without letting go, we ran out of the house, out into the street, laughing and crying at the same time.

And as we ran past Don Bartolo's store, then cut across the vacant lot, then headed to the church, past the tortilla mill, and Don Rubén's little house, everyone stared at our beautiful new clothes, and not once did anyone say, "Poor little orphans." Our neighbors admired our pretty clothes and shoes from afar, not knowing that by the time we got home our feet would be covered with blisters.

8

The Man Behind the Glass

Mᴀ ꜰᴀᴛʜᴇʀ ʜᴀᴅ told us about his dream house in the letters he'd sent to my mother from El Otro Lado. The house was made of brick with a shiny concrete floor and tall wide windows to let in the sunlight. The walls were painted the color of Mami's blue eye shadow, and it had three rooms.

Papi's dream house had a television, a stereo, a refrigerator, and a stove. It was a house with electricity, gas, and running water, and maybe even an indoor bathroom, one with a shower that made you feel as if you were standing in the rain on a sticky, hot summer day. That was the house that my father dreamed of.

Back then, I didn't know that Guerrero was the Mexican state with the most people emigrating due to the scarcity of jobs. I hadn't known that a year before he left, my father had already been leaving home to find construction work in Acapulco, Mexico City, even as far as Mazatlán, Sinaloa, until eventually making his way farther north.

At first, he had lived in California's Central Valley and had slept in an abandoned car while working in the fields harvesting crops, just as he had done in his youth. Eventually he left to try his luck in Los Angeles, where he was fortunate enough to find himself a stable job as a maintenance worker at a retirement home.

Four years after my father left for the United States, and two years after my mother left, the construction of our house finally began. Back then, I interpreted this to mean one thing—Papi and Mami would soon be back!

Abuela Evila gave my father a piece of her property, which meant that our house was going to be built right next to hers. It wasn't something Mago, Carlos, and I were happy about. Who wanted to live next to Abuela Evila? Not us. But because it would cut down on the final costs, it was the only option my parents had. Besides, as he would later tell me, my father had helped his parents pay for the mortgage on their property with the wages he had earned since he was nine years old. Really, it was only fair for him to get a piece of that land. If only he had realized he was making a mistake, building a house on a property that was not under his name.

Workers came early one morning to tear down the outhouse and the shack in which I was born. Both the shack and the outhouse were made of bamboo sticks, so it didn't take long to get rid of them. I stood there watching, sad that my little shack was being destroyed. Mago put an arm around me and said, "Just think about what is going to be built right there on that spot."

The workers returned the next day and the day after and the day after and began to lay the foundation, and after that, the walls. As soon as school let out, Mago, Carlos, and I would run down the hill to help out as much as we could. Abuelo Augurio handed each of us a bucket, and we carried bucketfuls of gravel and mortar. Carlos worked especially hard. He liked working side by side with Abuelo Augurio. He wanted our grandfather to be proud of him for being quick and steady, not like us girls who were too slow and clumsy with the bricks and the buckets of mortar. But Abuelo Augurio didn't pay much attention to Carlos.

We scraped our fingers carrying bricks. At night we couldn't sleep from being so sore, but every day we put all of our energy into building our house, and when our fingers hurt too much, or our knees wanted to buckle under the weight of the buckets of wet mortar we carried to the bricklayers, we would tell ourselves that the faster we worked, the faster we would have a family again. That thought gave us strength.

But it wasn't long before the workers stopped coming. By the time February came to an end, and Carlos turned nine, the workers were nowhere in sight. Abuela Evila said our parents had no more money, so the house had to wait. We stood by the door every morning before going to school, hoping to see the truck that brought the construction workers bumping and jerking its way down the dirt road. Then we headed to school, where all we did was look out the window and sigh the hours away, leaning our sorrow on our elbows.

By the end of the week, Mago stopped looking down the dirt road. She pushed Carlos and me up the hill and told us that it didn't matter anyway. She said that no matter how many bricks and buckets of mortar we helped carry to the bricklayers, the house would never be done because it was just a foolish dream, just as silly as our dream of having a real family again.

"It will get finished!" Carlos said. "They will come back!" He took off running up the hill, and by the time we got to the gate of our school, he was nowhere in sight.

When we got back from school, I went inside my grandfather's room to look at the Man Behind the Glass. "How much longer?" I asked him. "How much longer will you be gone?" As always, there was no answer.

9

Tía Emperatriz

SCORPIONS HAD ALWAYS been a part of our lives. We were taught by Mami to check our shoes before putting them on in the morning and to search our bedcovers at night to make sure there were no scorpions in the folds. We had to shake our clothes before putting them on. We couldn't lean against walls. We couldn't reach into the wardrobe or drawers without fear of being stung by a scorpion hiding in the dark.

But at night, while you're sleeping, there's nothing you can do to keep a scorpion from crawling up onto the bed or, as in Abuelita Chinta's case when she died in 2002, you can't keep a scorpion from falling from the ceiling and stinging you.

So the night I woke up screaming for Mami, I recognized the pain right away from the two previous times I'd gotten stung. My right butt cheek burned as if I'd been branded by a red hot poker like the cows at the dairy farm down the road from my grandmother's house.

"Mami! Mami!" I yelled.

"Nena, what's wrong?" Mago asked.

"Scorpion," I said.

Mago ran out of the room to get help. Carlos jumped out of bed and stayed by my side but didn't touch me, as if he were afraid the scorpion would sting him, too. My grandfather kept on snoring and didn't wake up to help.

"Mami!" I cried out again. My mother didn't come to my side. Instead, it was my aunt who came running into the room, asking me where it hurt.

The scorpion was hidden on the collar of my dress, and when Tía Emperatriz pulled it off, I felt another sting on my neck. The pain spread up, pulsing in waves from my neck to my shoulders and up to my face.

"Mago, go slice an onion and get the rubbing alcohol!" Tía Emperatriz said. Mago ran to the kitchen while my aunt and Carlos hunted for the scorpion because the locals believed that if you killed the scorpion that stung you, its venom wouldn't be as powerful. But they couldn't find it.

"What's all the fuss about?" Abuela Evila said as she stood by the door. When Tía Emperatriz told her about the scorpion, Abuelita Evila glanced around the room. "There it is," she said, pointing to the straw-colored scorpion crawling high up on the wall, barely visible in the weak light from the bare bulb hanging above us. Everyone gasped as it squeezed its flat body through a crevice between the adobe bricks and disappeared from sight.

Tía Emperatriz rubbed alcohol over the stung areas and then tied the onion slices on them with strips of cloth. Tears bathed my face, and I felt as if a thousand hot needles were piercing my body. My face, my hands, and my feet were becoming numb. She sent Mago back to the kitchen for an egg, which she then forced me to swallow. It felt like a big ball of mucus sliding down my throat. Tía Emperatriz said the raw egg would dilute the venom. Back then I didn't know any better than to believe this, so I made the knot in my throat loosen so the egg could slide down.

"We need to take her to the doctor," Mago said as she sat next to me and squeezed my hand.

"There's no money for that," Abuela Evila responded.

"The venom might not do much harm, now that she's eaten the raw egg," Tía Emperatriz said. "Besides, look at you, Mago, when you've been stung, it's as if nothing happened."

"But that's because my blood is hot and strong," Mago said proudly. "And I'm a Scorpio, so scorpions don't do anything to me. But please, Tía, take Reyna to the doctor."

"There's no money," Abuela Evila said again.

"I'll keep an eye on her tonight," Tía Emperatriz said. "If she's still not well in the morning, I'll take her in. ¿Está bien?" Mago nodded. "Now, go back to bed, you two." Tía Emperatriz picked me up and took me back to the living room where she slept on a bed tucked in a corner of the room. For privacy, she'd hung a curtain from the rafters. She lay down next to me, and I eventually fell asleep in her arms.

In the morning, the whole room spun around me. I couldn't get up, and every time I tried to, I felt like vomiting. I wondered if this was how my grandfather felt when he was drunk. Abuelo Augurio liked to drink mescal, which is made from the heart of the maguey plant. When he would come home from the fields, he would sit outside on the stone steps taking sips out of his flask while watching the people go by on horses and on foot. He would call out to his friends and ask if they wanted a drink. When the smell of chorizo and boiling beans reached his nose, he would take one more sip of the mescal and make his way to the kitchen, holding on to the wall so that he wouldn't lose his balance.

That morning, I was moving just like my grandfather, zigzagging two steps one way, one step the other way.

Tía Emperatriz missed work to look after me. I felt as if I had a guitar inside my head. She held me tight by the waist and walked me to the outhouse, but with every step I took the guitar strummed and strummed, the vibrations sending waves of pain that bounced inside my brain.

"She needs to see the doctor, Amá," Tía Emperatriz said to Abuela

Evila. "She's burning up with fever. Let's not take any chances. If anything happens to her, Natalio—"

"He and Juana chose to leave their children behind," Abuela Evila said as she cleaned the beans. "I didn't ask for this. Look at me. I'm seventy-one years old. Do I look like I need to be taking care of three young children on top of the one I'm already looking after?"

"They left so that they could build themselves a house, Amá," Tía Emperatriz said.

"They won't come back. Trust me." Abuela Evila took her money bag out of her brassiere. "Look at María Félix. It's been nine years, and every time Élida asks her when she's finally coming back, she gives her excuses as to why she can't yet. But that's all they are. Excuses. And then it's me who has to dry the tears, who has to find ways to lessen the pain."

While my aunt and I waited by the dirt road for a taxi, I couldn't stop thinking about my grandmother's conviction that my parents were not coming back. Despite my dizziness and shivers, I was excited about the taxi ride, since I rarely got to ride in a car, or go anywhere outside of La Guadalupe. On the way to the doctor, I asked Tía Emperatriz if she thought Abuela Evila was right. "Do you think my parents won't come back?"

"I don't know, Reyna," Tía Emperatriz said. "From what I've heard, El Otro Lado is a very beautiful place. But here . . ." She waved her hand for me to look outside the cab window. I know now what she had wanted me to see back then: the banks of the canal lined with trash and debris floating in the water, the crumbling adobe houses, the shacks made of sticks, the children with worm-pregnant bellies running around with bare feet, the piles of drying horse dung littering the dirt road, the flea-bitten stray dogs lying under the shade of trees, flies hovering above them. But what I saw back then I saw through the eyes of a child—a child who had never been anywhere, a child who was still innocent enough to see past the things later in life she could not. What I saw were the velvety mountains around us, the clear blue sky, the beautiful jacaranda trees covered in purple flowers, bougainvilleas crawling up fences, their dried magenta petals whirling in the wind. I saw the cobble-stone street leading up to the beautiful La Guadalupe church, papel picado of all colors waving above the street.

"Don't you think there's beauty here, too?" I asked Tía Empera-triz. She looked out the window and didn't answer. As the cab made its way to the heart of the city, I continued to think that there was beauty everywhere around us. But when the cab stopped in front of el zócalo, where I saw mothers and fathers strolling about holding hands with their children, I realized that it didn't matter what I thought of Iguala.

Without my parents here, it was a place of broken beauty.

Though I felt better after the shot, Tía Emperatriz said I should sleep with her that night. I lay on her bed and watched her towel-dry her hair. She always bathed in the evenings because she said it helped her sleep better. She climbed into bed and turned off the light. It felt so strange to have a woman's body next to mine. In the two years my mother had been gone, I'd forgotten what it felt like to sleep with her.

I listened to my aunt's soft breathing. I wished I could close my eyes and snuggle next to her. I wished I could bury my face in her hair that smelled of roses. But instead, I moved to the other side of the bed, as far away as possible. I put my finger in my belly button and thought of my mother.

Mago would sometimes say, "I don't see Tía as my mother. She's more like an older sister to me." And yet, when we walked through the gates of the school for our parent-teacher conferences, Mago would put her arm through Tía Emperatriz's and look as proud as could be. She insisted Tía Emperatriz pick up *her* report card first. When we entered her classroom, Mago's classmates and teacher looked at Tía Emperatriz with admiration. She looked so elegant in her red high heels, pretty blue dress, and stylish haircut.

"Is that your mother?" one of the students asked, because for a moment everyone seemed to have forgotten that our mother was very far away.

"She's our aunt," I quickly said.

Mago glared at me.

Just because she takes care of us when we're sick, makes us pretty dresses once in a while, combs our hair up in ponytails without pulling on it, wants to know what we learned in school, notices when our underwear is full of holes and needs to be replaced, sees the dirt behind our ears and cares enough to make us bathe, that doesn't mean she could take Mami's place, I told Mago afterward.

"I said she's like an older sister to me, okay?" Mago yelled.

And yet she was not happy when two months earlier we'd learned of Tía Emperatriz's secret: she had a boyfriend. We were perched in the guamúchil tree when a taxicab pulled over and stopped right underneath us. As they kissed, Carlos and I covered our mouths and tried not to giggle, but Mago was shocked. They never saw us up there. We were very quiet, and they were too busy kissing to pay attention. Tía Emperatriz didn't want Abuela Evila to know she had a boyfriend. She started wearing skirts a little above her knee, but when she came home she lowered them so that Abuela Evila wouldn't see. Up from the tree, we could see her wipe the makeup off her face before coming into the house.

Abuela Evila never approved of any of my aunt's suitors, so my aunt was already considered a spinster. She was going into her thirties, and women there start getting married as soon as they become señoritas, even to this day.

"You should be happy for her," I told Mago as we watched Tía Emperatriz sneak out of the house to see her boyfriend.

"If she leaves, then what's going to happen to us?" Mago said.

"Mami and Papi are coming back soon," I said.

"Wake up, Reyna. Look over there, do you see that?"

I turned to look at Papi's dream house. A foundation, one unfinished wall, exposed rebar. The house looked as fragile as the skeleton of the dead sparrow Mago and I once found in the vacant lot, which Mago said had been spit out by a snake.

"They aren't coming back until that house is finished," Mago said. "It's taken Papi four years to build a foundation and half a wall. How long do you think it will take him to build the rest?"

On Monday I returned to school. It was Mother's Day, my third Mother's Day without Mami. The students in all grade levels were doing arts and crafts projects. In my class we made a bouquet of tulips using egg cartons, which we cut out and shaped before painting them red, yellow, or pink.

El maestro gave us pink paper so that we could make a card for our mothers. It was hard for me to write YO AMO A MI MAMÁ, as we were told to do. I folded the paper in half and then snuck it into my book.

I thought of the day I learned to spell "Mamá." We were doing phonics, and el maestro wrote on the board MI MAMÁ ME MIMA. MI MAMÁ ME AMA. We had to repeat after him as he pointed to the words. "Mi mamá me mima. Mi mamá me ama." *My mama spoils me. My mama loves me.* My throat began to close up, and I wiped the moisture from my eyes. When he said to write the sentences ten times I couldn't stop my hand from shaking as I wrote the words down. And then I started to rearrange the words so that they formed a question: ¿ME AMA MI MAMÁ? *Does my mama love me?*

If so, why is she so far away?

As Mago, Carlos, and I walked home after school, we talked about the projects we had made. Mago's class had made carnations with red yarn. Carlos's class made posters using finger paints. He made a big heart that read "Te Quiero Mucho," but he hadn't written the name of the person he loved, either.

"Let's give them to Tía Empera," Carlos said. "Mami isn't here anyway. She won't find out about it."

"We could give them to Abuelita Chinta, next time she comes," I said.

"Tía Empera is nice to us," Mago said.

"And *today* is Mother's Day. Who knows when Abuelita Chinta is going to come," Carlos said.

"We could save them for Mami," I insisted. "We'll give them to her when she returns."

In the evening, Tía Emperatriz came home with a bouquet of flowers for Abuela Evila. She also brought rotisserie chicken for dinner.

It wasn't until after her bath that Mago said we needed to decide what we wanted to do. When we couldn't agree on anything, Mago stood up and said, "I'm going to give her my carnations. Do whatever you want."

I glanced at the photo of Papi, wishing for the thousandth time that we had a photo of Mami, too. I was forgetting what she looked like, smelled like, felt like. I couldn't remember the sound of her voice, the way she laughed. Every time I closed my eyes to remember, I would hear Tía Emperatriz's laughter. If I took a breath, I would inhale the fragrance of Tía Emperatriz's shampoo that smelled of roses.

I went to the living room where my aunt was drying her hair. "Tía, we want to give you this," Mago said as she shyly handed the bouquet of yarn carnations to her.

"And this," Carlos said, handing her the poster that read "Te Quiero Mucho." I stood back. I held on to my bouquet of tulips and hid behind Mago.

"Oh, my goodness," Tía Emperatriz said. "What a sweet surprise!" She took Mago's and Carlos's presents. I clutched Mago's dress so hard that she yanked it away. She pushed me toward Tía Emperatriz.

It was so difficult for me to completely give myself over to my feelings for Tía Emperatriz. As much as I loved her, there were two possibilities hovering in the horizon that would separate me from her. Either my parents would return soon or she would marry and leave to have children of her own. Either way, I would lose her. After having already lost both my parents, how could I bear to get attached to someone I would lose as well?

But she's here now, I had told myself that evening, and so I walked to her and offered her my gift.

"Here, Tía," I said. "I made this." I couldn't bring myself to say "for you" because it wasn't true.

"Thank you so much for this, niños," Tía Emperatriz said, giving us each a hug. As we went back to our room, I looked back at Tía Emperatriz, who was putting our art projects on her nightstand. I ran back to give her one more hug.

"Thank you, Tía," I said, and I went back to my room and dreamed of roses.

10

Elizabeth and Mami,
recently arrived in Mexico

"¡Apúrate!" Mago said as she stopped to wait for me. I walked faster to catch up with her and Carlos, being careful not to spill any more water from the buckets I carried in each hand, but they were already half empty.

"Why do we need to carry our own water from the well?" I asked again for the hundredth time. "Why can't we use what's in the water tank?"

"Because our grandmother is a bitter old woman," Mago said. "And let's not complain today, or she won't let us go with our aunt."

That afternoon, Tía Emperatriz was going to take us to the movie theater to watch *La Niña de la Mochila Azul,* starring Pedrito Fernández, who was really cute, and both Mago and I had a big crush on him. School had ended the previous week, and we got really good grades, so the movie was Tía Emperatriz's present to us. This was my first time going to the movie theater, and I couldn't wait.

When we finally made it home from the well, I only had a little water left in my buckets, my ankles were raw from being scraped by the buckets, and my palms were red and blistered.

But I thought about Pedrito Fernández, and I could already hear him singing my favorite song: *La de la mochila azul. La de ojitos dormilones* . . . I was humming this song as we walked through the gate. I stopped when I saw a woman standing in the patio holding a little girl in her arms. The woman was wearing a burgundy dress and golden high-heeled sandals that glittered in the sun. I couldn't see her face very well because she had big dark sunglasses on. Her hair was permed and dyed red. She looked like a TV star. The little girl in her arms was dressed in pink ruffles and lace. She was a chubby baby, her cheeks so puffy it seemed as if her mouth were stuffed with cotton candy. *This little girl must have a lot of good food to eat, wherever she lives,* I thought. I'd never seen such a healthy-looking baby before.

"Well, aren't you going to say hello to your mother?" the woman asked with a smile.

We stayed by the gate, holding our buckets.

"Don't just stand there," Abuela Evila said. "Go get your things ready."

Tía Emperatriz walked over to us, took my buckets, and whispered, "Go give your mother a hug."

We still didn't move from the gate. I clutched Mago's dress and hid behind her. Mami didn't look like the mother I had tried so hard not to forget during those two and a half years.

"Look at you kids, you've grown so much!" she said. When she took off her sunglasses and I saw those eyes that were also Abuelita Chinta's eyes, I could no longer deny that she was my mother. Carlos ran to hug her. I waited for Mago, to see what she was going to do so that I could do the same. But she just stood there clutching the handles of her buckets. Élida left my grandmother's side and went into the house without another glance.

"Where's Papi?" Mago said. "Is he back, too?"

"No, he's not back. Now go and get your things so that we can leave," Mami said.

"We're leaving right now?" I asked. I looked at Tía Emperatriz.

"Of course," Mami said. "Don't tell me you want to stay here?"

When we didn't say anything, Tía Emperatriz said, "We'll go another day, niños. Do as your mother says."

"I'll get our stuff," Mago said. She put a hand on my shoulder and then went inside the house while Carlos and I stayed with Mami.

"I'm nine now," Carlos said. I was three months away from turning seven, but I didn't want to tell her my age because I kept staring at the little sister we had never met before. *She really does exist. She really is real.*

"Ven acá, Reyna," Mami said. I went to her, and I let her hug me with one arm. I hesitantly wrapped my arms around her waist, feeling as if this were a dream and she would disappear any minute. I looked at the hand she had around me and saw the silvery scars that ran the length of her index, middle, and ring fingers. It took me a second to remember that when she met Papi, and up until she was pregnant with Carlos, she'd had a job at a tortilla mill and one time her hand had gotten caught in the grinder as she was stuffing the dough into it. She had almost lost her fingers. That was why she switched to selling Avon. I hugged Mami tighter, as many more things I had forgotten about her returned to me.

The little girl pulled my hair, and I cried out.

"Betty, no!" Mami said.

I moved out of the little girl's reach and massaged my scalp. Mago returned with our things stuffed into two pillowcases, and we said our goodbyes. We didn't hug our grandmother. But we thanked her for letting us stay at her home and for taking care of us.

"Well, at least there'll be three fewer mouths to feed," she said, as if the food she had given us those two years and a half had come out of her own pocket, and not from my parents' hard work.

"Ay, Amá, you'll never change, will you?" Tía Emperatriz said. She opened her arms, and we ran to her and hugged her.

"Come on, it's getting late and my mother is waiting for us," Mami said.

"Bye, Tía," Mago said to our aunt.

I looked at Tía Emperatriz. There were many things I would have liked to say to her, but when I glanced at my mother, I knew it wouldn't be a good idea to say anything but thank you. Mami narrowed her eyes as she looked at me, and I wondered if she knew I had betrayed her while she was away.

"Come back and visit," Tía Emperatriz said as she walked us out to the gate.

Élida stayed in Abuela Evila's room and didn't come out to say goodbye.

"Wait! The photo," I said as we were leaving. I ran back into the house. Even though I had memorized every part of his face, I couldn't leave the Man Behind the Glass.

Mami hailed a cab, and the three of us sat in the back. Mami and her little girl took the front. We had so many questions to ask her but didn't because the taxi driver started a conversation with Mami.

"You're coming from El Otro Lado, aren't you?" he asked.

To this day I still don't know how it is that people always seem to know when someone has just gotten back from the United States. Do they smell differently? Speak differently? Or is it their clothes?

Mami laughed and told him yes. "I just got back last night," she said.

"Did you like it? Is it as nice as people say?" the taxi driver asked.

"Oh, yes. It is beautiful," Mami said. "A truly beautiful place."

"So why did you come back? I mean, with our economy in the toilet, everyone is leaving for El Otro Lado, not the other way around."

Her little girl started to cry, and Mami didn't answer.

Despite our sadness at leaving Tía Emperatriz and missing out on the movie, we were thrilled that our mother had returned. We kept waiting for her to say that she had missed us, but she'd hardly said a word to us. We got off at the main road and walked the rest of the way to Abuelita Chinta's house in single file behind Mami. The air smelled of smoke as trash piles burned on either side of the train tracks. Abuelita Chinta's house was the only one on the block made of bamboo sticks. It was covered with cardboard soaked in tar on the outside, and the roof was made of corrugated metal. The neighbors' houses were made of brick and cement. The prettiest house belonged to Doña Caro. Her husband, Don Lino, was a welder. He made good money and his family had a refrigerator and running water. Abuelita Chinta didn't have those things, but she had a stove and electricity. She bought water from the next-door neighbor and carried it home in a bucket.

Sixty feet from Abuelita Chinta's shack, to the west, was a canal that sometimes overflowed during the rainy season. Perpendicular to the canal were the train tracks which served the El Río Balsas Railway up until the 1990s, when the government privatized the railroads and the train from Iguala was suspended. But back then, the trains would come by carrying iron ore, grain, sugar, salt, fuel, cement, fertilizers, and passengers. The bamboo sticks of my grandmother's shack rattled like maracas when the train passed by. It was especially scary at night because everything was quiet, except for the barking of the neighborhood dogs, when all of a sudden the train would come rushing by with its whistles and roaring engines.

Doña Caro was sitting outside her house combing her long, gray hair. When she saw my mother, she said, "Juana, you're back." I wanted to scream that yes, Mami was back, and we would no longer be the little orphans!

How is Papi?

Tell us about the U.S.

What did you do while you were there? Is it true what people say?

Did you miss us?

Does Papi miss us?

Why didn't he come back with you?

"Why don't you kids go outside to play with the new neighbors?" Mami said without answering our questions. She said she had something to tell us, but that now was not the time. Only Carlos listened to her and went in search of kids to play with. Mami handed Mago her little girl and told her to take care of her while she and Abuelita Chinta prepared dinner.

Mago refused to take the baby.

"She's your sister," Mami said.

"She's your daughter," Mago said, and ran out of the house.

"Reyna, you take care of her."

"But—"

She put her little girl on my lap, and I did as I was told. I didn't want to watch this little girl. But Mami was back, just as I had hoped for, and it was better if I behaved or she might decide to leave again.

My grandmother's shack was just one big room. (Unlike Abuela Evila's, this house had no interior walls, so privacy was hard to come by.) A curtain separated the front from the back part of the house, and that is where my grandmother had stored our belongings from our old house, like my parents' bed, the broken refrigerator, the dresser. In the middle of the shack was the dining table. To the right hung a hammock from the rafters where my uncle, Tío Crece, slept. Abuelita's bed was on the left side of the dining table. The kitchen area was in the front part of the house. Next to the stove was a small table full of saints, candles, and flowers. In the center was a portrait of my dead grandfather.

I sat on Abuelita Chinta's bed and watched her and Mami make dinner. Finally we would start having real meals. Meals that were more than just beans and tortillas. I was so happy about the food that for a moment, I forgot I was supposed to be mad about watching Elizabeth, or Betty, as Mami said we should call her youngest daughter. My little sister. A complete stranger. She was a year and three months old. She looked at me and smiled. Part of me wanted to smile at her. Part of me wanted to hold her in my arms and smell her scent of baby powder and milk, but I didn't do it. Instead, I studied her face, and I was jealous that she was prettier than me, even at her age. I was jealous that her hair was curlier than mine, and her eyelashes were thicker and longer than mine, and her eyes were not slanted like mine, but instead were round and framed by those thick, dark lashes that made it seem as if she were wearing eye makeup.

But then I looked at her skin. She was very dark, this little girl. And it made me feel glad that she was so dark. I had heard people say that in El Otro Lado there were a lot of golden-haired people, with eyes as blue as a summer sky and skin as white as a pig's belly. But this little girl, who was born in that special, beautiful place, was almost as dark as the Nahuas, the indigenous people who came down from the hills to sell clay pots at the train station.

Mami had forgotten I was there and didn't whisper as much as before. Now I could hear a little of what she was saying to Abuelita Chinta. Something about another woman. A fight she had with Papi. She was making green salsa, and as she talked she smashed the roasted green tomatoes with the pestle so hard the juice splattered on her dress. But she didn't care. She said she hated Papi and never wanted to see him again.

"I'm going to get back at him, Amá. I swear."

"Hush, Juana. Don't say such things. He's still the father of your children," Abuelita Chinta said.

"But it can't be true," I stammered. "Papi can't love another woman."

Mami looked up, startled, and when she realized that I was in the house with them—and that I'd been there all along—she got furious.

"What are you doing standing there? Go outside and don't come back until I call you, you hear!"

Betty started to cry. Tears stung my eyes, but Mami didn't care about our tears. "Get out!" she yelled again, and I ran out.

Carlos was playing marbles with the boys, but Mago wasn't play-

Abuelita Chinta's shack

ing jump rope with the girls. Instead, she was all alone, perched up on the metal thing used to change the direction of the train tracks. I carried Betty in my arms and struggled to hold her up. Her cheeks might have looked as if they were stuffed with cotton candy, but she weighed more than a sack of corn.

Mago was staring into the distance, past the huizache trees, and when I looked in her direction, I saw the towers of La Guadalupe Church near Abuela Evila's house sticking up like two fingers. Behind the towers, the Mountain That Has a Headache touched the sky.

"Do you miss her?" I asked.

Mago glanced at the mountain one more time and then jumped off the track-changer. "Who, Mami? But she's back," she said. "And why were you crying?"

I started crying again. I didn't know why I still felt that familiar emptiness inside when I looked at the Mountain That Has a Headache even though my mother was back.

Carlos came over to us, smiling and pointing toward the house. "Can you believe she's here?" He took a deep breath and said, "Finally, everything is going to go back to how it was before she left."

Mami stood at the door and told us to come inside. As I looked at her in the doorway, beckoning us to come in, I knew why the emptiness and the yearning were still there. Carlos was wrong.

The woman standing there wasn't the same woman who had left.

11

Papi and Mami as a young married
couple, with Mago and Carlos

IN AUGUST, two months after my mother had returned from El Otro Lado, the peso was devalued for the second time that year due to the national debt crisis. What little money my mother had brought with her was quickly spent. She found herself the head of the household and with very few options of how to make a living. After two years of earning dollars, it was difficult for her to readjust to the hardships brought on by Mexico's unstable economy. But what was harder for her was to have to explain to everyone who knew her why she had come back. As the taxi driver had said, everyone was leaving, not returning. I didn't realize back then how difficult it must have been for my mother to look at her friends and admit that her husband had indeed left her for another woman, just as they had once teased her that he would.

I often found her talking with my grandmother in whispers. But when Mago, Carlos, and I asked her for details of those two and a half years that she was gone, she would say little. So all we knew at that point was that my father had left her for another woman, but back then we still didn't know how he'd gone about it. We wanted to know what it meant that he was now with someone else? Did it mean he would not be coming back? Did it mean he had given up on the dream house? Did it mean that he would start a family of his own with that other woman and forget about us? Did it mean we would never see him again?

"It means he's washing his hands of us," my mother said. "It means we will starve here in this miserable place, and he will be too busy tending to his new woman to give a damn!"

"Papi wouldn't do that," Mago said. "He'll come back."

Out of all of us, Mago was the only one who harbored any hope that Papi would not forsake us. My mother's broken promise—that she'd be gone only a year—had caused a rift between them, so Mago's loyalty to my father remained strong. He had been gone for so long that in his absence he had become bigger than life in Mago's eyes. But regardless of how much she had changed, I was too happy to have my mother back to cling to the hope of seeing my father again. And I was angry at him. I didn't have a single memory of him and Mami together—of all of us together—and I felt cheated out of the family I yearned to have. Why did he have to go and fall in love with someone else? I wanted to know. Hadn't Mami always done what he had asked of her? Hadn't it been enough that she had followed him to El Otro Lado and left us behind?

And now he had returned to us a different version of my mother, one who was bitter, heartbroken, and weighed down by the knowledge that she had four children to support and was on her own.

Not too far from the train station is La Quinta Castrejón. Although it has now deteriorated and is no longer the fancy place it once was, back in its day it was frequented by wealthy people. It was on the outskirts of my grandmother's colonia, La Ejidal, which was as poor as could be. But La Quinta Castrejón sat there amidst the poverty, teasing us, reminding us of what we couldn't have. It was surrounded by a block wall lined with broken pieces of soda bottles that glinted in the sunlight like the jagged teeth of a beautiful but deadly beast. There was a long driveway that led to the reception hall and pools. The driveway was lined with palm trees, the only palm trees in the neighborhood, like soldiers standing guard. Inside there was a large swimming pool with a high diving board and smaller pools for little kids. There was a playground with swings and slides and a seesaw. Weddings and quinceañeras were held in the reception hall every weekend. Later, when the middle class was almost entirely wiped out as a result of the debt crisis, those parties became less frequent, causing La Quinta Castrejón to lose its glamour and be mostly forgotten.

But at the time, that hadn't happened yet, and Mami decided to try her luck there.

"That place is immune to the recession," Mami had said. "People still have to get married. And inflation can't stop young girls from turning fifteen."

Mami had been unable to find a job, and she did not want to sell Avon anymore because she wanted to avoid her old clients and their mocking glances as much as possible. So we started to sell things at La Quinta Castrejón on the weekends.

On Saturday, after a lunch of alphabet soup and tortillas, Mami prepared the merchandise to be sold that night. I wondered what kind of party would be taking place. Mago said it would be a wedding. I thought it would be a quinceañera. We placed a bet and the loser had to clean the outhouse the next day.

Around five o'clock Mago, Carlos, and I left the house with Mami. Betty stayed home and cried. She wasn't allowed to come. Mami wanted her to come along. She wanted all of us to come so the guests at La Quinta Castrejón could see she had four mouths to feed and take pity on her and buy from her. But the first night we came to sell, Betty cried and cried because the loud music and the laughter and chatter of the people inside kept her from falling asleep. The night was cold and we were shivering because our sweaters were too thin to keep out the chill. But Mami refused to leave even though everyone was inside the hall dancing and having a good time. She said that soon the party would be over and they would come back out and buy more cigarettes or gum, maybe even a bag of potato chips if they felt like a midnight snack.

Then the next day Betty had a fever and a cough. Abuelita Chinta scolded Mami as if she were a little girl, saying that it was the night's dampness that had made Betty sick, and what would we do if she came down with pneumonia?

Mami said, "She's an American, that's why she's so fragile." Because Mago, Carlos, and I have thick Mexican blood running through our veins and neither the dampness nor the chill of the night would make us ill, we had to come along. I didn't mind it so much. It meant we would get to spend time with Mami and see the beautiful dresses the quinceañeras and brides would be wearing.

We got to La Quinta Castrejón and were disappointed to see there were already other mothers setting up their stands. They had all their kids with them, too. The winner was the mother who brought along five kids, the youngest tied to her back with a rebozo. Mami cursed under her breath and began to set up her stand. She put out the mint and caramel candy, little bags of peanuts and roasted pumpkin seeds, cigarettes and matches. Mago and I helped her with the stand while Carlos walked around the parking lot offering to watch people's cars in exchange for tips.

Mago and I watched a limousine approach. I held my breath and prayed that it was a quinceañera, first because I loved quinceañeras and second because I didn't want to clean the outhouse the next day if I lost the bet I'd made with Mago. I prayed to the saints and held my breath until the driver opened the door of the limo, then I saw the young girl in her puffy pink dress and glittery tiara emerge, her escorts at her side. Mago was too mesmerized by the girl who seemed to be floating in a pink cloud to get mad that she lost the bet. We watched this young girl and her escorts walk into the reception hall while everyone clapped for her and congratulated her for becoming a mujercita, a little woman.

Soon all the guests were inside, and we were out in the cold night shivering and blowing puffs of warm air into our hands. It was the middle of the rainy season, and the sky was thick with rain clouds. Once in a while we would see lightning flashing over the Mountain That Has a Headache. Mami paid no heed to the weather. She kept glancing at the other vendors. She rearranged her goodies as if trying to find just the right way to display them. A man came outside to buy a pack of cigarettes, and he looked at Mami and at Mago and me. I put on my sad face, just like Mami had told me to do. But I knew that no matter how hard I tried, I was almost seven years old, too old to compete with the baby nursing at his mother's pitiful small breast. The man looked like a prince with his suit and tie. He bought his cigarettes from the woman and even gave her an extra tip, for her children, he said, and then went back to the party.

I didn't look at Mami because I knew she was angry, at me, at the man, at the mother with her five children, at Papi for putting her in that situation, at herself for leaving El Otro Lado in a moment of desperation. "I should have stayed," she would say to Abuelita Chinta sometimes. "He left me there on my own, and I knew no one, but I should have stayed. There were jobs. Maybe not great jobs, but at least we weren't starving. And here in Mexico, with the cost of everything going higher and higher, how are we to survive?"

I leaned against the wall and tried not to think about that beautiful place she yearned for. Mami picked up her tray of cigarettes and gum and decided to go inside the reception hall to offer them to the guests. Sometimes she got kicked out; sometimes, if the hosts were kind, they would let her stay for a bit.

Mago and I got up and walked over to look at the pool. There was a chain-link fence from the reception hall to the ticket office to keep people out, but we didn't need to go inside. From out there, we could see the pool clearly, shining like a blue jewel. By the ticket office was a white poster listing the admission prices. Mago helped me add up the numbers because I hadn't yet learned to add big numbers in my second-grade class. The cost of swimming here, for my siblings and me, plus Mami, was two days' worth of meals.

"Your father worked on that pool," Mami said from behind us, startling me. I turned to look at her, expecting her to be angry at Mago and me for leaving the stand unattended. I was waiting for her to yell at us, but instead, she said, "Your father tiled that pool."

We turned back to the pool and admired the navy blue tiles going all around the edge and covering the inside. "Papi did that?" I asked with awe. I had known Papi worked in construction, but I'd never really known, until that moment, which projects he had worked on around the city.

"I remember that he came home after work and told me that as soon as the pool opened, he would bring me here to swim." Mami put her hand up on the chain-link fence and curled her fingers around the metal wire. She put her forehead right up against the fence and looked at the pool. "Your father said that as a thank-you gift, the owner had allowed the workers to come for a day to enjoy the pool, free of charge. So he brought me here. Imagine that? I don't know how to swim, but your father does. He held on to me the whole time. I was so afraid, but not once did he let me go . . ."

I turned to Mami and saw the blue water reflected in her teary eyes. I wanted to tell her what Mago had told me once before. Memories are yours to keep forever. I wanted to tell her that as long as she held on to those special moments with her and Papi, they would always be hers—that other woman, whoever she was, couldn't take them from her.

But Mami had already wiped her tears. She had already looked at the stand and noticed we hadn't sold anything that night. She was walking away with brisk steps, her hands clenched into fists, yelling for us to come and tend the stand or there would be no money for food tomorrow. "I can't do everything by myself," she said angrily. "You kids are old enough to help."

I didn't move away from the chain-link fence. I heard the music drifting out into the cold night. It was finally time for the waltz. I looked at the pool Papi had tiled with his own hands and imagined myself dancing to El Vals de las Mariposas with him. In my mind's eye, he was holding me tight, whispering in my ear how proud he was of me for becoming a little woman.

"Get away from there," Mami said as she pulled on my ear. She dragged me away from the pool and the pretty tiles, and I went back to tend the stand with Mago. Soon it was midnight and the rain was starting. The guests came out and rushed to their cars without another glance at our goodies. Carlos and the other boys ran from one car to another, trying to collect their tips from the guests for watching the cars. Some guests ignored the boys' outstretched hands and hit the gas pedal too hard. I worried for Carlos as I saw him jump out of the way to avoid being hit.

"This is the last time we come here," Mami said as she started to throw all the goodies into a bag.

"It'll be better next weekend, Mami," I said. "Maybe next week the guests will be different."

But Mami wasn't listening. She threw the bags onto our shoulders and folded the metal table. Just as the rain began to pour, we rushed down the long driveway. We slid on the mud, our legs getting splattered by the procession of cars. The guests turned right onto the paved street to go back to their fancy homes, and we turned left and stumbled on the dark dirt road toward Abuelita Chinta's shack. Mami wouldn't slow her pace even though we were gasping for breath and our legs were burning and our sides were hurting. She stared straight ahead and didn't look back.

I know now that she wasn't fleeing the rain. She was running away from the glittering pool and its blue tiles, from the memory of my father and her wading in the water, arms intertwined, from the pain of knowing that even though he had held onto her in the pool of La Quinta Castrejón, he eventually had let go of her, in a place just as beautiful and frightening. El Otro Lado.

12

Mami in the United States

Two and a half years after my mother went to live in the United States, my father told her that he didn't love her anymore, and that he no longer wanted to live with her.

"And where am I to go?" my mother asked, holding tight to my little sister because she was the only family my mother had in that strange and beautiful country.

The irony was that in her worst nightmares she had pictured my father leaving her for a golden-haired, blue-eyed gringa. But the woman who stole her husband was a paisana, a Mexican from the state of Zacatecas. What was it about her he liked? my mother had wondered. Was it that she was educated and was a nursing assistant, unlike my mother, who was only allowed a sixth-grade education? Or was it the fact that this woman was a naturalized U.S. citizen and could speak English, unlike my mother, who as hard as she tried, couldn't seem to make sense of the strange words that rolled off the tongues of Americans? Did my father see that woman and her American privileges as a way to a bigger future, a future that my mother, with her limitations, couldn't give him?

Whatever it was about that woman, my mother hadn't been able to stop herself from thinking that perhaps Abuela Evila was right: she just wasn't good enough for him.

And then came his ultimate betrayal. At the end of the week he tossed her out of the apartment, but did not allow her to take Betty. My mother's first thought had been to go to the police, but she was afraid of being deported, and if that were to happen, then surely she would never see her daughter again. She wanted to go back to Mexico, back to the place she knew, back to her mother, back to us—her children—away from my father, but she couldn't leave like this, with no money and no daughter. Everyone would scorn her for coming back worse off than when she left.

Every day she would go to the babysitter's house to visit my little sister. My father had told the babysitter he would hold her responsible if anything happened to Betty, and because she was terrified of my father, the babysitter never took her eyes off the baby. But when my mother came knocking, the babysitter didn't have the heart to tell her she couldn't see her own child, and so she let her into her house. But not once did she let my mother take Betty out.

But on Mother's Day, while Mago, Carlos, and I were debating about whether or not to give our art projects to Tía Emperatriz, my mother was rushing to the babysitter's house because it was her special day and she wanted to spend it with her daughter. Betty reached for her as soon as she saw her. My mother sat in the living room with the baby and looked outside at the beautiful sunlight.

"Let me take her out," she asked the babysitter. "It's such a nice day today, and I want to take my little girl to the park and buy her an ice cream."

"You know I can't do that, Juana," the babysitter said. "Natalio will kill me if he finds out I let you see her, let alone take her out."

"Only an hour," my mother said. "I only ask for an hour. Please, it's Mother's Day today."

The babysitter finally agreed. "You promise you will bring her back in an hour?"

"Yes, yes, I promise," my mother said.

And she had not meant to break her promise, but half way back to the babysitter's house something had bubbled up inside her. Her blood boiled at the thought of that other woman preparing her daughter's bottles, giving her a bath, tucking her into bed, singing her to sleep. She imagined Betty growing up thinking the other woman was her mother. She became jealous of the woman who had already taken her husband from her, and she swore that she wouldn't let her take her baby's love away from her as well. And him, how could he have let go of her in that most frightening place where he knew she was all alone and he and Betty were the only family she had there? So she turned around and walked in the opposite direction, never once looking back.

The events culminated with something so horrible that even now, I still can't fully believe it. My father, in a moment of rage, his blood boiling with alcohol, went looking for my mother with a gun. Was he planning to shoot her? My father would later say no, his intention had been to scare her. But whatever the truth may have been, someone did get hurt. An innocent bystander had tried to defend my mother when he saw my father bullying her on the sidewalk in front of Tía María Félix's apartment, where my mother had sought refuge. My father wanted Betty back. My mother refused to hand her over. Betty was crying uncontrollably while both her parents had their shouting match over who got to keep her. My father's new woman waited in the passenger seat of the car, and her presence enraged my mother even more. It made her hold on to Betty with all her might. The bystander and my father got into a fistfight when he tried to break up my parents' argument. The gun accidentally went off, and the man was shot.

Luckily for my father, the man did not die. Luckily for my father, he was allowed voluntary deportation, instead of getting thrown in prison. Within a week, he had managed to sneak across the border and resumed his life in the United States as if nothing had ever happened.

The story my mother told us back then did not include as many details, and it wouldn't be until I was a young woman that I would hear the full story. But still, the thought that Papi had tried to shoot Mami was something so horrible it was almost too much to be believed. It was straight out of a Mexican soap opera!

"She's exaggerating," Mago said after we'd heard the abbreviated story. Whether Mami was exaggerating or not, we couldn't be sure, but either way we became fiercely loyal to her. Even Mago, as doubtful as she was, tried to please Mami and was careful not to mention Papi whenever she was around. Yet it wasn't long before we discovered that our loyalty and our love wouldn't be enough. Mami was distant with us, indifferent in many ways. Sometimes, her eyes would widen in horror, and she would shake her head as if trying to rid herself of the memories that haunted her. Then, she would look at us, but not really see us. She was looking for something we—her children—could not give her. We didn't know yet what exactly that was, but we soon found out.

By November, my mother had given up on selling at La Quinta Castrejón and had found a job at a record shop. She would usually get home around seven, when it was already dark. The road in front of my grandmother's house was made of dirt and covered with so many potholes and rocks that taxicabs and combis—public minibuses—wouldn't come near the house. Mami would have to get off at the main road and walk the eight minutes to Abuelita Chinta's house in the dark since there were no streetlights.

One evening, Abuelita Chinta sent Carlos to wait for Mami at the main road and walk her home. Usually, it was Tío Crece who waited for Mami, but he wasn't home yet and we were sure he was at the cantina drinking his wages away.

Carlos was terrified of walking across the bridge over the canal in the dark. "La Llorona is out there crying out to her children," he said.

"Don't be afraid," Abuelita Chinta said to Carlos. "Just make sure that when you come to the canal, you pray a Hail Mary and an Our Father. Make the sign of the cross before you walk across the bridge."

Mago and I sat on Abuelita Chinta's bed and turned on the radio. We didn't have a TV, but the radio had some nice programs like *Porfirio Cadenas: El Ojo de Vidrio*, a soap opera about a highwayman seeking to avenge his father's death. But my favorite program was storytime, where we got to hear fairy tales like "Cinderella," "Hansel and Gretel," and "The Three Little Pigs."

Mami came home by herself. "Where's Carlos?" we asked.

"I don't know. He wasn't waiting for me tonight," Mami said.

I peeked out the door. Nothing was out there but the train tracks, the gurgling canal, the lonely whistle of the last train announcing its departure from the station.

"Let's go look for him," Mago said.

We made our way to the canal, but we didn't see anyone coming across the bridge. I sat on the train rail and waited. I listened to the crickets singing their sad songs. The canal gurgled. The wind rustled the branches of the guamúchil trees. The fireflies were playing peek-aboo among the bushes, and I wanted to get up and chase them, trap them in my cupped hands and set them free inside Abuelita Chinta's house where they could glow above us like stars. But I didn't want to leave Mago's side because La Llorona might get me if I went out too far.

Finally, we saw a small figure making its way toward us from the other side of the bridge.

"Where were you?" Mago asked.

Carlos walked past us with his head hanging low.

"So where were you?" Mago asked again as we rushed to catch up to him.

"Nowhere."

"What do you mean, nowhere? We were worried about you."

"Leave me alone," he said. He went into the house and didn't answer Mami when she asked him about his whereabouts. He didn't want to eat dinner. He went to lie down on his cot and didn't speak to us for the rest of the evening.

In the morning, Carlos was still in a bad mood. We usually walked to school together, but that day he left without us. He didn't meet us for lunch. When we came back from school we tried to get him to tell us more jokes about Pepito, but instead he ignored us and stayed out all afternoon playing soccer in the vacant lot with his friends.

"What's gotten into him?" Mago asked me as she stirred the beans.

"I don't know," I said. I took a drink of cool water from the clay pot in the kitchen and ran back outside where my friends were playing jump rope.

I loved Abuelita's street. In the evening, the rays of the setting sun would paint the dirt road the color of baked clay. All the neighborhood kids came out to play. The train tracks provided lots of fun. We had contests to see who could jump over the most ties or who could balance herself the longest on the tracks. Sometimes we put pieces of scrap metal on the tracks and after the train swished by we would run to pick up our flattened shiny metal. Women would sit outside their homes on wicker chairs, embroidering cloth napkins or reading a magazine while listening to boleros on the radio. In clusters or alone, men returned home from work. Some came from the cornfields covered with sweat and dirt, with their machetes hanging at their sides from strings of rawhide. Others came from the train station, looking like ghosts, covered from head to toe with the powder that seeped out of the cement bags they loaded and unloaded all day long.

I would imagine those men's wives and kids waiting for them at home. I pictured the women clapping balls of dough into tortillas and cooking them in the comal. I could smell the beans boiling, the meat frying, the chiles and tomatoes roasting before being turned

Abuelita Chinta's street

into salsa on the molcajete. I could see the fathers washing themselves before sitting down at the table to eat dinner with their wives, sons, and daughters. If Papi hadn't left, that is how my evenings would have always been, I would tell myself.

While I made mud tortillas with my friends Meche and Cheli, Carlos and his friends would go wait for the evening train, and as soon as it came, they would run after it, grab ahold of it to climb on, and then ride it all the way to the train station, where they then would have to run back for our favorite part of the evening, when Doña Caro's husband came home.

Don Lino was the only person on our street who owned a vehicle. All of us kids would stop what we were doing as soon as we heard the quiet hum of the motor in the distance.

"Come on, let's go!" Don Lino's son, Jimmy, yelled. "Here comes my papi!" We all ran down the road to meet Don Lino and climb on the back of his blue truck, which rocked side to side, groaning as it went. We pretended we were on a ship being tossed in a storm.

When Mami got home, Betty, as usual, ran to her wanting to be picked up.

"Only refried beans and a chunk of cheese?" Mami said. "That's all we're eating tonight?"

"There are people who won't be eating dinner tonight, Juana. Let us be thankful," Abuelita Chinta said as she scooped the beans into our bowls.

"I can't believe your father doesn't send any money for you kids," Mami said to us. "He's probably spending it on that woman!"

"Juana, we'll be okay," Abuelita Chinta said. "You're here now with your children. I'm sure that's enough for them."

"You're right, Amá. Things are going to get better really soon."

I wanted to reach out and hold Mami. I wanted to tell her that I'd rather eat beans for the rest of my life as long as she was with me. But the look she gave me scared me. It was almost as if she hated me.

"You look just like him," she said to me. I glanced at the Man Behind the Glass, and for the first time, I was not happy about having his features. I didn't want Mami to look at me like that, a look full of pain, anger, hatred. I wanted to grab the Man Behind the Glass and toss him onto the railroad tracks so the train would shatter him. So that Mami wouldn't look at him, and look at me, and then think we were one and the same.

Abuelita Chinta set the bowl of beans on the table and ruffled my hair. "Why don't you kids go buy some sodas for our meal? When you come back, the beans won't be so hot."

We took the money and left.

"So what's the matter with you?" Mago asked Carlos as we were coming back from the store.

"You're going to get mad if I tell you."

"Just spit it out."

We stopped walking. We were already near the house, and we didn't want to go inside just yet because then we wouldn't be able to talk.

"Mami has a boyfriend," Carlos said.

"What?" Mago and I said at the same time.

"I saw her. I saw her with a man." He told us that the previous night many combis had come and gone, but without Mami. Because he was afraid of standing there in the dark alone, putting himself in danger of getting beaten or killed by some crazy person, he climbed up the tree near the tortilla mill. Minutes later, a taxi pulled up right under the tree and Mami and a man got out. The taxi left, and as soon as it did the man pulled Mami into his arms and kissed her on the mouth.

"They kissed for a long time," Carlos said. "I didn't know what to do. I didn't want Mami to get mad at me. When they were done kissing and hugging each other, the man hailed a taxicab and left. Mami made her way to the bridge, and I wanted to run to her and walk with her, but instead I stayed up in the tree. I didn't want her to know I had seen her."

We continued on our way before Mami or Abuelita Chinta came looking for us. What did it mean that Mami had a boyfriend? I wondered.

At dinner, I could see how much Mago was struggling to keep from shouting that we knew Mami's secret. She had a scowl on her face, and whenever Mami said something to her, Mago just grunted in response.

"¿Qué te pasa?" Mami asked again.

Then Mago couldn't hold back anymore and said, "Mami, who was that man?"

"What man?"

"The man you were kissing by the main road."

Since she was holding Betty on her lap, it was hard for me to see the expression on Mami's face. She buried her face in Betty's hair, as if hiding from our accusing eyes.

"Well, since you already know, I might as well tell you," she said finally. "He sells car insurance next to the record shop. But at heart he's a wrestler. He does Lucha Libre on the weekends and he's very good—"

"Who cares? What is he to you?"

"Don't talk like that to me, Mago," Mami said, looking over Betty's head. "Anyway, I might as well tell you now. I'm going away with him."

"What?" we all yelled. Betty started to whimper at hearing our angry voices.

"Juana, what are you saying?" Abuelita Chinta said.

"Francisco has gotten a contract to fight in Acapulco, and he asked me to go with him. I've accepted."

"But you can't go!" Mago yelled. She got up so suddenly, her chair toppled over. "You can't!"

"I won't be gone for long. Now sit down and stop yelling at me."

"You said that the last time," Carlos said. "And you were gone two and a half years."

"Mami, don't leave us again," I said as I rushed to her side.

"And what about us?" Mago said. "What's going to happen to us?"

"You'll stay with your abuelita. She'll watch over you."

"Juana, you can't do this," Abuelita Chinta said. "It isn't right."

"When Papi hears of this, that you're leaving us again—" Mago said.

"Don't you dare bring up your father. There's nothing between us anymore. Don't you kids understand that? He tried to *kill* me."

"You're making that up," Mago said. "He wouldn't have done that. And if he did, maybe, maybe it was all your fault!"

Mami stood up and headed over to Mago, ready to beat her.

Abuelita Chinta quickly got in between them. "Juana, you need to think things through."

"I have, Amá," Mami said. "And I've made my decision."

∞

When Mami left, she didn't even have the courage to tell us. When we got home from school the next day, we found Betty in tears. Abuelita Chinta told us that our mother had just left with the wrestler. "They've gone to catch a taxi over by La Quinta Castrejón," she said.

Betty's sobs were deafening. Mago, who had always shown her dislike for Betty in many ways, was the one who picked her up and held her. Carlos and I bolted out the door, hoping that Mami and the wrestler might still be waiting by the main road. At seven years old, I found myself running to catch up to my mother and beg her not to leave me for the second time in my life. Carlos ran faster than I did, and by the time I got to the main road, he was bent over, crying. There was no sign of Mami anywhere.

13

Tío Crecenciano

AFTER MY MOTHER left, Carlos became terribly ill. Abuelita Chinta said he was suffering from sorrow. He had fever, headaches, nausea, and vomiting. He lost so much weight he really did look like a skeleton now. I thought about that song Élida liked to sing for him, *La calaca, tilica y flaca. La calaca tilica y flaca.*

While Mago and I sat around his cot, watching him wither away, all I could think of was the empty road where my mother had vanished. I wondered if Carlos was thinking about it, too. I wondered if he was replaying that moment in his feverish mind, as I was.

"It's all her fault," Mago said as she reached to hold Carlos's limp hand. "I hate her."

"Mago, don't say that," I said, but a part of me felt she was right. I didn't know what was wrong with my brother, but I also felt sick. Even though I wasn't physically ill, inside I was burning. I felt as if I had a scorpion inside of me that was stinging my heart again and again. I wanted to reach inside my body and yank the scorpion out. Stomp on it. Or kill it with my bare hands.

When Carlos was in his thirties, we would finally learn the medical term for what he had—hepatitis. Even if we had known this back then, it wouldn't have made a difference. Mago would still have blamed it on our mother, and Abuelita Chinta would still have said, "They can call it what they want, sadness in any other form is still sadness."

My hot-blooded Scorpio sister would never succumb to something as silly as sadness. She reacted in the only way she knew how.

A few days before my mother left, Tío Crece's dog had five puppies we were not allowed to touch. Tío Crece said he was planning to sell them and didn't want us messing with them. I wondered why anyone would want to *buy* a dog, since there were so many homeless dogs out in the street you could take home with you for free.

Tío Crece made a little bed for them in a cardboard box. They were tiny and their eyes were still closed. When we tried to pick them up, the mother dog growled at us. We looked at the puppies snuggling with their mami, and I couldn't believe that I actually felt jealous of them. Mago looked at the puppies and their mother with the same intense jealousy she had Doña Paula and her two sons. When I reached out to her, the look of yearning on her face was quickly replaced with a scowl.

After lunch, Tío Crece's dog went out and didn't come back right away. The puppies whimpered and cried from hunger.

"Do you think we can give them a tortilla soaked in bean juice?" I asked Mago as we washed the dishes on the washing stone.

"Let me see what I can find for them," she said. She went into the house and left me to wash the dishes by myself. Then she came out and made her way to the back, where the puppies were. I couldn't see what she had in her hands, but it didn't look like tortillas to me.

I dried my hands and went to the back. "What are you doing?" I asked.

Mago was holding a can of jalapeños and was offering a hot pepper to one of the puppies, as if it were a teat. "Stop that!" I yelled. "You'll kill them."

"So what?" she said. "They're just dogs."

"Mago, stop!" I said, crying. Mago pushed me away.

"You better leave, before I hit you," she said.

I turned and ran into the house, yelling for Abuelita Chinta to come. Except she wasn't there, and I remembered she was going to do a body cleansing for my friend Meche's mom. I ran to get her, but by the time we got back to the house, it was too late.

Finding the puppies dead, Tío Crece went into a rage and chased after Mago, ready to beat her. Abuelita Chinta, as usual, grabbed the broom and chased after him. "Leave her alone, leave her alone!" she said, hitting him with the broom.

Abuelita Chinta and I put the dead puppies in a sack and tossed them into the vacant lot where people burned their trash. For the next several days, on our way to el mercado, we would catch a whiff of the stench of their rotting bodies.

Because of his illness, Carlos missed over a month of school, and his grades, which were not great to begin with, plummeted.

"I'm not going back to school," Carlos said when Abuelita Chinta told him he was well enough to return.

"Of course you are," Abuelita Chinta said. "How can you learn otherwise?"

"I'm not," Carlos said. "I'm going to flunk fourth grade, anyway. So what's the point of even trying?"

"Mijo, don't talk back. When your mother returns, I don't want to have to tell her you did not behave."

Carlos was sad and angry about failing school, and he did something he had never done before, and he never did again—he yelled at our grandmother. "Your daughter is never coming back! She doesn't love us!"

Tío Crece rushed at Carlos, and I thought he was going to hit him. Instead, he grabbed him by the arm and pushed him out the door. "Come on," my uncle said. "Let's go find work."

"Crece, that isn't a good idea," Abuelita Chinta said as my uncle sat on his bike and Carlos climbed onto the pegs on the back axle.

Abuelita Chinta, Betty, and I watched my uncle maneuver his way down the dirt road with his black dog at his side and my brother standing on the pegs. Carlos turned to look back and waved. Mago had left early for school to work on a project for her class. I knew she would be angry when she found out where Carlos was. I was scared for my brother. I didn't want him hanging out with our crazy uncle. I didn't want him learning to become a man from Tío Crece. But who else would he learn it from, I asked myself as I glanced at the Man Behind the Glass. Not from *him*.

The story I heard as a child was that when Tío Crece was eighteen, he had many admirers. One woman in particular was desperately in love with him, but he didn't feel the same. One day, when he was at work unloading the freight cars at the train station, she had come by with lunch and a gourd of cold water for him. But it wasn't plain water. She did witchcraft on him by giving him agua de toloache, a drink made of water mixed with jimsom weed and menstrual blood meant to make the person who drinks the water fall desperately in love. My uncle was carried home by his coworkers. He stumbled into the house, talking nonsense, his skin burning hot. He had hallucinations, and Abuelita Chinta spent all night by his side, trying different remedies to counteract the poison. Tío Crece didn't fall in love with the woman. And he was never the same after that.

Back then I had never heard of schizophrenia, and so I had believed, without question, that my uncle's life had been ruined by witchcraft. When we came to live at Abuelita Chinta's house, my uncle was about to turn thirty, and no woman in town would look at him twice. The handsome young man he'd once been was gone. His curly black hair was often matted and oily from not showering. His teeth were beginning to rot. His clothes were torn and dirty. Instead of a belt, he wore a rope around his thin waist to hold up his pants. The only thing that remained the same were his eyes, beautiful brown eyes the color of syrup, like the kind that covers the pancakes vendors at el zócalo sell. Sometimes, when the craziness left him for brief moments, and he showered and put on his best clothes, I would catch glimpses of the man he could have been, and I would feel sad for him.

Not even a week after Mami had left, Tío Crece said to me, "Te doy un peso por un beso," while holding out a shiny coin. A peso for a kiss, he said. His breath reeked of alcohol. I looked at the coin my uncle was holding out to me, and I thought about the candy I could buy with it. My mouth watered at the thought of a pulpa de tamarindo, the candy melting in my mouth in an explosion of bitter, sweet, and tongue-burning hot.

When I didn't respond, Tío Crece leaned back and laughed. "My niece is smart. You don't want a little peso, do you? Está bien, how about this?" He held out four more coins to me. I held my hands behind my back, the fingers tightly laced together, but I didn't know how long I could resist. I glanced at the outhouse in the farthest corner of the backyard, and I wished Mago would hurry up and pee.

"Ándale, take them. What's a little kiss compared to what you can buy with this?" He offered them to me again, and I watched how they sparkled in the sun.

"Nena, what are you doing?" Mago called out to me.

"Nothing," I said right away.

Tío Crece laughed. "I'm just keeping my niece company," he said. Then he walked away.

"Stay away from him, Nena," Mago said as she took the sponge from me. "He's crazy."

From that moment on, I tried to avoid Tío Crece as much as I could, but it was hard to do so in a small shack that had no interior walls. Mago and I had to be extra careful when he was around. He would lie on his hammock reading a dime novel that had a picture of a woman with big chichis and butt cheeks the size of watermelons. He would stick his hand down his pants and play with himself, not caring that we could see him.

For the rest of the day, while I was in school, I kept thinking about my brother and Tío Crece. I was imagining the worst. What if Tío Crece went into a crazy rage and beat my brother for no reason? What if he got mad at him and left him stranded somewhere else and Carlos couldn't find his way back? What if he taught my brother to say dirty things to girls and to drink tequila?

"Abuelita, you should have stopped him," Mago told our grandmother as soon as we got home from school and noticed that Carlos wasn't home yet.

My grandmother didn't say anything. We all knew that when it came to Tío Crece, there wasn't much one could say or do.

In the evening, Mago, Betty, and I listened to the story of Hansel and Gretel on the radio. I felt sad for the little boy and girl as I imagined them out there in the dark forest all alone, trying to find their way back home. I understood their fear all too perfectly. How could their father leave them out there to fend for themselves?

Carlos and Tío Crece came into the house looking dirty and sweaty, but with smiles on their faces. Tío Crece handed my grandmother two bags from which she took out five dead turtledoves, an iguana, and ten ears of corn.

"Where did you get all this food?" Abuelita Chinta said as she set it out on the table.

"My nephew here is pretty good with his slingshot," Tío Crece said. Carlos smiled so big, you could see his two front teeth and the tiny one in between them, but he didn't pull his lips closed and bite them, as he always did to keep himself from smiling big and showing his teeth.

As Abuelita Chinta and Tío Crece prepared dinner, Carlos sat with us at the table and told us all about his adventures. He said he and Tío Crece found some work at the train station first and loaded and unloaded the cargo from the freight cars for half a day. From there they went all along the highway and side roads picking up dried cow and horse dung and putting it into a sack. Then they went to sell it to the brickmaker. From there they snuck into a cornfield, but my uncle wouldn't let Carlos pick the corn because of the scorpions that crawl up the stalks. Instead, Carlos's job was to put the corn into the sack as my uncle cut it.

"Mago, our uncle is like you," Carlos said. "He got bitten by a scorpion in the field, but it didn't do anything to him!"

From then on, Carlos and Tío Crece became inseparable. As crazy as Tío Crece was, he was the only male role model Carlos had, and he figured a crazy uncle was better than nothing. Unlike Abuelo Augurio, who had wanted nothing to do with Carlos, Tío Crece didn't say no to Carlos when he asked if he could tag along when Tío Crece ran errands. They went to gather wood together. Tío Crece would put Carlos on the back pegs of his bike, and they would go to the bakery to buy sweet bread for our evening cup of cinnamon tea. Sometimes on weekends they would take day trips together and come home with fish they had caught at the Lagoon of Tuxpan.

Mago would say, "Don't spend so much time with him, Carlos." But Carlos would shrug and happily climb onto my uncle's bike and wave bye to us as Mago and I headed to school, where all we did was worry about the time Carlos spent with Tío Crece. We didn't want him picking up any bad habits from him, especially drinking. Mago said that was how little boys begin drinking—when their fathers give them sips of their own beer until eventually they start buying them their own. I would later learn this had happened to my father.

"Remember, he isn't your father," Mago would tell Carlos. "Don't get too close to him."

"Stop telling me what to do," Carlos would say to Mago sometimes. "You aren't my mother."

Looking back on it now, I realize that this was the beginning of Carlos's independence from Mago. My mother's second abandonment had forced him to grow up. And that meant that he no longer needed a little mother. He needed a man to look up to. He needed a father, and the closest thing to that was Tío Crece.

A few weeks later, Tío Mario arrived, and we were happy for his visit. But Tío Crece was not happy. He always felt threatened when other men were around, and his brothers were no exception. During the few days Tío Mario was there, Tío Crece was in a bad mood. He even hit Carlos. In the morning he had made Jell-O cups for Carlos to sell, but my brother didn't sell many. In the evening, as he was walking home with the tray still full, Carlos, who was terrified of walking across the bridge in the dark, had run across and tripped, sending the Jell-O flying in different directions. Tío Crece flew into a rage and beat Carlos.

The day before his departure, Tío Mario and Tío Crece went to the local bar. Tío Crece was moody enough when he wasn't drinking. Didn't Tío Mario know his brother turned into a demon when he was drunk? Sure enough, that night we woke up hearing a commotion outside. We looked out the door, and in the moonlight we saw Tío Mario and Tío Crece by the train tracks, yelling and shoving each other.

"Calm down. Calm down!" Abuelita Chinta said as she rushed outside. Tío Crece pushed past her and came into the house. He grabbed a machete and ran back out, the blade glinting silver in the moonlight. "I'm going to kill you!" he yelled. As Tío Crece ran with the machete up in the air, Tío Mario put his hands up.

"Brother, calm down," Tío Mario said. But Tío Crece swung his machete, and Tío Mario pulled out the knife he always carried in his pocket for protection.

"Por el amor de Dios, hijos míos, don't fight. Please, stop this!" Abuelita Chinta cried.

Carlos said, "Tío Crece, please, put the machete down."

Tío Crece cursed and spat. I was almost expecting to see foam coming out of his mouth. He reminded me of the dog with rabies Don Lino had killed with his gun a few days before.

The neighbors came out but did nothing to stop my uncles from killing each other. Tío Crece sprang toward Tío Mario. I closed my eyes at the sound of metal against metal, their hard breathing, the shuffling of feet. The dogs barked even louder. Tío Mario cried out. I opened my eyes to see him grab his shoulder. Tío Crece's machete had torn his shirt, but there was no blood, as far as I could see.

Angry now, Tío Mario lunged at Tío Crece and drew first blood. Tío Crece touched his cheek where the knife had cut him.

Suddenly, Carlos pushed Tío Mario and put himself in between them. "Don't kill Tío Crece!" he yelled.

Tío Crece's machete hovered in the air. Mago yelled at Carlos to move out of the way. Tío Mario's knife pointed at Tío Crece. Abuelita Chinta shoved Carlos aside and stood there with her outstretched arms looking like La Virgen de Guadalupe herself. "Kill me, kill me, but not my son!" Abuelita Chinta yelled.

They're going to kill my grandmother! They're going to kill my brother! Mago and I rushed to Abuelita's and Carlos's side. Finally, Tío Crece seemed to wake up from his drunken hallucination. He dropped his machete to the ground and stumbled away, back to the house.

Carlos rushed after Tío Crece. When we went inside, Tío Crece was passed out in his hammock and Carlos was sitting by his side, looking like a dutiful son.

"Don't ever do that again!" Mago told Carlos and smacked him hard on the head. "Why would you risk your life for *him*? Are you going crazy, too?"

When we woke up the next morning, Tío Mario was gone. Abuelita Chinta no longer allowed Carlos to go look for work with Tío Crece. Instead, she made him go to school with us. As we were crossing the bridge, Carlos turned around and waved bye to Tío Crece, who was making his way down the dirt road alone, with only his black dog at his side.

14

Abuelita Chinta

IT WAS JUNE, the end of the school year and the beginning of the
rainy season. Mago, Carlos, and I rushed home after school just as
the clouds burst and the raindrops started to splash down. The thirsty
earth soaked up every drop of rain. Abuelita Chinta greeted us with a
cup of hot chocolate, which, though made with water and not milk,
was delicious because she was there at home, waiting for us, asking
us about our last day of school, about what we learned, smiling at us
with her gap-toothed smile that looked just like my own. I breathed
in the scent of hot chocolate and wet dirt, the smell of Abuelita's

almond oil and epazote, and all those scents swirled together with the melted wax and withering flowers on her altar. I took another deep breath and became dizzy with all the smells of home.

She left us drinking our hot chocolate and went out into the rain to visit my aunt, Tía Güera, whose baby girl, Lupita, was ill with the evil eye. Mago, Carlos, Betty, and I sat at the table listening to the rain.

"It sounds as if God is throwing pesos on our roof all the way from Heaven," I said.

"And what if each raindrop was a coin? What if trees did have money for leaves?" Mago asked. "Papi would still be here with us."

I imagined him sitting at the table, sipping hot chocolate, sitting so close I could easily reach out and touch his hand.

Carlos turned to Mago and said, "Tell us something about Papi that made you happy. Anything."

Mago blew into her clay cup and sipped her chocolate. "Well, there's that one time when we were living at Don Rubén's house . . ." she said. She closed her eyes and stayed quiet for a while, as if she was remembering it all and was enjoying the memory, wanting to keep it for herself for just a little bit longer before sharing it with us. "It was the day before the Day of the Three Wise Men. I remember he came home that night looking suspicious. Mami had put us to bed earlier than usual, and of course we had protested. But she insisted that we must be good kids if we wanted Los Reyes Magos to bring us presents. So we jumped into bed and you two fell asleep. But I did not. I pretended to, but I kept my eyes slightly open and waited for Papi. When he came home, he grabbed Mami and took her outside to the backyard. The next day Mami woke us up and took us outside. Papi said that somewhere under the bushes, we would find what the Wise Men had brought us.

"To you, Carlos, they brought a red truck, and to you, Nena, a baby doll that could wink its eyes."

"And what did they bring you?" Carlos asked.

"To me they brought colored pencils and a drawing pad."

"And me? What did they bring me?" Betty asked.

"You weren't born yet," Mago said. "But maybe on the next Day of the Three Wise Men they will bring you a doll, a beautiful Barbie made in the U.S., just like you."

Carlos said he imagined Papi driving a big white van all the way from El Otro Lado, and heading back to live with us. "The van would be full of boxes and boxes," Carlos said. "With lots of clothes, and toys, and a brand-new bicycle for me."

"What about us?" Mago asked.

"Well, he would bring you dolls and a toy kitchen set."

Mago waved her arm. "Forget that, I want a bike, too."

"And I want skates," I said. I didn't care if I wouldn't be able to skate on the dirt roads.

"I want a tricycle," Betty said.

We were quiet after that. Mago glanced at the Man Behind the Glass and sighed. "He will come back for us. I know he will."

I clung to Mago's words. With Mami gone again, our father was the only hope we had, however small that hope was. Despite what had happened between them, we were still his children, weren't we? He wouldn't forsake us, would he? We needed to believe in something, for what would happen once we lost our faith in both our parents and had nothing left to hope for?

Abuelita Chinta came back soaking wet, her legs covered in mud. She held her sandals in her hands and told us she had to walk barefoot all the way from the main road because everything had turned to mud, and she didn't want her sandals getting ruined. Carlos grabbed one of the pots we put under a leak in the roof. It had been raining so hard that the pot was already full of water, perfect for Abuelita Chinta to wash her muddy legs with.

She took some pieces of dried cow dung Tío Crece kept in a sack and lit them on the ground so that the smoke would keep the mosquitoes away. Soon, the house smelled of burnt grass. "They're going to eat us alive!" she said. We'd been so busy talking we hadn't even noticed all the mosquitoes in the house. Abuelita Chinta sat at the dining table, and Mago heated up the rest of the hot chocolate for her so that she could warm herself up. Mago turned on the radio just in time to catch another episode of our favorite radio-novela, *Porfirio Cadenas: El Ojo de Vidrio.*

"*¿Por qué se hizo criminal el Ojo de Vidrio? La borrascosa juventud de*

Porfirio Cadenas, cómo perdió uno de sus ojos, y por qué tuvo que seguir la vida criminal, perseguido por sus poderosos enemigos . . ." We sat there and listened to the radio. But halfway into the story the power went off and we all groaned. Now the only light we had came from the candles on Abuelita's altar. And the only thing we could listen to was the harsh sound of the never-ending rain.

I asked Abuelita to tell me a story about Mami. What was she like when she was a child, I wanted to know.

"Your mother was a tough girl," Abuelita Chinta said. "Tough but also very impulsive. I guess that's the way she still is." She laughed at a memory that came to her, and I begged her to share it with us. My grandmother said that there had once been a donkey in the neighborhood that had no owner and was so wild nobody would go near it. My mother, who was twelve at the time, had gotten it into her head that she would tame the donkey, then she would set up her own business delivering water from the community well, as she'd seen other donkey owners do. She and Abuelita Chinta could ride the donkey to the fields to deliver lunch to Abuelito Gertrudis, and so she would spare her poor mother the long walk. They could also use the donkey to carry wood from the hills, and they could sell its dung to the brickmakers or dry them and burn them to keep the mosquitoes away at night. All this she was imagining would happen if she could just tame that donkey.

So as she was walking home from school with her friends one day, she spotted the donkey near her house. It was too busy munching on wild grass to notice her. "I'm going to ride that donkey," she declared. Her friends laughed and said she couldn't do it. Many of the boys had tried and hadn't been able to even get close enough to the donkey, let alone ride it. No girl had ever tried. But my mother had it in her head that she would do it and good things would come of it. And so she did. She rode the donkey for thirty glorious seconds. Thirty seconds of triumph before the donkey reared on its hind legs and sent her flying up into the air. She was still dreaming about the water delivery business she was going to start, so she didn't feel the pain of the impact as she landed on the ground, her arm twisted at an odd angle.

From then on, her friends teased her about the donkey. Her broken arm took a long time to mend, but even after it had, they wouldn't let her forget that she had failed. She wished they would remember those thirty seconds of triumph.

"Your mother thinks she has failed again," Abuelita Chinta said as she finished her story. "And she thinks everyone else thinks so, too."

The rainy season brought more mosquitoes than usual. They swarmed around us, biting us. Abuelita Chinta had a mosquito net hanging around our bed, but it was old and peppered with holes, so the mosquitoes could get in and bite us all night long. Luckily, the rains also brought an explosion of frogs, hundreds of them hopping from place to place, croaking and eating the mosquitoes swarming around. We chased the frogs and tried to push them back to the canal, where they wouldn't bother anyone with their constant croaking that echoed throughout the neighborhood. In the evenings, the fireflies came out, and we caught them and put them in a jar. We brought them into the house and set them on the table to light up the house. Dragonflies swirled around us, and Carlos and his friends chased them around with their slingshots and had a competition going for the one who could kill the most dragonflies. I hated them for that. Dragonflies are beautiful, and I didn't want to look at Carlos's outstretched hand, proudly displaying a dead dragonfly on his palm, the still wings shining in the sun like stained glass.

I loved the summer rains. I loved it when the rains were gentle, and I could smell the sweet scent of wet earth. Everything was green around me, wildflowers grew along the train tracks, and the clouds gathered at the peaks of the mountains like soft, cushy pillows. But halfway through the summer, the heavens burst wide open.

For days and days the rain poured on us with no end in sight. Thunder shook the bamboo sticks. We didn't have enough pots and buckets to catch the rain dripping through the roof. Then one day it didn't matter.

We woke up in the middle of the night to discover the shack had flooded. Soon, our bed was underwater. The only one who didn't get wet was Tío Crece, who slept on a hammock hanging from the rafters. He slept there all night long, while Carlos, Mago, Betty, Abuelita

Chinta, and I sat on the small dining table and waited for morning. Mago held Betty in her arms and kept her warm while the rest of us shivered and leaned against one another as we drifted in and out of sleep.

We spent the whole morning getting the water out of the house in buckets. Our sandals got stuck to the muddy floor and sometimes we would fall into the water. We hung our clothes on top of bushes and on the rocks by the train tracks to dry. The mattresses steamed under the sun. The neighbors put a few of their belongings out to dry, too, although their houses hadn't flooded as much. Their homes were made of concrete and brick, whereas Abuelita's house, with its flimsy walls made from bamboo sticks, was like a sieve.

When we finally got all the water out of the house, we took our buckets to the train tracks and filled them up with gravel. We went back and forth from the train tracks to the house, throwing handfuls of gravel on the floor as if we were planting corn for next year's crops. Finally, the dirt floor was firm enough and no longer muddy.

Throughout the week, we heard news about the damage the floods had done. The river that ran parallel to the train tracks had flooded, the water spilling onto the bridge and making it impossible for cars or people to get across to go to el mercado, the bus station, or el centro. The neighborhood next to ours was completely underwater. It was built on lower ground, and the people who lived there had to stay on the roofs of their houses. People navigated through the streets in makeshift canoes, and the corpses of their chickens, pigs, dogs, and cats floated in the water. Luckily, not many people had died, but the rainy season wasn't yet over and you never knew what other tragedies it would bring.

Early one morning, someone knocked on our door and called out to my grandmother. "Doña Jacinta, Doña Jacinta!"

Abuelita Chinta crossed herself at her altar before opening it. I did the same, hoping it wasn't any more bad news. Abuelita Chinta opened the door and we stood behind her, wondering what other havoc the floods had caused.

"¿Qué pasa?" Abuelita Chinta asked. It was the son of one of Tío

Gary's neighbors. He bent over to catch his breath. He was barefoot, and not only did his legs look as if they were dipped in chocolate, but his hands and arms as well. I wondered how many times he'd slipped as he ran over here. "Catalina," he said. "The river."

"Ave María Purísima," Abuelita said, crossing herself.

Tío Gary lived across from the train station in a shack similar to our own. The river raged just thirty feet behind his shack. Catalina was his five-year-old daughter. When we got to Tío Gary's house, all his neighbors were outside, whispering to one another, crossing themselves again and again. Abuelita Chinta didn't go into the shack. She hurried to the river's edge. The waters had receded enough to be contained within the river bank, but the current was still swift and strong, dragging with it branches, broken chairs, clothes, pieces of wood. Farther down the river I saw several men who were holding on to a rope they'd tied to a tree to keep the current from dragging them away.

"The current is still too strong," Abuelita Chinta said.

Catalina's mother, Tía Lupe, shuddered in pain. Her tears rolled down her cheeks nonstop, as if the river itself had gotten inside her body and was spilling out. Tía Lupe said, "There's still hope. Catalina might have survived. She might have gotten hold of something to float on. She might have been saved by someone down the river." No one contradicted her.

I listened to the neighbors whisper the details to every newcomer that arrived. They said my five-year-old cousin had wandered off that morning and went to play by the river. Catalina's legs got so muddy she decided to wash them in the river, but the bank was slippery, and she fell in and was whisked away by the current. The neighbor's child went to get help, but when help came she was nowhere to be seen. Tío Gary, who worked at the train station unloading the freight cars, came home as soon as he heard what had happened.

"They've been out there all day," the neighbors said. "And so far have found nothing."

In the evening, we made our way home. Only the four of us went. Abuelita chose to stay and lead prayers all night long.

That night Mago and I couldn't sleep. "Tell me a story," I said to Mago.

"Which one?" she asked.

"Whichever one you want," I said. I just didn't want to think about Catalina. I didn't want to think about the river. I didn't want to think about her mother's tears.

"Once upon a time there were three little pigs . . ." Mago began.

As I listened to the story, I thought about Papi's dream house. Maybe it wasn't so foolish to want to live in such a house. Look at the little pigs. The ones who got eaten were the two who lived in shacks of sticks and straw. And the one who survived the big, bad wolf had a brick and concrete home, just like the one Papi wanted to build for us. Maybe that's why Papi had wanted such a house, to protect us, to shelter us from the horrors waiting just outside our door. I fell asleep with a prayer on my lips for Papi to finish his dream house one day. Then he could finally come back, take us there, and keep us safe.

The next day, Tío Gary and his friends made their way down the river again. We stood by the bank and watched them get smaller and smaller. Inside Tío Gary's house, all the women were back to praying. Mago, Carlos, Betty, and I stayed outside with the rest of the kids and found ways to entertain ourselves. We made mud tortillas. We wrote our names on the wet dirt with a stick. But our eyes always returned to the river.

Then the men finally came. Their heads hung low, their backs bent over. They dragged their feet over the muddy dirt path that paralleled the river. And in Tío Gary's arms we saw her, Catalina. Her limp arms hung at her sides. Everything became a blur. I wiped my eyes again and again, but the tears never stopped. Nobody touched Catalina except her mother and Abuelita Chinta, who pulled dried leaves and twigs out of Catalina's wet hair. Tío Gary said she was tangled up in the branches of a fallen tree.

They hung Catalina by her feet so that the river would drain out of her. We all kneeled and prayed, and not once did I take my eyes off my cousin's bloated body, and I shuddered at seeing her like that, hanging by her feet, like the chickens at the meat section in el mercado, just as cold and lifeless. I was gripped with a fear so great, it made my stomach churn. *What if something happened to me, Mago, Carlos, or Betty? What if, by the time Papi finishes his dream house, there's no one left for him to keep safe? Or what if he never finishes it, what if he never returns, and we are left here to face the wolf all on our own?*

15

Abuelita Chinta and Betty

A WEEK AFTER the new school year started, Mago's dream came true. She was chosen to be a flag bearer, an honor given to the sixth graders with the best cumulative grades. The only problem was that she would need a special uniform. We hardly had any money to eat, let alone to buy fabric and pay a seamstress to make a uniform.

"We have a few weeks yet," Abuelita Chinta quickly said at seeing Mago's crestfallen face. "We'll come up with the money, somehow."

Back then, Mago had loved school more than anyone I knew. Even more than I did. Sometimes at night, when everyone else was sleeping, she would tell me about her dreams of going to technical school and being a secretary one day. Being a secretary had also been my mother's dream. Mago put her fingers in the air and pretended to type on an invisible typewriter. I closed my eyes and I pictured her dressed in a pretty silk blouse and black skirt with a slit in the back, the kind secretaries in soap operas wear. I imagined her boss, a handsome lawyer, telling her she was the best secretary he'd ever had. Then they would fall in love. "Where will I get the money to pay for technical school," Mago wondered, "when we don't even have money for my flag-bearer uniform?"

Mago envied Doña Caro and Don Lino's children. Don Lino made good money as a welder, and his kids didn't have to worry about paying for school. Their oldest daughter was a kindergarten teacher. Lemo, who was fifteen, was learning to be a welder, like his father. Alba, who, at thirteen, was a year older than Mago, was already talking about going to nursing school in a few years. And little Jimmy, who was eight years old like me, didn't know what he wanted to be yet, but when Doña Caro said her little boy was going to be the mayor of Iguala, no one laughed. If Abuelita Chinta had said the same thing about Carlos, I know the whole neighborhood would have bent over with laughter. "Him? The little orphan?" they would have said.

Abuelita Chinta did her best to look after us, but she didn't earn much as a healer. It was hard for her to feed four children and herself. What little food she bought she distributed evenly among us. Sometimes she went without food and made sure that we were fed first. Money wasn't the reason she tended to the sick of body and mind. But because she was a respected healer, people would sometimes bring her fruit from their trees, guavas, oranges, plums, and she would give them to us. If someone gave her a tablecloth as a gift, she would use that cloth to make dresses for us, saying that her table had no use for such things.

"She's too old for this," Mago said as we watched Abuelita Chinta make her way down the dirt road to do a cleansing. Mago shut her textbook.

"What's wrong?" I asked her.

"What's the point?" Mago said. "Why study so much when we all know I won't finish school. I should just quit now and get a job. Put some food on the table."

"Don't say that!" I said. "You have to finish school. One day, you'll be a secretary. You'll have a good job. You'll make us all proud."

Mago was almost a señorita—almost because she was twelve and her body had not yet begun to bleed, but she kept praying it soon would. She was turning into a pretty girl. Her breasts were starting to grow and the boys were noticing. But Mago was very self-conscious about the way she looked, especially about her scars.

"I'm ugly," she would say while looking at herself in the mirror.

La Quinta Castrejón had a big grove of mangoes at the rear of the lot, behind the beautiful hall for parties and the swimming pools. The owner of La Quinta was called El Cuervo, the crow, because he dyed his hair black, always dressed in black, and owned a black car.

Carlos and some of his friends decided to take a trip to the grove to help themselves to some of those mangoes. Their first attempt was successful, and Carlos came back with a bucketful of small mangoes. We gobbled them up with chili powder. "Next time," Carlos said, "I'll bring more mangoes. You can sell them at the train station, Mago. Maybe then you'll have enough money for your uniform."

The next time Mago and I went with Carlos and his friends. One of the boys was put in charge of looking out for El Cuervo while the rest of us climbed up the trees. I didn't go up too high because I was afraid of heights. But the mangoes within my reach were tiny. Higher up, mangoes the size of a man's fist hung like giant Christmas decorations. Carlos kept going higher and higher up the branches. Mago told him not to go too high, but Carlos didn't listen. The bigger the mangoes, the more we could get for them at the train station, he told her.

"¡Ahí viene el Cuervo! Quick, get out. The Crow is coming!" At hearing this, we jumped down from the trees. Mago grabbed my hand and together we rushed to the hole in the fence. We turned to look behind us and gasped at seeing that Carlos was still up in the tree. Because he had climbed too high, he was now struggling to get down. We heard El Cuervo's car crunching the gravel on the dirt path as he drove into his property.

"¡Apúrate!" Mago hissed at Carlos. He jumped down from the last branch and his bag broke. All the mangoes rolled in different directions. By then the kids we came with were running toward the train tracks, rushing home. But Carlos was busy picking up his mangoes and there was El Cuervo, unlocking the gates, ready to come in.

"¡Déjalos!" Mago yelled. But Carlos wouldn't leave the mangoes. He scrambled to pick them up and used his shirt to hold them.

"Hey, get off my property!" El Cuervo yelled. A gunshot rang out. We pulled Carlos out of the hole in the fence and ran as fast as we could back to Abuelita's house.

"Don't ever go back there again, you hear?" Mago said. "It was a bad idea. I should never have let you come!"

"I'll be more careful next time," Carlos said.

"I said no!" Mago hit Carlos on the arm and took off running.

"But your uniform . . ." Carlos said, but Mago was already long gone.

We came home to find Abuelita Chinta and Mago sitting around Betty on Abuelita's bed. Abuelita Chinta was making a paste with the sap and pulp of aloe vera leaves. Mago was putting a wet cloth on Betty's face, who was crying uncontrollably.

"What happened to her?" I asked.

"I was boiling water," Abuelita Chinta said between sobs. "For her bath."

Every few days, Abuelita Chinta would send Carlos, Mago, and me to bathe in the canal. The water was the color of coffee, and once in a while a piece of horse dung would float by, but it was fun to play in the water. Betty, as the youngest, bathed at home. That day, as Abuelita Chinta was carrying a pot of boiling water outside to mix the hot water with the cold water in the bucket, she lost her grip on the pot, and the boiling water splashed down on Betty's face.

Betty's cries were deafening. Mago took off the wet cloth so that Abuelita Chinta could apply the aloe vera paste, and I gasped at seeing Betty's red face. Her skin looked as if it were melting.

"Let's take her to the doctor, Abuelita," Mago said.

"We have no money," Abuelita Chinta said. "And I don't know when your mother is going to call. But you're right, Mago, your sister needs a doctor. She's in too much pain, and I don't think my remedies will be enough."

"But you're a great healer," I told Abuelita Chinta. "You can heal anything, can't you?"

Abuelita Chinta put her hand on my arm and said, "No, mija. There are many things I cannot cure. I couldn't heal my son. I couldn't heal your mother's broken heart. And now, I can't even help your little sister."

Mago stood up. "I'll be right back," she said, and then left.

Mago came back with money she had borrowed from Doña Caro. She picked up Betty and carried her out of the house. We followed behind her. Abuelita Chinta hailed a cab, and we squeezed in. It was a long, painful ride. I put my hands over my ears to block out Betty's cries. By the time we got to the emergency room, huge blisters had popped all over Betty's face, some oozing a pinkish liquid that mixed in with her tears. We were at the hospital for many hours. The doctor put a yellow ointment on Betty's face and wrapped her head with gauze. He did the same to the areas on her arms and chest that had gotten burned.

Mago barely had enough money left over to buy the medicine the doctor had said to buy. "We're going to need more money," she told Abuelita Chinta as we walked out of the pharmacy. "This medicine won't be enough. And we need to do things right. I don't want my little sister getting any scars on her face."

In the morning, Mago left early and didn't tell us where she was going. She came back with news that she'd gotten a job at the train station, selling quesadillas at one of the food stands. "I'm starting there tomorrow," she said.

"But what about school?" Abuelita Chinta asked.

"I'm still going to go. I'll go to my job after school. Maybe it will be enough to pay for my uniform and buy Betty's medication."

Abuelita Chinta looked down at the floor and shook her head. "I'm sorry, my granddaughter."

"Don't be," Mago said.

The next day Carlos didn't come home with us after school. He claimed he had something to do and took off without another word. Mago and I hurried home because she only had about half an hour to do her homework. It was Mago's first day of work. Her job was to help out at Doña Rosa's food stand. As part of her wages, Doña Rosa promised to give her any leftover quesadillas.

Abuelita Chinta tried to feed Betty bean broth, but it was painful for Betty to open her mouth, and after a spoonful or two, she pushed the bowl away from her. Abuelita Chinta held her gently and kissed the top of her head. "I'm so sorry, mi niña. I'll never forgive myself."

"It wasn't your fault, Abuelita," I said quickly.

Carlos came home with great news. He'd gone to visit Tía Emperatriz to ask if she could make Mago her flag-bearer uniform. "She said to come pick it up next week."

"Thanks be to God," Abuelita Chinta said, crossing herself. *Maybe Mago doesn't have to work, after all*, I thought. But then I looked at Betty, who looked like a mummy with her face all bandaged up, and I remembered there was another reason Mago had looked for a job.

At dusk, Abuelita Chinta sent us to the train station to wait for Mago. "It will soon be dark, and it is not safe for your sister to walk home by herself," she said.

Carlos and I put on our sandals and left. We had a competition to see who could balance on the rail the longest. Soon, we heard the rumbling of the approaching evening train, and we turned to see it snaking its way through the hills, shaking the leaves of the guamúchil trees along the tracks. The conductor blew the whistle as Carlos and I scrambled out of the way. We rushed down to the dirt path and ran alongside the train.

When we got to the station, most of the passengers had gotten off the train, and the few that were continuing on to Cuernavaca or Mexico City were boarding. We sat on a bench and watched Mago go from passenger car to passenger car carrying a tray of hot chicken

Iguala's train station

quesadillas, offering them to the people who were sitting in their seats, waiting for the train to depart. The whistle blew, the conductor yelled, "¡Váaaaamonoooooos!" but Mago was still inside the train. Last-minute passengers hurried to get on. "Come out, come out," I said under my breath. The train started to move, and Mago was nowhere in sight.

I stood up and rushed over to the train. "What are you doing?" Carlos said as he ran after me. The train slowly began to pull out of the station.

It would be so easy, I thought, *for Mago to stay on the train. She could decide to leave this place and not come back. She could finally say that enough was enough, that she was tired of being our little mother.* My breath caught in my throat, and I found myself rushing to the moving train, walking alongside of it, searching desperately for my sister. "Mago! Mago!" I yelled, tears already streaming down my face. Then finally, Mago appeared on the landing of the last passenger car with an empty tray and jumped off just before the train sped up.

"I thought you were leaving me," I told her reproachfully. She laughed and ruffled my hair.

"Never," she said. We stood by the train as it rushed past us in a blur.

16

Abuelita Chinta

Mami's sister, Tía Güera, would usually come over during the week to visit Abuelita Chinta. She and my grandmother would take two plastic chairs and sit outside the shack. I dreaded my aunt's visits. She would call me over to delouse my hair. It was excruciating getting deloused by her. She seemed to get too much pleasure out of hunting for the little suckers, and she would pull out whole strands of hair along with the lice. At this rate, I would tell myself, I'm going to go bald!

It was also excruciating to have to listen to her talk. My aunt would do her usual complaints: "Ay, Amá, I don't have any money to buy food and my husband drinks his wages away." Or "Ay, Amá, there's a sharp pain in my stomach that won't go away, and I think someone is doing witchcraft on me." Or "Ay, Amá, why is my husband such a drunk? Maybe you can make him a remedy so that he can stop." Or, "Ay, Amá, how hard life is. Why does my husband stay out all night long, saying he's working, but then comes home smelling of some other woman's perfume?"

"Let me make you a tea of flor de azahar," Abuelita Chinta would say to Tía Güera once she was done listening to my aunt's complaints. "It's good for the nerves." I wanted to ask Abuelita Chinta if she had anything for my poor scalp, which by then would be throbbing with pain.

But one day, just as they were about to go inside the shack, Doña Caro came out of her house and called out to my grandmother.

"Doña Jacinta," she said as she walked over to us. "Juana called this morning, but you weren't home."

Mami would sometimes call us at Doña Caro's house to tell us she had wired money so that Abuelita Chinta could go pick it up at the bank. The phone calls were rare, but nevertheless, every day we would stop by Doña Caro's house to check if our mother had called. Abuelita warned us about annoying Doña Caro, but we couldn't stop ourselves from inquiring about the phone call.

"I'm afraid something awful has happened," Doña Caro said. "Juana and the wrestler got into a car accident, and he's dead."

"And my daughter?" Abuelita Chinta asked. I grabbed her hand and I leaned against her.

"She was in the hospital. She said to tell you she's coming home."

"Is Mami really hurt?" I asked Doña Caro.

"Nothing serious, child. Just a cut and some bruises," she said, then she turned and went back to her house.

For the following days, all we could think about was our mother, and the thought that we had come so close to losing her would keep us up at night.

∞

Years later, my mother would tell me the story of the wrestler, of how she had not meant to fall in love with him, but this is the way things happen sometimes, especially when you're hurting from a broken heart. He worked next door to the record shop.

He told her, "I only sell car insurance during the day. At night, and on the weekends, I'm a luchador. I dream of one day becoming a great wrestler, like the legendary El Santo."

That's when she began to think of him as more than just the man who worked next door. That's when the small things he did for her—like bringing extra tacos to share with her during lunch, buying her popsicles from La Michoacana across the street, watching the record shop for her when she needed to make a quick run to the bathroom—became much bigger in her eyes. A luchador! There was more to this man, Francisco, than met the eye, after all. But a wrestler? Who would have thought?

She liked the way he stood next to her, as if ready to protect her from any harm that came her way. And being a wrestler, he could protect her from anything. Anyone. When he took her to a wrestling match and won, she decided that Francisco would be the man to save her. From what? She didn't know. All she knew was that my father had let her go, that he had come after her with a gun, and ever since that day, she'd felt as if she were trying to stay afloat, with nothing to hold on to. Francisco would be her way out of the sorrow and fear that threatened to engulf her every waking hour. When he asked her to go with him to Acapulco, she didn't think twice about it.

But then, as she lay with her head against the shattered windshield of his car and saw him slumped over the steering wheel, unconscious, she realized that even he, with all his strength, couldn't save her.

During the two weeks after Mami's return, I would wake up to the sound of crying. In the thin moonlight streaming through the gaps between the bamboo sticks, I saw her sitting in her bed, trembling as she sobbed. We hadn't known how to comfort her or what to say, so we stayed away. She stayed away from us too, and only once did she try to hold one of us—my little sister. Yet when she reached for Betty, my sister cried and held her arms out to Mago.

"Why are you crying? I'm your mother," Mami said. But Betty just

cried harder, and Mami had no choice but to give her back to Mago.
She didn't try to hold her again.

"You have to give her time," Abuelita Chinta said. "You've been
gone for many months, Juana."

"I came back, didn't I?" Mami said. The truth is that she had come
back, but would she have done so if the wrestler hadn't died? Would
she have come back if my father hadn't left her for someone else? We
didn't know the answers to our questions, and we were afraid to ask.

In the morning, Abuelita Chinta gave Mami a cleansing. She sent
Carlos to the neighbor's down the street to buy an egg while she gathered the rest of the items she would need: the bottle of almond oil,
a bunch of epazote from her garden, a cigarette. Mami lay down on
the bed. Abuelita Chinta sat next to her on the edge and began to rub
Mami's body with the almond oil. My grandmother prayed under her
breath as she did this. She took the egg from Carlos and then rubbed
it on Mami's head, being careful not to touch the bandaged area on
Mami's forehead where she had gotten cut. Then she rolled the egg
on her chest, arms, hands, legs, and feet so that it would absorb the
impurities inside my mother's body and soul. Mami kept her eyes
closed as my grandmother gently tapped the branches of the epazote
all over her body.

Finally, Abuelita Chinta lit a cigarette and blew puffs of smoke all
over Mami. The smoke settled over Mami like an invisible blanket.
The cleansing was so soothing that she fell asleep, and Abuelita Chinta
sent us all outside to let our mother rest.

"Hopefully now her soul can be at peace," Abuelita Chinta said.
I crossed myself at the altar on my way out the door and prayed for
Mami to wake up without any more sadness weighing her down.

The next day, Mami sent Carlos to the neighbor's house to buy water
from them on credit so that she could bathe. For the first time since
she'd been back, she stood in front of the mirror to put on makeup.
She pursed her lips, and I imagined that she was kissing Papi through
the mirror. With the bright red color on her lips, hot pink cheeks, and

dark blue eye shadow, Mami became a different woman, and I could almost see that other mother—the one she was before she left—peeking through.

She combed her black hair with her fingers and wrapped a bandana over her head to cover the area where the doctors shaved her hair to stitch up her cuts. She opened the dresser and took out the nicest dress she had, the burgundy dress she wore that bittersweet day when she picked us up at Abuela Evila's house after she'd arrived from El Otro Lado. Then she sprayed on perfume that smelled of jasmine.

"Well, wish me luck," she said to us as she left the house, and the four of us knelt at my grandmother's altar and prayed for Mami to find a job.

She came back with a smile on her face. Don Oscar, her former boss, had given her back her old job at the record shop, although she would have to work the afternoon shift. "But a job is a job," Mami said, smiling, "and beggars can't be choosers." Even Betty, only three, seemed to know it was a time to celebrate because when Mami reached out for her, Betty jumped into Mami's outstretched arms.

Mami said, "Let's go to el zócalo." We washed our dirty feet and faces as quickly as we could and then went to the main road to catch a taxi. Unlike Abuela Evila, Abuelita Chinta would take us there once in a while. She never made us feel as if we were her prisoners. But we hadn't been there in years with our mother.

Mami asked the taxi driver to drop us off at my aunt's house. She lived downtown, close to everything. Tía Güera and my cousin Lupita came with us to el zócalo, and while she and Mami sat on a bench and talked, we played hide-and-seek with the other children. Across the street was the San Francisco Church, and food vendors lined the sidewalk, shaded by the tamarind trees. People sat on the benches located around el zócalo, some reading the papers, others talking, some watching us children play. I thought about how painful it had been to go there with Abuelita Chinta because I would see all those mothers and fathers sitting on the park benches watching their kids play.

How different it felt that day! While I ran and laughed and chased the kids around el monumento a la bandera, I would glance at the bench where my mother was sitting with my aunt, and I would wave at her because I wanted to make sure I was not just imagining her. When she waved back, I felt as if I were flying because it was so good to know that I was not dreaming.

On Mami's first payday, she came home and said, "Let's go to a matinee." I'd never been to the movies, and I was still sad about the day we didn't get to go see *La Niña de la Mochila Azul* with Tía Emperatriz, but that day we hurried to put on our best clothes.

We went to the theater, and Mami bought us a bag of popcorn smothered in chile sauce. We sat in the middle section, and we fought over who was going to sit next to Mami, but the fight didn't last long because Mami said the youngest kids got to sit by her, which meant Betty and me! So I sat on her left, Betty on her right, and Mago and Carlos sat farther out. I knew Mago was mad because she stuck out her tongue at me right before the movie started.

The movie we watched was called *Mamá, Soy Paquito.* It was about a boy who was very poor and lived with his mom, who worked very hard to take care of him. But one day his mom died, and Paquito was left all alone and everyone treated him badly because he was a little orphan. His father didn't live too far, but he might as well be living as far away as El Otro Lado for all the good it did to Paquito to have his father so close. His father was very rich. I thought about the distance between me and Papi, and I thought it was the same for Paquito. My father was far away, but Paquito was a world apart from his father because that is the way things are, between the rich and the poor, even if they live side by side.

I cried when Paquito went to his mother's grave and sang her a song and promised to be a good boy. I glanced at Mami and saw that her eyes were as watery as mine. She reached up to touch her bandana. I wondered if she was thinking what I was thinking. If she had died in that car crash, what would have happened to us?

I leaned my head against Mami's arm, and she reached out and played with my hair.

Then a few weeks later, Mami came home full of excitement. She said, "The government is giving away land!" and hurried to gather the things she thought we would need to become squatters.

So Mago carried Betty, Carlos carried a rope, I carried a blanket, and Mami led the way with a shovel and a flashlight in her hands.

We hurried to keep pace with Mami as we headed to the river. On the other side of the river was a grove of mangoes and tamarind trees. We came to a big meadow. There were people there already staking out their piece of the land the government was going to give away. Mami chose one of the few available spots, and she had Carlos gather some branches to use as posts. Once they were in the ground, we tied the rope from one post to another to create one big square. Mami walked into the middle of the square, put a blanket down, then sat and smiled. "Here is where we're going to live," she said. "I'm going to show your father that I can build my own dream house, too."

Mago, Carlos, Betty, and I sat next to Mami. All around us were families, who, like us, were there because they also had a dream. They were building tents out of torn sheets, cardboard, branches, and pieces of corrugated metal. Some had a fire going and were cooking a meal out in the open. I caught a whiff of beans, and my stomach growled. We hadn't brought a single thing to eat.

"So what happens now?" Mago asked.

"We wait," Mami said. "They didn't say when exactly the government officials are going to be coming by to give us the deed to the land, but it shouldn't be long. For now, we can't go anywhere or we'll lose our spot."

I turned to look behind me. The river was only about fifty feet away. I thought of my cousin Catalina. I didn't want to live this close to the river that cut my cousin's life short. I thought of La Llorona, and how she always roams rivers, canals, and creeks. I didn't want to live anywhere close to water.

"I'm hungry," Betty said.

"Me, too," Carlos said.

"Me, too," Mago and I said. Mami shook her head at us.

"Think of this as an adventure," Mami said. She grabbed a stick and got up. "Here is where my room will go. Where do you kids want your room to be?"

Mago got up and ran to a spot. "Here, over here, so that I can get a nice view of the river."

Carlos said he wanted his room to face the mountains.

"Do I get my own room, or do I have to share it with Mago?" I asked.

Mami said, "You can have your own room."

So I got up and walked around and thought about where I wanted my room to be. I chose the spot next to Carlos because I didn't want a view of the river. But I did love the mountains.

"And here is where the kitchen will be, and the living room," Mami said, tracing the lines on the dirt with her stick.

But we could not be adventurous for long with an empty stomach. We sat under the hot sun with nothing to eat or drink. Finally, Mami couldn't take our complaints anymore, and she got up and said, "Let's go home so you can have your dinner, but only you girls. Carlos, you will stay to guard our land."

Carlos groaned. "But I'm hungry, too."

"Don't you dare go anywhere, not even to use the bathroom. I'll come back with food and water for you."

As we headed down to the tracks, I turned to wave goodbye to Carlos. He didn't see me. He was sitting on the ground scratching the dirt with a stick. I wondered if he was drawing the furniture for his bedroom. He wiped his forehead once and kept on scratching the dirt.

Because he was the only male in our little family, Mami appointed Carlos the head squatter, which meant he was responsible for watching our land. On the days that followed, Mago and I went to school while Carlos stayed by himself down by the river. He built himself a tent using branches, an old blanket, and pieces of cardboard Tío Crece found outside Doña Chefa's store. As soon as we got back from school, Mago and I rushed over to Carlos with food. By the time we got there, Carlos was about to pee himself. He rushed into the nearest bushes while we laughed.

"Why won't they hurry up and give us the land?" Carlos asked. "I don't want to be here much longer."

"Is it really scary?" I asked him. Carlos had been sleeping out there by himself at night. Mami wouldn't let Mago or me stay with him because we were girls. Sometimes, Tío Crece would come over with his dog to keep him company, but he never spent the night. He said he might be crazy, but he was not crazy enough to be sleeping out in the open and on the ground where a scorpion, a centipede, or a tarantula could crawl on him and sting him. "I have my hammock at home," he said.

Mami checked on Carlos as often as possible. She would bring him caramel candies, lollipops covered in chili powder, comic books, and a bag of little green soldiers to help him pass the time.

"Any time now, mijo, just be patient," Mami would say.

"I'll be patient, Mami," Carlos replied. Now that we had our mother back, we wanted to make sure that this time we would keep her with us.

Then Abuelita Chinta said, "Juana, this is ridiculous. It's been two weeks already. How much longer are you going to keep that boy out there in the middle of nowhere?"

"For as long as necessary," Mami said. "A thing like this requires sacrifices. You know that, Amá."

Soon, Carlos got sick with a cough and Abuelita Chinta said it was the midnight chill and the morning dew that was getting into his lungs.

"What will you do if he catches pneumonia?" Abuelita Chinta asked.

"He won't. Any minute now, we'll get the deed and we'll have our own land."

Mami sat at the kitchen table with us as we did our homework. She asked me for a piece of paper and my coloring pencils. Then, just like a little girl, Mami drew a picture of a house. She even drew sunflowers and trees and a rainbow over the house. She proudly showed us her artwork and then she went over to the wall to hang her picture.

I thought about the three little pigs story, of that brick house that had kept the third pig safe. I wanted so much for Mami's dream to come true. What if she were right? What if she really could show Papi that she could build a dream house of her own?

"Any day now," Mami said to no one in particular.

But the next day Carlos was worse. He coughed so much the other squatters complained they couldn't sleep at night because of his coughing. "Take the boy home," they would tell Mami. She bought him some cough syrup and a little jar of VapoRub and every day before going to work, she would check on him. Abuelita Chinta watched with worried eyes, until finally she said, "Come on, mijas, let's resolve this problem once and for all." We went with our grandmother to the river and by then Carlos was burning up with fever. He was sleeping on the ground on top of his blanket and his arms were wrapped around his legs. He had wet himself and flies buzzed all around.

"Come on, mijo, let's go home," Abuelita Chinta said as she picked him up. Even in his feverish state, Carlos refused to get up.

"No, no, no. I want to help Mami with her dream house."

I wanted to stop my grandmother from ruining our chance at such a house, but at the sight of my brother I knew that the price would be too high if anything happened to him. He was so weak it wasn't hard for us to pick him up. Between my grandmother, Mago, and me, we took my brother home where my grandmother immediately set out to cure him.

When Mami came home, she ran over to the river to save her land, but by then new squatters had moved in. She came back home in tears.

"I'm sorry, Mami," Carlos said. He buried his head in the pillow and coughed for a long time.

"Maybe we'll get it next time," I said.

Mami didn't say anything. She yanked her drawing off the wall where she had hung it on a nail and looked at it for a long time. Just as I fell asleep, I thought I heard the sound of paper being torn to shreds.

17

Betty, Mami, Mago, Tía Güera, and
Lupita at Mago's graduation

MAGO AND I stood by the tracks watching the train rumble past us. Mago said, "That train could take us to El Otro Lado."

"Really?" I asked, taking her hand as we started walking toward downtown. Carlos walked on the tracks, bending down once in a while to pick up bits of gravel.

"You should see, Nena," Mago said, "how many people at the train station are heading to El Otro Lado. I've asked them about the journey, and it doesn't seem so bad. They ride the train to Mexico City, transfer to another train, and ride it all the way to the border. We could save up some money, buy the train tickets, and go."

"But how would we find Papi?" Carlos asked, joining us.

"We'll ask around when we get there," Mago said.

"My teacher says Los Angeles is very big," Carlos said, shooting a rock at a bird with his slingshot. He missed.

"But what about Mami?" I said. "Would we leave her here?"

"Why not?" Mago said. "She's left us again, hasn't she? She won't care whether we leave or not."

"Yeah, but—" I said, ready to defend Mami. I was still thinking about that drawing she had torn into shreds.

"But what?" Mago said.

"I don't know. I just wish things were different," I said.

We walked the rest of the way downtown in silence, on our way to Mami's work.

Not long after the government had finally given away the land Mami so desperately wanted, she decided it would be best if she went to live with Tía Güera. Back then my aunt had lived downtown, a few blocks away from my mother's work. Mami started staying over at her apartment a day or two during the week. Then it became three days, then four, until finally she packed up her clothes and said she was moving in with my aunt. Since she would get out so late from work, the public minibuses weren't running by then, and Mami had to take a cab home. "The cab fare is seven times the bus fare. That's money we can use to buy food," she would say. "Also, I'm frightened of walking home at night on these dark streets. What if something happened to me?"

"I can walk you home," Carlos said, holding tightly to his slingshot.

"Mijo, you're only ten years old. I don't think a robber would be frightened of you and your slingshot," Mami said.

We begged her to stay with us. We promised we would be good, but Mami shook her head and said it was for the best.

By then, my memory of Papi had become a wisp of smoke. Sometimes I would forget that I had a father, and whenever I remembered him, the memory of him did not hurt. It did not take the breath out of my body or sting me and fill me with pain like the venom of a scorpion.

But the thought of my mother living apart from me made my body tremble, my teeth clench in my mouth, my eyes burn as they did whenever we had no money to buy gas and I would have to fan the hot coals in the brazier as our meal slowly cooked.

If she hadn't returned from El Otro Lado, Mago said I would have already forgotten her, the way I'd forgotten Papi. Little children are blessed with short memories. But my mother's constant comings and goings wouldn't let me forget her. Instead, they increased my longing for her even more.

She visited us on Sundays, and every time she left us, Carlos, Mago, and I would keep ourselves from running after her. Betty chased after her like a little duckling. We were left behind to comfort our little sister, to hold her while her tears subsided, to make funny faces and stick out our tongues, do cartwheels and handstands, sneak into the neighbor's yard and steal juicy guavas and mangoes to sweeten the bitter memory of the one who came and went.

Since my grandmother didn't have a refrigerator, we had to go to el mercado every day to buy the ingredients for that day's meal. But first we had to stop at Mami's work so she could give us money.

Whenever we walked there, we would be out of breath and our feet would be hurting. It would take us forty-five minutes to get there and another forty-five to get back. Mago could get there by herself on the combi, but she didn't like going alone and we couldn't afford the bus fare for us all, so we walked. Mago thought I should stay home, that it was too far for me to walk, but I wanted to see Mami more often than four days a month and so I would come. And I wouldn't complain about my feet hurting because if I did Mago would stop bringing me. She had been less patient with me. With us all.

Usually Mago would go in there and wouldn't even talk to Mami. She would just hold out her hand for the money and then quickly leave the record shop, and all I could do was turn around and wave a quick goodbye to my mother.

But one day, when we went inside, Mami wasn't alone. Her boss, Don Oscar, was there, and his son was there, too. I knew he was his son because he looked just like Don Oscar, and Mami was always talking about Don Oscar and his family, about the three record shops they owned and the money they had. I saw Mago wiping the dust off her face with her hand. But she couldn't do anything about the dust that covered her feet.

"Hola, niños, how are you?" Don Oscar said. We said good afternoon to him and his son, who was about Mago's age. "Mago, your mother tells me you've done very well in school. I'm very proud of you."

"Thank you, señor," Mago said.

"Mago, I asked Don Oscar to be your godfather for your graduation, and he's accepted. Isn't that great news?" Mami said. She came and put an arm around Mago's shoulders. My sister tried to skirm away from Mami, because even though it was the most amazing news we'd heard in a long time, Mago was still too angry at Mami for leaving us again.

"Thank you, señor," Mago said.

"We'll have the graduation party at my sister's house," Mami said. "It would be an honor if you and your family joined us, Don Oscar."

"Of course, of course," he said.

Mami gave us the money for our shopping, and she even gave us a few extra pesos so that we could buy ourselves a treat. Then we said our goodbyes. We walked out the door, and Mago stopped and turned to look at Oscar Jr. one more time. He smiled at her and she blushed all the way to el mercado.

"I think he likes you," Carlos said.

She blushed even more. "I don't think he would like someone like me," she said.

"Why not? There's nothing wrong with you," I said.

"Of course there is. I'm poor."

I thought about the movie we saw with Mami, of Paquito and his rich father. There was nothing wrong with Paquito except that he was poor. I told Mago I knew what she meant. But still, I thought about all those soap operas Tía Emperatriz liked to watch, the ones where tragically beautiful girls are saved from their miserable poverty by handsome rich men who fall desperately in love with them.

"Oscar can be your hero," I insisted. "He can save you."

Mago looked at me and said, "Papi will be my hero. *He* will save me. Save us all."

Don Oscar, his wife, and their three children attended Mago's sixth-grade graduation. They brought her three huge bouquets of flowers. She was the envy of the class because nobody else had gotten wealthy people for godparents. Everyone else's flower bouquets couldn't compare to the ones Mago got.

Mago wore her white flag-bearer uniform, which was the nicest outfit she owned. We all stood up and clapped for my sister when her name was called.

The party was held at Tía Güera's apartment building because it had a nice courtyard. To our surprise, Mami went out of her way to be nice to Mago. She even gave her a set of gold earrings that dangled from her ears. They looked too grown up on my twelve-and-a-half-year-old sister, but that was why Mago loved them—that, and because they were a gift from Mami.

That day was the first time in a long time that Mago didn't have to be anyone's mother. She didn't have to clean or take care of anything or anyone. For the first time, Mago could be a girl. Mami, Abuelita Chinta, and Tía Güera took care of the guests. They served the food and drinks. While the adults talked, we were free to run around the courtyard. We were very shy around Don Oscar's kids; even though they were our age, they belonged to a different class than us. They had beautiful clothes, they went to private schools, they spoke formal Spanish, and once in a while they giggled at the way we talked. Mago never stopped blushing when Oscar Jr. looked her way.

I didn't know that thirteen years later, I would return to Iguala during my junior year of college, and I would be invited by Don Oscar to celebrate Christmas with his family. I would find myself wearing clothes as nice as theirs. I would find myself not gawking at their two-story brick house because by then I would have set foot in similar houses in the United States. I would find myself sitting in their living room, and having Oscar Jr. and his sisters shove lyrics of their favorite American songs at me so that I could translate them for them. I would find myself telling them about my college courses after Oscar Jr. had told me about his last year at UNAM, Mexico's biggest public university. I would return to the U.S. more determined than ever, because even though I had drunk Bailey's with them, dined and sang English songs with them, my cousin Lupita, Tía Güera's daughter, was working for them as a maid. And I knew then, as I do now, that could also have been my fate.

18

Reyna, Mami, Mago,
Carlos, and Betty

A FTER MAGO'S PARTY, our relationship with our mother improved. We were like Hansel and Gretel. No matter how many times we were abandoned and left to fend for ourselves, we would always follow the crumbs back to Mami. As the months went by, she continued to visit us on Sundays, but the visits weren't awkward anymore, and she would often take us to el zócalo where she would treat us to a churro, a cup of crushed ice with tamarind syrup, or a corn on the cob. But there were times when I was afraid that one day, the crumbs would not be there to guide us back. I would see her sitting there on the bench at el zócalo, and instead of watching us play, she would be looking longingly at the couples strolling around hand in hand. I wasn't old enough to understand that Mami was two people in one: a woman who wanted to be loved by a man, and a mother who wanted to do right by her children. But the look on her face was enough to alert me to the conflict inside her. When men passed by and glanced at her, sometimes even stopping to ask her for the time, it terrified me. It made me want to hide her, turn her into Rapunzel and lock her up in a tower, away from men's prying eyes.

When the Christmas season finally arrived a few months later, las posadas took my mind off my worries. The Christmas season is something that all of us kids looked forward to, when our bellies would be stuffed like piñatas with peanuts, jicamas, candy, oranges, and sugarcane. Beginning on December 16th and ending on the 24th, churches all over Iguala did reenactments of the difficult journey Mary and Joseph took as they traveled from Nazareth to Bethlehem looking for shelter. The evening would end with a party at someone's home, where participants would be offered hot fruit punch, tamales, buñuelos, and a goodie bag. Sometimes we would even get to break a piñata.

At dusk, Carlos, Mago, Betty, and I would hurry over to the church where everyone was meeting. There the "pilgrims" were given a candle. The procession moved out of the church gates, and we began to sing. In the front of the procession were the two boy attendants who held a wooden box with statues of Mary and Joseph. We stopped in front of a house and asked for shelter. *En el nombre del cielo os pido posada, pues no puede andar mi esposa amada.* When shelter was denied, the procession continued on to another house, where again, they wouldn't let us in. *Aquí no es mesón sigan adelante: yo no puedo abrir no sea algún tunante.*

We visited a few more houses until finally we came to the house that would give us "shelter," and we heard the words we'd been waiting to hear since the procession first started: *¡Entren santos peregrinos, peregrinos, reciban este rincón, no de esta pobre morada sino de mi corazón!*

Then we all rejoiced and put out our candles. The children clapped because finally it was time for the best part of the posada—the breaking of the piñata and the goodie bags. We would rush home and share them with our grandmother. Then we went to sleep with our bellies full of fruit and candy.

On the last day of the posadas, Mago, Carlos, Betty, and I went to the part of the town where the wealthy people lived, where Don Oscar and his family lived. In that neighborhood, beside the goodie bags, they would be giving out toys.

Because it would be a long walk in the dark, Abuelita Chinta insisted Tío Crece go with us. Mago and I didn't want him to come, but we also didn't want to walk in the dark by ourselves, so we said okay. He rode his bicycle alongside us. Sometimes, he would put Betty on the handlebars because she was small and tired right away. And it turned out that Tío Crece wasn't feeling crazy that night. Carlos told us jokes about Pepito, and Tío Crece laughed harder than any of us. He even had his own Pepito jokes, and Carlos memorized them to retell to his friends.

We walked for forty-five minutes along the dark dirt roads. By the time we got to the rich neighborhood, the posada was already starting. Our feet were tired from all the walking, but once we got in line, we felt as if we could have walked a hundred miles more for our free toys. Betty and I got a doll, Mago a porcelain tea set, and Carlos a car. We sat on the sidewalk playing with our new toys, eating the peanuts in our goodie bags and sharing them with Tío Crece, who wished he were still a kid and had gotten a goodie bag and a toy for himself.

The next day was Christmas, and Tío Crece found a large dry branch and sanded it until it was smooth. He then painted it white and filled a coffee can with wet cement and stuck the branch into it and waited until the cement hardened and the branch could stand on its own. Then he brought it into the house and told us, "Here is our Christmas tree!"

Abuelita Chinta would save the shells of the eggs she fed us all year long. She would make a little hole in the egg, empty its contents into the frying pan, and then wash the shell and put it in a bag. When Easter came around we would paint the eggshells, stuff them with confetti, and glue a piece of tissue paper on the opening. Then Abuelita would sell most of the eggs, but she would keep a few for us to smash on one another's heads, as is tradition.

Because we didn't have decorations for our tree, we used our eggshells. We painted them in different colors and hung them from our tree, which in the end no longer looked like a branch but a work of art.

Mago and I spent all morning cleaning the house. I sprinkled water on the dirt floor and swept it until it was as smooth as clay. When I was done, Mago used the broom to get rid of the spiderwebs on the ceiling and the walls. We dusted the furniture, wiped the chairs and table, and even went outside to sweep the dirt road. We wanted this Christmas to be special. Mami and Tía Güera were coming over in the evening, and we hoped that if we made the house look beautiful, maybe Mami would finally decide to come back to live with us. We loved spending Sundays with Mami, but seeing our mother only once a week was not enough.

In the evening, when we saw Mami and Tía Güera walking across the bridge, we ran to meet them. There was a man walking with them, and I thought it was my aunt's husband. I had seen him only once or twice, but when they got closer to the house, I knew it wasn't him.

"This is Rey," Mami said.

I turned to look at Mago and saw that her smile had completely vanished. I tried to hold her hand, but she pulled it away.

They came into the house, and I could smell the delicious scent of the roasted chicken Mami had brought. I looked at Rey. He seemed too young for Mami, and later I would learn he was in fact fourteen years younger than she. He was going on twenty-one, and my mother was two months away from turning thirty-five. How flattered my mother must have felt to have a twenty-year-old lusting after her, a woman who had given birth to four children and whose body was not what it had once been. If she had still harbored any insecurities after having been abandoned by my father for another woman, Rey came and helped her get rid of them once and for all.

She met him at the rotisserie where she worked a second job. Rey worked at a hardware store near the marketplace and would go in during his break to buy a meal. At the sight of him, I hated him. I wished his name wasn't the male version of my name. I didn't want to have anything in common with that man, and I especially didn't want to share my mother with him. Suddenly, the chicken didn't smell as good. Our Christmas tree was a branch, and it looked pathetic with all those eggshells. And who were we trying to fool by cleaning the house? No matter how hard we scrubbed, the floor was still made of dirt, the walls were still made of sticks and cardboard.

Abuelita Chinta said, "The children are hungry. They've been working hard all day. Please, let us sit at the table." That which I had dreaded for months now had finally come to pass. I felt my eyes burn with tears, but I quickly wiped them away. I couldn't ruin our Christmas dinner.

Mago, however, had no qualms about ruining our meal. We hadn't been sitting for a minute before she started to cry.

"What's the matter with you?" Mami asked.

"What's the matter? What do you think is the matter with me?" Mago yelled. "Why did you have to bring *him*? This is our night with you. It's Christmas. We don't need you to bring your boyfriends home!"

"I can bring whoever I want," Mami said.

Mago rushed at her, and for a moment, I thought she was going to hit our mother. Instead, she started kicking the chairs, pulling out her own hair, and screaming at the top of her lungs. It sent shivers down my spine. My sister had turned into a monster.

Tía Güera and Mami rushed to Mago and held her down, but Mago just screamed and screamed: "I want to die! I want to die!" They forced her onto Abuelita Chinta's bed, and Mami and Tía Güera pinned her down while Tío Crece grabbed a rope. Rey stood by the door and didn't say or do anything.

"I want to die. I want to die!" Mago shrieked. "¡Me quiero morir!"

"What are you doing?" Abuelita Chinta said.

Nobody listened to her. I held Betty and my cousin Lupita in my arms because Mago was scaring them. She kicked and screamed as if she were possessed by the devil himself. I watched Mami, my aunt, and my uncle tie Mago's ankles and wrists. Mago kicked her legs up in the air and hit Mami in the face before Tío Crece finally restrained her.

I had not noticed Rey had gone outside, but when I looked around, he wasn't there anymore. The screaming suddenly stopped, and when I turned to look at Mago, her eyes were rolling back, then her head hung limply to the side.

"She's fainted!" Abuelita Chinta said, making the sign of the cross. She rushed to her wardrobe where she kept her medicine and came back with a bottle of alcohol. "Look at what you've done, Juana! You should be ashamed of yourself." My grandmother started to cry as she tended to my sister.

Mami's hair was a mess. Her cheeks were stained with mascara and her hot pink lipstick was smeared across her chin. She rubbed her cheek where Mago had kicked her, and I could tell it was swelling. Mami said, "I'm leaving now. If she isn't going to welcome Rey into this house, then I won't stay."

"Juana, be reasonable," Abuelita Chinta said, drying her tears. "You shouldn't have brought that man here. Not tonight. The children wanted to spend this special day with you. Por el amor de Dios, Juana, son tus hijos."

"I'm sorry, Amá." Mami didn't look at us. She walked out the door and left. We sat on the bed, and finally Mago opened her eyes. She looked around and saw that Mami was gone.

"Come, children," Abuelita Chinta said. "The chicken is getting cold and we must not waste the food God has so kindly provided for us."

Carlos and I untied Mago's wrists and ankles, but we stayed there on the bed. Mago got up and headed to the opened door. I thought she was going to go outside and run to catch up to Mami, ask her to please come back. Instead, Mago slammed the door shut.

The next day, as she listened to songs from Juan Gabriel, Mago wrote a letter to Papi. But she couldn't find the right words, so she included lyrics from "Querida," which is about a woman, but the root of the feelings was the same—wishing for that loved one's return.

Iguala, Gro. 26 of December, 1984

Papá, don't get mad when I tell you this, but I can't stand this anymore. I think that when you come back you are going to find me dead and buried because I can't stand this life anymore. Papá, I don't know why you don't love my mom anymore if she hadn't done anything bad. She says you tried to hurt her, but I don't believe that, Papá.

Papá, every moment of my life I think of you. Look at my loneliness. Come. I miss you and cry still for you. Take pity on me. Tell me when you are going to return. Beloved. Come to me as I am suffering. Come to me as I am dying. In this loneliness. In this loneliness . . .

I love you with all my soul.
Magloria Grande Rodríguez

I took Papi's photo down from the wall and placed it on my grandmother's altar, next to my grandfather's picture. There the Man Behind the Glass was surrounded by San Judas Tadeo, El Santo Niño de Atocha, San Martín de Porres, San Antonio de Padúa, La Virgen de Guadalupe, and other saints I didn't know the names of. Maybe while we knelt at the altar to pray, the saints would *have* to deliver our words to our father, now that he was right next to Them. And really, there was only one prayer they had to deliver, only one thing we asked for—that he come back.

19

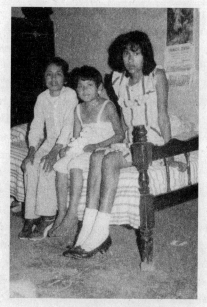

Carlos, Reyna, and Mago

ONE SUNNY DAY in May, when I was four months away from turning ten, my cousin Félix showed up at Abuelita Chinta's house and said, "Your father is going to call you in an hour. He wants to talk to you."

He turned around and ran off, and it took us a moment to recover from the shock. By the time we could speak, Félix was already hurrying across the bridge and turning the corner to head to the main road.

"Papi is going to call?" Carlos asked, and then the question turned into something else when he shouted, "Papi is going to call!"

We laughed and danced around in a circle. "Papi is going to call. Papi is going to call."

"But what are we doing? We don't have much time, let's go!" Mago said. Since Abuelita Chinta wasn't home to give us bus money, we had no choice but to walk to Abuela Evila's. My heart beat so hard against my chest, it hurt. I couldn't believe Papi was going to call. I couldn't believe that soon I would hear his voice.

Is he finally coming home? I wondered. We walked along the pere-férico, passing a mango grove and a sugarcane field. Finally, after forty-five minutes, we came to the entrance of my grandmother's neighborhood, La Guadalupe. I glanced up the hill at the familiar church towers. We stopped to rest by Don Rubén's house, which by then had been turned into a liquor store. The walls were white and a huge Corona bottle was painted on one side. I felt so sad to look at that little house, which was no longer a house but a place for drunks like Tío Crece.

"Come on," Mago said. She wiped her forehead and then picked up Betty. Carlos and I ran after her. Since I didn't want to be the last one to Abuela Evila's house, I ran as fast as I could, but my side hurt and my throat was dry and my head was burning from too much sun. Then I thought of Papi, and I picked up my pace again. I could kiss Juan Gabriel. It seemed that the lyrics of his song had finally touched a chord in Papi. Thank goodness Mago had thought of using them in the letters she had written to him not only in December, but in the past few months as well.

Abuela Evila's house finally came into view.

"What should we tell him?" Mago said as we stood outside our grandmother's gate. There was so much to tell him, but how much time would we have before Abuela Evila snatched the phone from us?

"Let's just tell him we miss him," Carlos said. "I think he has something he wants to tell us, don't you think? Or why would he be calling us, after all this time?"

We knocked on the gate and waited. Then Élida came out and smirked. She glanced at us and shook her head. "You could have at least changed out of those rags," she said. "Look at you, you look like beggars."

"So what?" Mago said. "It's not like he's going to see us like this."

Then my cousin Félix poked his head out the kitchen doorway and laughed. He whispered something to Élida, and then Élida laughed, too. We walked past them and went into the living room. I wondered what could be so funny.

Nobody had to tell me who the man sitting on the couch was. I thought about the eight-by-ten-inch photo I had placed on my grandmother's altar. He had put on weight. He wore glasses now. Instead of black-and-white, he was in color, and I could see that his skin *was* the color of rain-soaked earth. There he was, the Man Behind the Glass, in the flesh.

Papi

"Go say hello to your father." Tía Emperatriz came up from behind us and pushed us toward him. I didn't want to go. All I wanted was to run away, run back to Abuelita Chinta's house, far away from him. I didn't want to see that look on his face. All those years staring at his photo, wishing that his eyes were not looking to the left but instead were looking at me. All those years wishing to be *seen* by him. And here he was, looking at me, but not really seeing me. He couldn't see past the tangled hair, the dirt on my face, my tattered clothes. He couldn't see the girl who had longed so much for this moment, to finally meet her father.

I knew he was ashamed by what he saw. What a cruel joke Félix played on us by not telling us the truth! If he had, we would have bathed and changed our clothes before going to my grandmother's house. Instead, I had to stand before the father I hadn't seen in almost eight years, looking like a beggar. I touched my hair, and I knew it was matted and oily. When was the last time I bathed? I wondered if he could see the lice that at that very moment were running around on my scalp. I had an overwhelming urge to scratch, and I bit my lips and tried not to move.

Papi hugged Mago, Betty, and Carlos and then called me over. I had no choice but to go to him. He hugged me too briefly, too hesitantly, the way one would hug an acquaintance's child, as if out of obligation. Looking back on it now, I understand how awkward it must have been for him as well. We were strangers to him, too.

He introduced us to the woman standing by his side, whom I hadn't noticed until then. My eyes were focused on him, only him.

"This is Mila," he said.

I looked at the woman who had broken up my family. I wanted to yell at her, to say something mean, but I couldn't think of anything to say. Instead, I compared her to my mother. She wore her wavy black hair in a stylish cut, whereas Mami, ever since she returned from El Otro Lado, had worn hers short, like a boy, but permed into tight curls, and dyed a rusty red. Mila was light-skinned and wore makeup in soft colors such as peaches and browns, unlike Mami's dark blues, purples, and hot pinks that didn't go well with her olive skin.

The woman was wearing white pants and a pink blouse, and white sandals with straps. Mami was always wearing flowery dresses like the kind Abuelita Chinta wore. I suddenly wished to see Mami wearing a pretty pair of white pants. I wished that the woman before me didn't look younger than my mother, even though she was five years older. I wished her skin wasn't so light and smooth looking, so different from my mother's sunburned face lined with wrinkles.

I wanted to kick myself for thinking those thoughts. I was betraying my mother. I told myself I should hate that woman, not admire her clothes or makeup or pretty skin.

"I'm starving," Papi said. "Let's eat."

He gave Tía Emperatriz money, and she went to buy a pot of menudo at the nearest food stand. Out of the suitcases, he took out three dolls, one for me, one for Mago, and one for Betty. They were life-size baby dolls with blue eyes that closed when they were laid down, and opened when stood up. I buried my face in my doll's hair and smelled the scent of plastic, the smell of a new toy. He gave us girls a couple of dresses and Carlos got jeans and three shirts. This time, he had gotten our size right. He looked at our feet. I put one foot behind the other, ashamed of my old sandals. He said he hadn't known what our shoe size was, so he hadn't brought us any. He promised to buy us new shoes the next day.

We played with our new dolls. Mago, who was going on fourteen and claimed to be too old for baby dolls, was more than happy to play with Betty and me, just to spite Élida. Papi didn't give Élida anything, and part of me was glad. Now she knew how we had felt when her mother had visited from El Otro Lado and didn't give us a single present. But part of me wanted Papi to be different than Tía María Félix. I wanted him to be kinder to his niece.

Soon evening came and he still hadn't told us why he was there. I waited for him to tell us that he missed us. I waited for him to say he was sorry for being gone for so long. I watched him sitting on the patio with his new woman, laughing at something she said. I felt the sting of jealousy burning sharp like a scorpion sting, and I thought of Mami. Just briefly, I understood how she had felt. For a moment, I understood her anger.

We spent the night at Abuela Evila's house. In the morning Papi shaved Carlos's hair to get rid of the lice. He even gave him a bath, as if my brother were a little kid, but he said Carlos was in need of a good scrubbing. He took us girls to the hair salon and told the hairstylist to cut our hair short. I wanted to protest. I wanted to tell him no. But when I looked at him, I was afraid he would disappear if I angered him. I was afraid he might leave again and never come back. So I sat still and closed my eyes when I heard the hissing of the scissors. I cried silent tears about losing my hair once again.

"Look at all the lice," the hairstylist said to her coworkers. Papi picked up a copy of the newspaper on the seat next to him and hid behind it. Mago sat with Betty on her lap, waiting. When the hairstylist was done with me, it was Betty's turn. She cried and kept moving her head and Mago had to hold her still. When the hairstylist was done with Betty and asked Mago to sit down, Papi said, "Not her." I looked at Mago, and I was so angry I could spit at her. On our way home we stopped at the pharmacy, and Papi bought special lice shampoo and made us wash our hair with it as soon as we got home.

"You didn't have to cut my hair," I said.

"It'll grow back, Chata. Don't worry." My anger disappeared immediately at hearing Papi call me by the special nickname he had given me when I was little.

Later, he inspected the house he had built for us. We were sur-

*Reyna and family in front
of the dream house*

prised to see it almost finished; it just needed the windowpanes installed. As we walked from room to room, we told him how we'd helped to build this house by carrying the gravel and the mortar buckets and bricks. "Which is going to be your room?" Mago asked him. Papi didn't say anything.

In the evening, when Papi reached into his suitcase to grab his pajamas, he found a big surprise. A dozen baby scorpions and their mother came tumbling out to the floor when he took out his pajama pants. I screamed and jumped onto the couch. He stepped on the scorpions and killed them.

"You could've been stung," Mila said, glancing around the floor to make sure he had killed all the scorpions, and then she added, "How soon do you think we can go home?"

Go home? I wondered. *But this is his home.*

As if reading my thoughts, Mago said, "Our house is finished now. He doesn't need to leave again." She turned to him and said, "Right, Papi? You're staying now, aren't you?"

Papi looked at Mila and then at us. "Let's talk about it later. ¿Está bien?"

"Why don't you tell them now, Natalio? Tell them you aren't staying," Mila said.

"All right," he said. He sat us down on the couch and said, "Well, you see, kids, I've decided I can't come back here. Even though the house is finished, there are no jobs here. If I come back, we'll still live in this miserable poverty, ¿entienden?"

"But the house is finished, Papi. We'll be safe there," I said.

"We don't eat much," Carlos said. "You wouldn't need to make a lot of money to feed us. Mago already has a job at the train station. I could get a job, too. I'm old enough."

"No!" Papi said. "You need to go to school. All of you need to stay in school, you hear? Negra, what is this about you working already?"

Mago stayed quiet. He looked at her, waiting for her to say something. Finally, Mago stood up and said, "Abuela Evila was right all along. Excuses, that's all you have to give us. Excuses as to why you can't come back." She ran out of the living room crying.

The next day, Papi told us he would be leaving in a few days. Mila would be flying back because she was a naturalized U.S. citizen. Since he had no papers, he would hire a coyote to take him across the border.

"I'm not coming back here," he said to us. "I have a new life in El Otro Lado. I don't want to give up that life, but I know it isn't fair for you not to have a father. I thought your mother was taking care of you, but now I see that she isn't. I don't have enough money to take all of you with me. I can take only one of you."

Tears gathered in my eyes because I didn't want to hear what he was going to say next. I knew who he had chosen.

"I'm going to take Mago with me. She's the oldest, and she won't have as much trouble running across the border with me."

"You can't take her," I said. "You can't take her."

"Why not?" he asked.

"Because she's all I have."

Mago put an arm around me. I held on tight. I had survived being left by my father. I had lived through my mother's constant comings and goings. But if Mago left me, I didn't think I could survive. I looked at him, and I wished he had not come back. I wished he had stayed where he was. I wished he were just a photograph hanging on the wall. I would've preferred that to losing my sister. Why did he have to come back, only to leave again, and not just that, but take away the only person who truly loved me?

"And what about me, Papi?" Carlos said. "I can run really fast. Just ask my friends. They can never catch me when we play soccer. I'd leave la migra in the dust! Take me with you, Papi."

Papi put his hand on Carlos's shoulder. "You're right, Carnal. You could probably manage the crossing as well as Mago. I'll take you with me. But you, Chata, I cannot."

"How could you split us up?" I asked Papi. "How could you take them away?"

"I don't want to separate you," he said, bending down to look at me. "I will come back for you, Chata. I promise that as soon as I have some money I will come back for you."

I shook my head, unable to believe him. "The last time you left, you were gone eight years, Papi," I said.

Papi looked down and didn't say anything.

We returned to Abuelita Chinta's house that evening because Papi didn't want us to miss school.

"You'll still be here tomorrow, won't you?" Mago asked. We were afraid that while we were gone, he would pack up and leave, never to return again.

"Of course I will, Negra," he said.

At school my classmates wanted to know all about him. They asked painful questions I didn't want to answer. "Is he finally moving back here?" they asked. "Or is he taking you with him?"

I didn't want to tell them the truth. I didn't want to admit that Papi didn't want me. He only wanted my sister and my brother. So I started to lie. "Yes, my papi is taking me to El Otro Lado with him. Goodbye, my friends. I will miss you." I could see the look of envy in their eyes.

"You're so lucky, Reyna," they said to me. By the end of the school day, I was starting to believe the lies myself. But then I was suddenly afraid. When my classmates found out I wasn't going anywhere, they would make fun of me so much I knew I would die of shame because they would never let me forget that my father had not wanted me. Like my mother, I was afraid of people knowing that I had failed.

After school, when we got to Abuela Evila's house, Papi and Mila were sitting on the patio with my grandmother. He called us over, and I was the first to rush to his side.

"Papi, you have to take me back to El Otro Lado with you," I said.

"Why is that?"

"Because I told my friends you would, and I have said goodbye to all of them! I'll die of shame if they know that I lied, Papi. Please take me with you."

He laughed. Mila didn't laugh. She glared at me.

"She's a stubborn one, isn't she?" Mila said.

"You leave her here with me, Natalio, and I will teach her some manners," Abuela Evila said. "This girl needs to learn that bad things come to women who don't know their place."

Mila looked furiously at my grandmother. Abuela Evila had not liked the fact that in the days Papi and Mila had been there, not once had Mila offered to help with the cooking or to wash the dishes. After the meals were over, she usually stood up, along with Papi, and left the kitchen to go sit on the patio or watch TV.

"It's different for women in the U.S.," Mila said. "Over there, women aren't treated like servants."

"I won't go with you if you don't take Reyna," Mago said. "I mean it." I looked at my sister's face, and on it I saw the conflict inside her. I knew she was dying to go. More than anyone, it had been she who had yearned for him all those years. But destiny had also made her become my little mother, and unlike my mother, Mago's maternal instincts won over her need to save herself. "I'm serious, Papi," she said.

"M-me, too," Carlos said, halfheartedly.

Papi reached his hand out to me, and I took it. "You really want to go live with me?"

"Sí, Papi. Please take me with you."

"All right, then in that case, I will take all my children back with me."

"But, but where in the world are you going to get the money?" Mila said.

"We'll borrow it," he said. "Beg everyone we know."

Papi said he would need money to pay a smuggler for the four of us—me, Carlos, Mago, and him. Betty could fly back with Mila since she was a U.S. citizen. For a brief moment, I felt the familiar jealousy I'd felt when I had first heard of my American sister. Being born in the U.S. was a privilege I wished I had had. That way, I wouldn't need to sneak across the border like a thief. I thought about the time Mago, Carlos, and I had tried to steal mangoes from El Cuervo's grove, and how frightened I had been of his gun. I felt a shiver run through me.

"Will they shoot at us?" I asked as we listened to Papi talk about the crossing, the people called la migra. I could hear the fear in his voice.

"No, Chata, no. No one will shoot at us," he said as he sat me on his lap. "Don't be afraid." But I saw the way he glanced at Mila before hiding his face in his beer.

The next day, Mago and I went to give Mami the news. Papi didn't want to talk to her himself, claiming that Mago might have a better chance of convincing her to let us go. He knew Mami had not forgiven him for what he'd done. At the sight of him, who knows what might have happened. As it was, Mago and I had a hard time convincing her to let us go. Fortunately, Tío Gary had come to Abuelita Chinta's house just in time to talk some sense into my mother. He said, "You aren't taking care of them, Juana, why deny them the chance to go to El Otro Lado? Besides, our mother is too old to be taking care of your kids. Let them go, Juana. It's for the best. Don't deny them the opportunity to have a better life."

"Fine," Mami said. "If they want to leave with him, so be it." She turned to look at us and said, "Tell your father that he can't have Betty."

My father was furious. "That's why I couldn't be with her anymore," he had said when Mago had delivered Mami's message. "She has never had a good vision of the future." He turned around and looked at us. "I know I promised not to separate you, but if your mother won't hand over Betty's birth certificate, I won't be able to take her. She's too little to run across the border."

Mago was holding Betty's hand. Papi reached his arms out and put Betty in his lap. "You hear that, mija? Your mother is keeping you from me."

Betty had just turned four in March. Like me, she had no memory of him and this was why, as he held her in his arms, she squirmed away and returned to our side. "I want my mami," she said.

"You see what your mother has done to me?" Papi said. "She has robbed me of my youngest child. There are laws in the U.S. I could have gone to court, filed for custody. I would have had rights. Instead, your mother took off like a thief and came back here, stealing her from me. And now look, my own daughter doesn't even know me."

"You tried to shoot her, Papi," Carlos said. "Mami was scared."

Papi laughed. "She overreacted. I wasn't going to shoot her. And whatever happened to that man was an accident. An accident."

"If you had just listened to your mother, this wouldn't have happened," Abuela Evila chimed in. "I told you she was not good enough for you, Natalio. I told you she would be trouble. But you didn't listen."

"I will go talk to her one more time," Mago said, standing up. "If we're going with you, we can't leave our little sister behind."

Mago and I went to Mami's work. We walked into the record shop and saw Mami dusting the counter while dancing to a cumbia. We stood there and watched her, and I knew that this was a different side to Mami she didn't allow us to see. There she was smiling, dancing, singing, things I hadn't seen her do ever since El Otro Lado had taken her away. I thought that part of Mami was gone. But then I knew that it was there, except not when she was with us.

Mami turned and saw us standing there at the entrance of the store.

"You startled me!" she said, clutching her chest. She rushed to the stereo and turned down the volume.

"Mami, we want you to let Betty come with us," Mago said as she pulled me into the store with her. "We can't leave her behind."

"Well, as you've always said, Betty is my daughter, not yours, so I get to decide her fate," Mami said.

"Why would you separate us like that?"

Mami took a deep breath. "Mago, I don't want to fight with you. If your father wants to take you with him, then you should go. Going to El Otro Lado is a good opportunity, for you, for your brother, for Reyna."

"So, why won't you let us take Betty, too?" I asked.

Mami looked away and didn't answer. Later, I would come to realize that her decision had come from stubbornness. Pride. If she had allowed my father to have Betty, it would have meant that he had won.

"Come on, Nena, let's go," Mago said. We went out into the busy street, and I turned to look behind me. Mami stood there at the door of the record shop and waved goodbye. Too soon, I couldn't see her anymore through the crowd of people rushing down the sidewalk. In my head I could still hear the song Mami was listening to. I could still see her dancing in the record shop, her lips curved into a smile. I pulled my hand from Mago's and stopped walking. *What if I stay? Could Mami be that woman, the one in the record shop, when she was with me? Could she finally start being the mother she was before she left? Maybe she could, maybe she would, but if I leave, then I'll never know.*

"Nena, you coming or what?" Mago said as she stood there holding out her hand to me. I turned to look at Mago, and at the sight of her I knew I could not survive being separated from her. Back then, she had still been *my* Mago. Hers was the first face I saw when I woke up and the last when I fell asleep. How could I think of staying, when knowing that if I did, I would lose the one person who had always stood beside me?

I ran to take my sister's hand, choosing not to follow the crumbs back to my mother.

I thought of Mami dancing in the record shop, and I promised myself that was how I would always think of her, and I would try to forget that other mother, the one who left and left and left.

20

Helicopter over the U.S.-Mexico border

Oᴜʀ ꜰɪʀꜱᴛ ᴛᴡᴏ attempts across the border were failures. Even now I blame myself. I was not used to walking and running so much and so fast. To make things worse, I had woken up with a toothache on the morning of our first attempt, and my father didn't have anything to give me for the pain. Around noon I began to get a fever, and the pain became unbearable. My father ended up carrying me on his back, but still, it wasn't long before a cloud of dust rose in the distance, and before we knew it a truck was heading our way. We rushed into the bushes, but the truck pulled over and border patrol agents got out and told us to come out from our hiding places. We were sent back to Tijuana.

The second time we tried to cross, we had the same bad luck. Again, I couldn't keep up with the rest of them, and the heat of the sun's rays beating down on my head gave me a headache. Once, when we sat down to rest, I walked away to relieve myself in the bushes and found a man lying not too far from me. I thought he was asleep, but when I got closer to him, I saw the flies buzzing over him and the big bump on his forehead.

I screamed for help. Papi arrived first, followed by the coyote, and then Carlos and Mago. Papi told Mago to shut me up before la migra heard me.

"Is he dead?" I asked Mago as she took me away. "Is he dead?"

"He's sleeping, Nena. He's just sleeping," she said.

We got caught shortly thereafter, and I was glad because I couldn't get that dead man out of my head.

I am grateful now that back then I was too young to fully grasp the extent of the danger we were in. I am glad I did not know about the thousands of immigrants who had died before my crossing and who have been dying ever since.

After getting sent back twice, Papi said, "This is the last time, mijos." He sent us off to bed even though it was only two o'clock in the afternoon. But that night we were attempting our third—and final—border crossing, and Papi said we needed to rest as much as possible. We would be running through the night.

Papi lay down on the floor beside our bed and said, "If we don't make it this time, I'm going to have to send you back. And I will send you to my mother, since your own mother isn't doing a decent job of caring for you kids."

"No, Papi, please!" I said. The thought of going back to Abuela Evila's house filled me with dread. But I knew it was my fault. If I hadn't gotten sick the first time, we probably would have made it. If I had walked faster, run faster, not complained about the heat or my hunger, or hadn't constantly asked for water, maybe then we would have made it. If my molar hadn't been hurting me so much and had I not whined about the pain, maybe then we could have made it.

"I'm sorry, mijos. I'm going to lose my job if I miss any more days." He said he didn't have the money to keep paying for food and the motel. He had barely been able to borrow the money for the coyote to take us across the border, and there was almost no money left. Some of it had also been spent on our trip, which had been a very uncomfortable two-day bus ride where we had suffered from endless motion sickness. I don't remember how many times my siblings and I threw up.

"Don't make us go back there again," Mago said in a voice so soft I didn't think he'd heard her. But after a minute or two, Papi finally looked at us. I grabbed Mago's and Carlos's hands and squeezed them. I thought about going back to Abuela Evila's house, back to being an unwanted, parentless child, back to waiting, always waiting, to hear from Papi so far away in El Otro Lado.

He sighed and said, "This will be our last time. If we don't make it, you're going back. Now, go to sleep. You will need all your strength tonight."

But I couldn't sleep. I thought about the past seven days and how quickly they had passed. I thought about Mami, little Betty, my grandmother, and I couldn't help feeling torn about our situation. I was so happy that my father had not left me behind, but I was also sad about leaving my little sister. I felt as if we had abandoned her. The day we left for the bus station she had cried as we walked away. Abuelita Chinta had cried, too. I stopped at the canal to wave goodbye to them and part of me wanted to tell Papi I had changed my mind, that I *did* want to stay. But then I thought about Mago, and I knew I couldn't be without her. And I wanted to have a father. *Why does it have to be so hard?* I had to leave my mother, my little sister, my grandmother—so that I could have a father. But even that was in jeopardy. If we didn't cross that third time, I would lose him.

Please God, give me wings.

Papi woke us up at sunset, and we took a bus to the meeting point where the coyote was waiting for us. We crossed the dirt path, slipped under the hole in the fence, and immersed ourselves in the darkness that had quickly fallen around us. "Remember," Papi said, "this is the last time." He followed the coyote. We followed our father in single file: Mago, me, and Carlos at the end. We walked along a small path, the thin moon curved into a smile, and I thought that if the moon was smiling at us, it must be a good sign. Far in the distance, I saw two red lights, like evil eyes. I shivered.

"They're just antennas," the coyote said when Carlos asked about the lights.

I thought about the church pilgrimages we had taken with Abuelita Chinta a couple of times. *If I once made it through nine days of walking, surely I could make it now, couldn't I?* But hard as I tried, I couldn't lie to myself. This journey was similar to the pilgrimages because we were walking through bushes and hills, but I hadn't been afraid back then. At this moment, every muscle in my body was tense. Every noise, like the chirping of crickets, the wind rustling the branches of the bushes, the sound of our labored breathing, frightened me. I thought those sounds were coming from la migra. I thought that somewhere in the endless darkness, la migra was there, ready to capture us and send us back to Tijuana, and ultimately, back to Abuela Evila's house.

I kept my eyes on Mago's back as I sang the songs from the pilgrimage in my head. I thought about Abuelita Chinta, her gap-toothed smile, and I felt a pang of sadness just thinking about the fact that with every step I took, I was getting farther and farther away from her, Mami, and little Betty.

"Reyna, apúrate!" my father hissed. I sprinted to catch up to the group. I didn't even notice that Carlos had passed me.

At first, it sounded like a kitten purring. Then the sound got louder, and the coyote yelled, "¡Córranle!" In the darkness, I saw him take off without us. My father grabbed my hand and ran, too. I couldn't keep up with his long strides, and I fell flat on my face. He scooped me up and ran with me in his arms. Mago and Carlos followed close behind.

A light shone in the distance, and the purring got louder.

"What's happening, Papi?" Mago asked.

"Helicopter."

Carlos tripped on a rock, but Papi kept on running and didn't wait for him to get up. "Wait, Papi!" I said, but Papi was like a frightened animal. He scampered through the bushes trying to find a place to hide.

"Get down!" the coyote yelled from somewhere in the darkness. Papi immediately dropped to the ground, and we became lizards, rubbing our bellies against the cold, damp earth, trying to find a place to hide. Pebbles dug into my knees. I couldn't see Carlos in the darkness, and I cried and told Papi to wait, but he pushed me into a little cave created by overgrown bushes. Mago and I sat by Papi's side, and he held on to us tight while we listened to the roaring of the helicopter right above us.

The beams of the searchlight cut through the branches of the bushes. I yanked my foot back when a beam of light fell on my shoe. I wondered if the people in the helicopter had seen my foot. I tried to hold my breath, thinking that even the smallest sound could give us away. *Please God, don't let them see us. Please God, let us arrive safely to El Otro Lado. I want to live in that perfect place. I want to have a father. I want to have a family.*

Finally, after what felt like hours, the helicopter left. We could hear the chirping of the crickets once more, the howling of a coyote in the distance, and then we tensed up when we heard the sound of branches breaking.

Papi poked his head out of the cave and sighed in relief. "I'm sorry, Carnal." We came out, and Carlos and the smuggler were standing outside our cave. Carlos smiled, proud of himself for not getting us caught.

"You should have seen him crawl under the bushes," the smuggler said. "He's a real iguana, this one."

When we finally got across the border to a place called Chula Vista, we headed to the house of the second smuggler, the man in charge of driving us to Los Angeles. We got there early in the morning.

My father got in the passenger side of the car, and my siblings and I sat in the back. The smuggler, who was called El Güero, told us to lie down and stay out of sight. Papi said that even though we had succeeded in crossing, the danger was not over yet. We could easily get pulled over by la migra on our way to Los Angeles. So Mago and I lay down on the backseat like spoons and Carlos had to lie on the floor. My stomach growled. We had gone the whole night without food.

As we drove from Chula Vista to Los Angeles, I wished I could get up and see what El Otro Lado looked like. I wanted to see with my own eyes the beautiful place where I would be living from then on. I started to get motion sickness, and the only thing we could look at was the roof of the car, which wasn't very interesting. Then Carlos threw up and for the rest of the trip the car stank of vomit. Finally, the smuggler said we could get up for just a minute, to stretch, and what amazed me the most were the palm trees. I had never seen so many palm trees, and there they were, on either side of the freeway, whizzing by. The freeway was amazing, so enormous compared to the tiny dirt roads in my colonia. And the cars were clean and shiny, so different from the rusty old cars back home. I wanted the smuggler to slow down. I'd never been in a car that traveled so fast, and I knew that in a few seconds I would have to lie back down again. I wanted to take everything in. The last thing I saw when El Güero said to lie down was a pair of golden arches, and I wondered what they were.

"Can't we stop to get some hamburgers for my kids?" Papi asked the smuggler.

I'd never eaten a hamburger before, but I heard this was what people in El Otro Lado liked to eat. My stomach rumbled in anticipation.

El Güero shook his head. "Too risky."

He took out a bag from the glove compartment. I saw him put his hand in the bag and then put something in his mouth. He opened the window and spat. He did that several times, and my curiosity grew more and more, but I was too embarrassed to lean closer to see what he was eating. He must have remembered we were hungry because he said, "You kids want some?"

Mago said, "What is it?"

"Sunflower seeds." He rolled down the window and spat again.

Mago, Carlos, and I looked at one another. Sunflower seeds? Here we were, coming to the richest country in the world, and this man was eating bird food? In my town, I had never, in my whole nine years, seen anyone eat bird food before. I would have preferred one of those hamburgers.

"They're almost like pumpkin seeds," Papi said, urging us to take some.

To my amazement, Mago reached out her hand. She grabbed the bag El Güero gave her and then put a pile of seeds into Carlos's and my cupped hands. She took some for herself and gave the bag back to El Güero.

"Look, there's the exit to Disneyland," El Güero said, pointing out the window. Then he remembered that we couldn't see anything because we were still lying down. "You can get up now," he said. "I think we're safe now."

Mami had mentioned Disneyland and how sad she was that she never got to go while she was here. I hoped one day we would get to see it. I hoped one day I would get to do everything people said you could do in El Otro Lado, like speak English. We sat up and got ready to eat our sunflower seeds. I let Mago go first. She put the seeds in her mouth and chewed them. When she swallowed, she started to choke.

"You're supposed to remove the shell," El Güero said. "I forgot to tell you that."

I put a seed in my mouth and did what El Güero said to do, to crack the shell with my teeth and eat only the kernel inside. I wondered if it was my hunger, but those sunflower seeds tasted delicious. I sucked the salt off the shells before cracking them and eating the inside. My first breakfast in the United States was bird food.

Not too long after, Papi pointed to the tallest buildings I'd ever seen and said that was downtown Los Angeles. I thought about the map Mago had once showed me. I remembered that little dot labeled Los Angeles. It suddenly hit me that Mami and I had switched places, but the distance between us was just as big as it had been three years before.

"How far are we from home?" I asked Papi. "From Iguala."

"Home?" Papi said. "This is your home now, Chata."

I could hear the anger in Papi's voice, and I wished I could tell him that even though this was my home now, my umbilical cord was buried in Iguala.

The smuggler said, "Guerrero is about two thousand miles or so from here."

Two thousand miles was the distance between us and Mami. Between me and the place I had been born. Between me and my childhood, however painful it had been. I turned to look behind me as the car sped on. Mami had once said she didn't want me to forget where I came from.

"I promise I'll never forget," I said under my breath. We exited the freeway and arrived at our new home.

Book Two

THE MAN BEHIND
THE GLASS

Prologue

TWENTY-FIVE YEARS AFTER my new life in the United States began, my father was diagnosed with liver cancer. By then, my siblings and I had little communication with him. By then, he'd managed to chase us away. But as is often the case with terminal illnesses, broken families put themselves back together, and I began to find my way back to my father, although the journey—like the one I took across the U.S.-Mexico border—was not at all easy.

On Tuesday, September 6, 2011, the day before my thirty-sixth birthday, Mago, Carlos, and I found ourselves around my father's hospital bed listening to the doctor tell us he had done everything he could for him. The doctor said we should let our father go.

He didn't know about all the times I had already lost him. Back in Mexico, there was always the hope that he would return. But now there was no hope to cling to. If we let him go, he would not be coming back.

I turned to look at my father. He lay on his hospital bed, only 130 pounds of flesh and bones. His face was sunken in. His skin sagged from all the weight he'd lost. Once, his skin was the color of rain-soaked earth. Now, it was a dull grayish color—like in that black-and-white photograph of him I so cherished. I could tell that he was not here. His eyes were slightly open, and they were glazed over, looking into space, looking at nothing. I wanted him to *see* me. I had always wanted to be *seen* by him.

I couldn't follow all the cords and hoses that came in and out of him. I couldn't understand all the numbers on the monitors next to him. But the wavy lines that represented his heartbeat told me of the conflict within him. His mind had already gone elsewhere. Yet, his heart struggled to hold on. It was fighting a losing battle. His blood pressure was now down to sixty.

The doctor waited for our decision.

I looked at Mago, then at Carlos. Betty lived in Watsonville, a six-hour drive from Los Angeles. But even if she lived here she would not have come. My mother knew what she was doing when she did not allow my father to take Betty. So now it was Mago, Carlos, and I who got to decide our father's fate. Were they thinking what I was thinking? How shocking it was to see him like that. I wanted to remember him how he once was. Robust. Strong. Proud. Cancer had taken so much from him already. It had humbled him in a way I never imagined him being humbled.

"Okay," we said. Mago, Carlos, and I looked at one another and nodded, reassuring ourselves of our mutual decision. "Okay," we said again.

"I'm sorry," the doctor said. "It'll be over quickly. He won't suffer."

We stood around our father. The machines were disconnected one by one from his body. During the interminable twenty minutes that it took for my father's heart to stop beating, the years I spent with him flashed through my mind, from the moment I first laid eyes on him after our eight-year separation, to the first day I came to live with him, to the day I left his house for the last time, to now.

I reached to grab his hand, that hand that was the exact shape of my own, and I held on tight.

1

*Mago, Reyna, and Carlos, recently
arrived in El Otro Lado*

IT WAS SEPTEMBER. We had been in the United States for three
months. The following day, I would be starting fifth grade, Carlos
seventh grade, and Mago eighth grade. We didn't speak a word of
English, and we were frightened. But Papi wasn't worried about our
lack of English. He was worried about something else.

"Don't tell anyone you're here illegally," he warned us.

"We won't, Papi," we said.

"I'm serious," he said. "If you tell anyone anything about how you
got to this country, you can kiss it goodbye. You understand?"

Papi said we had broken the law by coming to the United States,
but back then I didn't understand much about laws. All I could think
of was why there would be a law that would prevent children from

being with their father. That was the only reason I'd come to this country, after all.

"And you three better do well in your classes, because if you don't, I won't wait for la migra to deport you. I'll send you back to Mexico myself!"

"We won't disappoint you, Papi," my sister, my brother, and I promised while nodding our heads.

Papi leaned back on his chair and took a swallow of his Budweiser. He put it down on the kitchen table and looked at us. First at Mago, then at Carlos, and then at me. I leaned closer to my sister, cowering under my father's gaze.

"I brought you to this country to get an education and to take advantage of all the opportunities this country has to offer. The minute you walk through the door with anything less than As, I'm sending you straight back to my mother's house."

Oh, no, not to Abuela Evila! I clutched my sister tighter.

"Don't worry about us, Papi," Mago said. "We won't tell anyone we're illegals, and we'll get good grades. We promise."

Carlos and I only nodded, too frightened to say anything.

"Está bien," Papi said as he finished his beer. "Well, off to bed. You have to get up early tomorrow. And I wasn't kidding about what kind of grades I expect from you."

We left the kitchen and went into the living room, where my stepmother was watching TV. Seeing us come in, Mila got up and headed to the bedroom, the only one in the apartment. Mago, Carlos, and I had been sleeping in the living room since we arrived from Mexico.

Our new home in the U.S. was in Highland Park, a predominantly Latino neighborhood in northeast Los Angeles. Mila and my father owned a fourplex apartment building on the corner of Granada Street and Avenue 50. We lived in the one-bedroom unit because Papi said he needed the rent money from the bigger units. "The first thing I have to do is pay back all the money I borrowed for the smuggler," he'd said.

Mago and I pulled out the sofa bed and lay down. Carlos slept on the floor. That night, though, because he was also anxious about the next day, he snuck into our bed. We huddled together while we listened to a helicopter flying very close to the apartment. For a moment, I forgot we were at the fourplex in Highland Park. I thought I was back at the border, running through the darkness, trying to hide from the helicopter flying above us. Once more, I felt frightened at the thought that if we didn't make it, we would lose our chance at having our father back in our lives.

"It's okay, Nena," Mago said, putting her arm around me. I snuggled against my sister, and thankfully the roaring of the helicopter faded away. "We're safe. Now go to sleep. It's a big day tomorrow."

I tried to do as I was told, but it was a restless night for me. I was not used to living in a noisy place. While living at Abuelita Chinta's shack, the nights had usually been quiet, except for the occasional barking of dogs and the passing of the evening train. But here, it seemed as if people never slept. Cars zoomed by on Avenue 50 at every hour of the day and night. Sirens echoed against the buildings. Police helicopters circled the neighborhood. Sometimes we even heard gunshots farther down the street from the gang members living nearby. The only familiar sound I heard at night was the lonely whistle of the midnight train, which made me yearn for my country and for those I'd left behind.

Since we had arrived three weeks before school ended, Papi didn't enroll us. He said to wait for the new school year, so we stayed home all summer. We didn't mind because mostly we just watched TV. Finally, we had unrestricted access to television, yet strangely enough, sometimes I would miss the radio and the fairy tales I'd liked to listen to. I didn't like that TV took away my ability to imagine what things looked like.

Mago, Carlos, and I would clean the apartment so that Papi and Mila wouldn't think we were lazy. We would sweep the carpet with the broom because the one time Mago had tried to use the vacuum cleaner it had swallowed up the bottom of the curtains, and we hadn't known what to do. The vacuum starting smelling as if it were burning, and we pulled and pulled, but it wouldn't let go of the curtain. Finally Carlos rushed to yank the cord from the outlet, and we were able to get the curtain out of the vacuum. After that we decided it was safer to sweep. We knew how to use a broom. The vacuum cleaner was going to take some time.

But my favorite thing about that summer was that we got to see the ocean for the first time. One day in July, my brother, sister, and I had hurried into Papi's red Mustang, and we headed to Santa Monica.

When we arrived at the beach, Carlos, Mago, and I took off running to the shore and stared at the endless ocean before us. The few pictures I had seen in books or magazines couldn't capture its immensity. Miles and miles of water glittering under the summer sun. I had never imagined the ocean to be like that. I breathed in the salty scent and stood there as the wind blew my hair around my face.

"Well, what do you think, kids?" Papi had said as he came to stand behind us.

"It's beautiful," we said.

While Mila and Papi made sandwiches, Mago, Carlos, and I lay down on the blanket to get a tan. Papi said we were dark enough as it was, especially his "Negra," Mago. But it felt so nice to lie there under the sun, listening to the waves and the chatter of the families around us. For the first time, I felt as if we were a normal family, a family with two parents, as I had often dreamed about. If anybody had looked at us, they would have said, "Look at that happy family."

Mago, Carlos, and I dug a hole in the sand and filled it up with the water we carried in a bucket. The hole was only big enough to put our feet into. We looked for seashells along the shore, stood at the water's edge, and felt the sand give under us, but we didn't go in deeper. We didn't know how to swim. In Mexico we hadn't been afraid to splash around in the canal when it was waist deep, but there at the beach, with all those waves crashing down every few seconds, and the cur-

Reyna, Carlos, and Mago's first time at the beach

rent pulling us in, it was hard not to be terrified of drowning in that beautiful, endless water.

Papi said, "You all better get in, or I'm going to take you home."

Carlos and Mago walked farther into the water, but I stood by Papi's side thinking about the time I had almost drowned in the canal and about my cousin Catalina being carried away by the river.

"Come on, Chata, go in," Papi said.

"I'm afraid, Papi."

He grabbed my left hand and said, "Come on, I'll go in with you." Together we walked into the foamy water.

"Don't let go of me," I said to Papi as I clutched his hand, my toes digging into the sand eroding from under me. I tightened my grip on his hand, a hand that was a mirror image of my own with its long, long fingers. Piano hands, although back then neither of us had ever touched a piano. I still couldn't believe he was real, that he was no longer just a photograph hanging on the wall.

"I won't let go, Chata," he said. I held on to my father's callused hand and walked deeper into the water with him. I closed my eyes and thought about the saints I had prayed to. I thanked them for that day. That was the perfect way to see the ocean for the first time—holding on to my father's hand.

As he had promised, never once did he let me go.

Throughout the summer, I had been looking forward to the day when I would start school. I couldn't wait to meet my teacher, make friends, get my own books. Mila said that teachers here don't hit their students like they do in Mexico. And best of all, she said that my teacher would not yell at me for being left-handed. "That stuff your grandmother told you about the devil is pure nonsense." When she said that, I started liking my stepmother, and I stopped being so afraid of going to school. I hoped that one day I would be like her, fluently bilingual and a U.S. citizen.

But early the next day, when Mago, Carlos, and I stopped at the corner to say goodbye, my apprehension returned. Aldama Elementary was up the street. Mago and Carlos had to take a bus to get to Luther Burbank Junior High School.

"Walk me there," I pleaded. "I don't want to go alone."

"It's only four blocks away, Nena," Mago said. "And Carlos and I are late enough as it is. We'll miss our bus."

"Don't be scared," Carlos said.

"Everything will be fine. We'll see you when we get home," Mago said, waving goodbye.

I watched Mago and Carlos rush down Avenue 50 to catch the bus on Monte Vista Street. I wished I weren't ten. I wished I were old enough to go to junior high with them.

I made my way to Aldama Elementary. Since Papi was here illegally, he'd said he couldn't risk losing his job by taking days off or arriving late to work just to walk me to my school. I stood outside for a long time and watched children walk in. Some of them came in with their parents. All of them were strangers to me, and I thought about Iguala. Back there I had known, by sight if not by name, almost every parent and kid that came to my little school.

Aldama was three times as big as my school in Iguala. I had no idea where to go. I was so used to being with my sister, having her show me what to do, that now I was completely lost. I couldn't go through this by myself. I couldn't walk into that big school all alone.

What if I went home? Would Papi know I hadn't gone to school? Would he spank me?

I didn't know what it was about Papi that sometimes he could be nice, and other times, like when he was drinking, he would become a different person, one who yelled and hit. That father scared me. That father reminded me of Abuela Evila, although she didn't need alcohol to bring about that crazed look in her eyes.

A bell rang, and soon everyone was inside. I peeked inside the main doors, and I was overwhelmed by all the doors, the hallway that seemed to never end. I felt as if I were looking at a repeating image in a distorted mirror. My school in Mexico didn't have hallways. It didn't have so many doors. Tears started to well up, and I was angry at myself for being such a useless coward. A mother walked by and asked, "¿Estás perdida?" At hearing the familiar Spanish words, I immediately confessed that I didn't know where to go.

She took me to the main office and there, the receptionist asked my name and called my classroom. A few minutes later, a boy my age came in. The receptionist said something to him and motioned for me to follow him.

The boy didn't say anything to me as we made our way down a long hallway. We entered our classroom and the teacher, a tall, pudgy woman with short blond hair, looked me up and down and asked me something in English. I wanted to kick myself for coming late. Now, I had to stand in front of the whole class and have everyone watch me while the teacher spoke to me in a language I didn't understand. I looked at my feet. My toes wiggled in the new tennis shoes Papi bought me from a place called Payless. I didn't like wearing tennis shoes. After ten years of walking around barefoot or in plastic sandals, my feet felt trapped inside the thick material.

"¿Sólo español?" she said. I looked into her eyes the color of the sea. I thought about our trip to Santa Monica, of Papi holding my hand. *Please, don't let go of me, Papi.*

"¿Español?" she asked again. At first I didn't realize that she had spoken to me in Spanish.

"Sí," I said, feeling relieved she spoke Spanish. The knot in my stomach began to loosen. "Me llamo Reyna Grande Rodríguez. Discúlpeme, maestra, por llegar tarde."

She shrugged and smiled. "No entender mucho," she said.

"Oh," I said, disappointed that she didn't speak that much Spanish. She pointed to a table in the corner and gently pushed me forward. There were four students there and a man with black hair which was spiked with so much hairspray it looked as if he were wearing a push broom on his head. He had a very skinny neck and a big Adam's apple that went up and down like a yo-yo when he swallowed.

"I'm Mr. López," he said in Spanish. "I'm Mrs. Anderson's assistant."

He had us introduce ourselves and asked me to go first. "Me llamo Reyna Grande Rodríguez," I said.

He glanced at his roster and then looked at me. "Here in this country, we only use one last name. See here," he said, showing me the roster. "You're enrolled as Reyna Grande."

"But I'm Rodríguez, too," I said. "It's my mami's last name."

He asked me to keep my voice down so that I wouldn't interrupt

Mrs. Anderson, who was speaking to a class of about twenty students. I wanted to tell him that I had already lost my mother by coming to this country. It wasn't easy having to also erase her from my name. *Who am I now, then?*

"I'm sorry," Mr. López said. "That is the way things are done in this country. From now on you are Reyna Grande."

The students at my table laughed. One of them said in Spanish, "But she's so little, how can she be a queen, and a big one at that?"

Mr. López told them not to tease. He asked them to introduce themselves next. There was Gil, María, Cecilia, and Blanca. They were from Mexico, like me, except for Gil who was from someplace called El Salvador. I didn't know where that was, but he spoke Spanish, too.

For the rest of the day, I stayed at the table in the corner. Mr. López taught us the English alphabet. It was difficult to pay attention to him when Mrs. Anderson was speaking loudly to her students. Most of those kids looked just like me. They had brown skin, black hair, and brown eyes. They had last names like González and García, Hernández and Martínez, and yet they could speak a language I could not. Mrs. Anderson didn't tell them to keep their voice down. Sometimes it was hard to hear what Mr. López was telling us. Then he couldn't hear what we told him because we had to whisper.

Whatever Mrs. Anderson was teaching the other students, it wasn't the alphabet. She wrote words on the board. Although I could recognize each letter in those words, I couldn't understand what they spelled. I watched her mouth open and close, open and close as she talked. I wished I could understand what she was saying. I wished I didn't have to sit here in a corner and feel like an outsider in my own classroom. I wished I weren't being taught something kids learn in kindergarten.

"Reyna, pay attention," Mr. López said. "Now, repeat after me, *ABCDEFG . . .*"

By the end of the day, I still hadn't fully memorized the alphabet and the numbers in English. I walked back home feeling scared. I thought about the trip to the beach, of Papi holding my hand. I wished things would always be like that for me. But they wouldn't be like that if I didn't do well in school. Papi had said so.

I wanted to make my father proud. It still bothered me—as it would for many years—that my father had not wanted to bring me at first, and because of that I had a desperate desire for him to one day say, "Chata, you've made me a proud father. I'm so glad I didn't leave you in Mexico and instead brought you here."

I felt as if I owed him something, as if there was a debt that needed to be repaid. The way I could pay it back was to make him proud of my accomplishments, because they would be *his* accomplishments, too. Even now, there are times when I think back on that moment when I begged my father to bring me to this country, and the knowledge that he *could* have said no still haunts me. What would my life have been like then? I know the answer all too well.

Since I got out of school before Carlos and Mago, Papi told me to go to the neighbor's house and stay there until Mago arrived to pick me up. I told him I had stayed alone before. He said in this country he could get in trouble if the police found out I was all by myself. Mrs. Giuliano lived right across the street from us. She was an old lady with hair like cotton and eyes the color of my birthstone, sapphire. Her sweet smile reminded me of Abuelita Chinta, although she had a row of perfect teeth, unlike my grandmother's gap-toothed smile. She didn't speak much Spanish, but she spoke Italian and English. She was the first Italian I'd ever met.

When she opened the door she said, "Buon giorno, bambina!" She smiled and pulled me into her house. It smelled of bread and garlic. "Hai fame?" Mrs. Giuliano asked. She pointed to the stove where she was making minestrone.

"Si, tengo hambre," I said.

I sat on the stool and she gave me a bowl of the soup. She asked me a question in both Italian and English, but I only understood the words scuola and school.

"No good," I said, shaking my head. "No pude aprender inglés."

"No capisci?" she asked. "Dare il tempo, bambina."

Tiempo? She was right, time is what I needed, but back then I'd thought that I would never be able to stop feeling as if I didn't belong in that classroom.

I wished I could tell Mrs. Giuliano that school wasn't the only place that was difficult to get used to. Although there were many good things we now had, there were also things we had in Mexico that we no longer had here. Mago, Carlos, and I missed our freedom. We missed being able to go outside to walk around the neighborhood and feel safe because everyone knew us. The only person we knew in Highland Park was Mrs. Giuliano. We didn't know anyone else, and because of the gang members in the area, Papi wouldn't allow us to go too far. Unlike in Iguala, kids here wouldn't go outside to play in the afternoons. Women wouldn't come out to embroider cloth napkins and talk to their comadres. Men wouldn't come out to have a beer with their friends and play a game of poker or dominoes. The streets here were empty except for the endless procession of cars on Avenue 50. There was no one to play with except one another.

But I didn't have the words to tell this to Mrs. Giuliano, and I was afraid their meaning would get lost in the translation, no matter how similar Italian and Spanish were. But she seemed to understand my unspoken words because she squeezed my hand.

After my meal, Mrs. Giuliano took me to her backyard where she kept chickens in a coop. As I helped her clean it, the smell of chicken poop and feathers reminded me of Abuelita Chinta's doves. The smell made me even more nostalgic for Iguala. I touched my belly button, and I remembered the bond that tied me to my mother and to my country.

Would it be so terrible to be sent back? Even though I liked this beautiful place, I still missed my home. It still called to me in different ways. A pigeon resting on the roof of the house, its coos traveling down the vent of the heater in the living room. I'd stop and listen, letting my mind travel back to Abuelita Chinta's shack, and I'd remember waking up to the cooing of her doves.

Mexico was also in a cup of hot chocolate, the steam curling up into the air. I would inhale Mexico through my nostrils. While at the supermarket with Mila, picking out vegetables and herbs, crushing cilantro leaves with my fingers, bringing a bunch of epazote up to my nose, I'd think of meals in Mexico, of a pot of beans boiling, of my grandmother adding epazote leaves for flavor.

Mexico was in the whistle of the midnight train traveling on the tracks that run parallel to Figueroa Street. I'd awaken to the sound of the train's whistle, and my body would fill with longing. When Mago and I cleaned the beans before putting them on to boil, we'd pick out the clumps of dirt and moisten them with our tongues to smell the scent of wet earth. I thought about the dirt floor of Abuelita Chinta's shack, of how we would sprinkle water on it before sweeping it, so as not to unsettle the dirt. If I returned to Mexico, then I could see my little sister, my mother, and my sweet grandmother again. I would also get to keep my two last names. I would be in a classroom where I understood what my teacher said.

But what about my dream of one day making Papi proud?

I stood there in Mrs. Giuliano's backyard feeling as if I were tearing in half. *Where do I belong?* I wondered. *Do I belong here? Do I belong there? Do I belong anywhere?*

I didn't know the answers to my questions, but I sat on the bench in Mrs. Giuliano's backyard and I took out my notebook. I traced the letters of the alphabet as I began to say them aloud, my determined tongue stumbling over the right pronunciation.

2

Mago on Halloween

THE DAY BEFORE my first Halloween in this country, Mila came home with a costume she had picked up at the store for me. The plastic mask had a string on it, and the eyes were cut out so that I could see through the holes. The costume was of a girl with reddish hair and a purple star on the upper part of her left cheek. The dress was made of plastic, and it had sleeves in the colors of the rainbow.

"Who is it?" I asked my stepmother.

"It's Rainbow Brite," she said.

"Who?" I asked.

Mila shrugged her shoulders and handed me the costume.

"And what exactly is Halloween?" Mago asked.

"It's just a day when kids get to dress up and go from house to house to get candy," Mila said.

"You mean people give out candy for free?" Carlos asked, looking up from the minicars he'd been racing on the floor.

Incredible.

I no longer had any reservations about putting on the costume of that girl named Rainbow Brite. Whoever she was, all I cared about was getting my free candy.

Mila had only bought a costume for me because she said Halloween was for little kids. But at hearing about the free candy, Mago and Carlos wanted a costume, too, never mind that she had just turned fourteen a week before, and he was almost thirteen.

"We don't have money for any more costumes," Mila said. "You can share your sister's candy tomorrow."

Mago and Carlos went to bed disappointed about not getting a costume. I hung mine on the door so I wouldn't forget it for school the next day.

When October began, Mrs. Anderson started giving us art projects to do, things like witches and black cats, ghosts and pumpkins made from poster and tissue paper. In Mexico, we would had been preparing for the Day of the Dead celebrations, and I would have been looking forward to eating Day of the Dead bread and visiting the graves of my grandfather and my little cousin Catalina. We would have been decorating our altar with candles and marigolds and plates of food for our dead relatives to enjoy. But here, there was nothing like that to be done. We cut out skeletons, connected the bones with clips, and hung them on our door to announce the arrival of this holiday called Halloween.

In the morning, I was awakened by Papi yelling. In the dim morning light streaming through the window, I saw Papi hovering over Carlos. The living room smelled of Old Spice, Papi's favorite cologne, and something else, like the smell of vinegar and rust.

"I told you to stop doing that!" Papi said. Carlos was sitting on the floor, where he slept. He pulled his covers up to his neck as he looked at Papi.

"I'm sorry, Papá. I won't do it again," Carlos said, cowering beneath his blankets. Now I knew what the smell was. Mago and I had been taking turns waking Carlos up at night so he could use the bathroom. Papi would spank Carlos when he had his little accidents, and because we didn't want our brother to get spanked, Mago and I would try to help him. But the previous night, neither of us had awakened him, and the inevitable had happened.

Papi went to the bathroom and turned on the water in the bathtub. He came back for Carlos. "I told you not to wet yourself again, and now you're going to pay for it."

"No, Papi!" Mago yelled.

Carlos didn't say anything. Papi whisked him up on his feet and dragged him to the bathroom. Mago and I rushed behind them. The next thing we knew, Papi was picking Carlos up as if he were a doll and tossing him into the bathtub, pajamas and all. Water splashed onto the floor and the walls and on Papi's blue work uniform.

"Wash yourself up!" Papi yelled. He picked up his car keys and headed to the door. Mila looked at us. Her mouth opened, as if she wanted to say something, but then she shook her head and followed Papi out the door. They left for the retirement home where she and Papi worked, he as a maintenance worker and she as a nurse's assistant. It had a fancy name—Kingsley Manor, which made me think of princesses and lords, not old people. But I guess that was the point.

Mago and I rushed to pull our brother out of the bathtub, where he was crying. Papi had only turned on the cold water, and Carlos shivered while we dried his hair and helped him out of his wet pajamas. He didn't stop shivering even after he was in dry clothes.

"He didn't have to do that," Mago said.

"He left me for years. How can he treat me like this now?" Carlos said between tears. Mago and I left the soiled covers soaking in the bathtub. We sat on the couch, not knowing what to do. I thought getting dumped into a bathtub full of cold water was worse than getting a spanking from Papi, even though his spankings hurt more than Abuela Evila's, not because he was a man and could hit harder, but because he was our father, our hero. Like Mago had once said he would be.

"Come on, Carlos, we're going to miss our bus," Mago said as she got up to get ready.

"I'm not going to school," Carlos said, his bottom lip quivering, tears threatening to come out again.

"Come on," Mago insisted. "You'll only make it worse. You know how Papi feels about school."

She and Carlos left to catch the bus, and I was left there with my costume in my hands, the excitement of Halloween gone. I put Rainbow Brite back on the hook on the door, and then I left for school.

When Mila and Papi came home, he didn't say anything about what had happened that morning. I wanted him to say he was sorry, but we'd lived there long enough to know that Papi never apologized for anything. He still hadn't said he was sorry for leaving us in Mexico for eight years. Instead, he just walked past us and headed to his bedroom to change out of his work uniform, which was dark-blue pants and a light-blue short-sleeve shirt that had the word "Grande" embroidered over the left pocket. His hair had streaks of white in it, and I wondered what he had painted at Kingsley Manor that day. He never told us much about his job, but I knew a few details, such as that the name of the paint he used there was *Navajo White*. I knew that because Papi painted the interior walls of the fourplex units that color, which he brought from work in buckets. Sometimes, I would hear Mila and him talk about their coworkers, or the old patients, and I wished I knew those people, too, so that I could feel included in their conversations.

"Why aren't you ready, yet?" Mila asked me. I'd been sitting on the couch with Mago and Carlos for most of the afternoon. None of us could enjoy the cartoons on TV, so we had turned it off.

"Trick-or-treating will be starting soon," Mila said. "And it only happens once a year."

"We aren't going," I said.

Mila stood there and shook her head. "I know what your father did was wrong, but try to understand him. It's been a long time since he has had to be a father. Give him time to adjust."

Mila handed Carlos a plastic bag. From it, he took out a white sheet which Mila got at Kingsley Manor. "We already washed the sheets, Mila," Mago said. "They're drying on the clothesline outside."

"Oh, that isn't why I brought this," Mila said, grabbing a pair of scissors. She told Carlos to stand up and put the sheet over him.

"What are you doing?" Carlos asked. Mila cut out holes over the area where Carlos's eyes would be.

"I'm making you a Halloween costume," she said. A costume? Out of a sheet? She walked him over to the closet door so Carlos could see it for himself. He turned to look at us. Mago and I giggled. My brother was now a ghost. It was amazing. From that year on, Mila always brought us white sheets for Halloween, and she never bought me a costume again. If I had known she would do that, I wouldn't have praised Carlos's ghost costume so much.

"Let me see what I can come up with for you, Mago," Mila said. We looked out the window and saw that kids were starting to come out of their houses with their costumes on.

Mila came out of her room with the wedding dress she had worn when she married her first husband. The satin had yellowed by then and most of the sequins had fallen off. Mila's older son was about seventeen years old, so the dress had to be older than that.

"I can't wear that," Mago said. "I'll ruin it."

"It's already ruined," Mila said. But the way she said it made me think she wasn't just talking about the dress.

It would take us years to piece together the story of Mila and my father. They met at Kingsley Manor. Mila was already married and had three children—two boys and a girl. Mila left her husband and children for my father. She wasn't planning on leaving her kids forever, just until she and Papi got settled into a bigger place. Mila's whole family shunned her for breaking up her marriage and leaving her children. Her husband wasn't able to take care of them by himself, so he dumped them at Mila's mother's house. Her mother took Mila to court and fought her for custody of her grandchildren, claiming abandonment. The judge asked the older son—who was in his teens—whom he wanted to live with. He chose his grandmother. So the judge gave Mila's mother full custody of all three kids, and Mila only got visitation rights. She also had to pay child support.

Back then we hadn't known all of the details, but the way Mila was handing off her wedding dress to Mago, knowing that she would have to throw it away once we got back, hinted at her dark secret.

"Try on the dress, Mago," I said. "If we don't leave soon, all the candy will be gone."

Mago went into the bathroom and came out looking like a bride, and blushing like one, too. After a good laugh at her expense, and taking pictures with Papi's Polaroid camera to send to Mexico, we got ready to go. Mila made us practice the words "Trick or treat. Trick or treat." The words were hard to pronounce, and we stumbled on the harsh sounds.

"Well, it will have to do," Mila said. She gave each of us a large plastic bag and told us to be careful. "Don't eat the candy until you get home. Your father and I need to make sure it's safe."

The holiday reminded me of las posadas in Mexico, except there we would only get a small goodie bag and only one house would give them out, but here the offerings were endless! My brother, my sister, and I walked from street to street, venturing into neighborhoods we had never been to. *"Treecotree! Treecotree!"* we yelled as we knocked on the doors of the Victorian and Craftsman homes scattered throughout Highland Park, and the doors of the apartment buildings where immigrant families lived. By the time we returned home, it was past nine and our bags were bursting with candy. We had to carry them in our arms because the plastic handles had long broken from all the weight, from the abundance only found in El Otro Lado.

Papi and Mila were sitting in the kitchen when we got home. We put our bags on the table and she and Papi looked through our candy, throwing away the ones that seemed as if they'd been opened before. Papi found a tamarind candy coated with chili powder in Carlos's bag. "I used to like these when I was your age," Papi said.

"Here is another one, Papi. You can keep that one," Carlos said.

"Thanks, Carnal." Papi gently slapped Carlos on the back as they ate their tamarind candy.

Mila and Papi

"REYNA, YOUR MOTHER is here to pick you up," Mr. López said, handing me a slip from the main office. I gathered my things and left. I ran down the hallway. *Is Mami really waiting for me? Has she come all the way from Mexico to find me? Does she miss me?*

When I entered the main office, Mila stood up.

"Ready?" she said, grabbing her purse. I followed my stepmother out the door, feeling stupid. I'd forgotten Mila was going to pick me up to take me to my dentist appointment.

For the past few months, I had been suffering from toothaches. They had become so painful, Papi finally had no choice but to deal with the problem. We didn't have dental insurance, and Papi said he and Mila didn't have money to pay dental fees, so Mila figured out a way around that. We would use her daughter's insurance.

As we drove, I looked out the window and wished it were Papi who was taking me to my appointment, but I understood that he didn't want to risk losing his job by taking days off, although that wasn't the only reason. Since he didn't speak much English, he felt uncomfortable going places. As a handyman, he was comfortable with a drill, paint brush, or wrench, and he could work in silence while his expert hands did the work. But outside of home and work, it was Mila who had to take care of everything that needed to be done.

As we neared the dentist's office, Mila reminded me of what to say. "Answer to the name Cindy," she said. "And remember that you're nine, not ten."

Cindy was ten months younger than I was. She was a lot prettier too, with long glossy black hair and beautiful eyes framed by thick eyelashes. She didn't come to the house very often, and when she came, she would stay by Mila's side and wouldn't talk to us or play with us. She wouldn't talk to Papi either and would pretend not to hear him when he said hello to her. At first I would get angry at Cindy for giving my father the cold shoulder, but then I would think about Rey, at how I had hated him on the spot for the simple fact that my mother had chosen him over me, and I could understand Cindy's behavior. After all hadn't it been the same for her?

The only difference was that Mila, unlike my mother, never gave up on her kids. I imagine now how it must have hurt her, to be standing there in the courtroom, fighting to get her children back, and that her older son had had it in his power to choose. And he had chosen not to go with her. But just because she had lost them that day didn't mean she had given up the fight. And she never did.

But Mila's conflicted relationship with her children would affect the way she treated us. She had been living with my father for three years when one day my siblings and I had ended up at her doorstep, three children she hadn't been expecting. Although she and my father had not legally married yet, she had become our new mother, whether she wanted to be or not. She was nice enough to us, although sometimes, especially when her own kids were around, she would go out of her way to treat her children a lot better. Now that

I'm a mother, I can understand the predicament she found herself in back then—leaving her own children, only to have to raise another woman's offspring. And yet, the sting of her indifference still hurts. She wasn't an evil stepmother, not like in the fairy tales I loved to listen to. But she also wasn't the mother I so desperately wanted to have. How could she be? I understand it now, but back then, I could not see past my need.

I had never been to the dentist in my life, and luckily we hadn't really had tooth problems. In Mexico we never had money for candy, but we also hadn't had money for things such as toothbrushes. We would have to scrub our teeth with our fingers coated with baking soda.

I couldn't help feeling a little afraid about going to the dentist. In Mexico, Abuelita Chinta had given me mint leaves to chew on when my molar started to bother me. I didn't think I was going to get mint leaves this time.

Mila and I sat in the reception area to wait. I glanced at the pictures of a turkey, a pumpkin, and a pilgrim's hat taped on the door. There were similar decorations in my classroom. Mila fidgeted in her seat. Once in a while she would pat her wavy black hair. I found myself admiring her skin, as I'd done many times. It was two shades lighter than my own, and it looked good in soft pinks and peaches. Her makeup, as always, was perfect. She had roses blooming on her cheeks and her lips were glossy. She had a faint scar from her nose to her upper lip because she was born with a cleft lip, but that didn't take away from her looks. Mila wasn't beautiful, but she was pretty and she was classy.

The dentist's assistant came out and called out a name. When I didn't answer, Mila nudged me and stood up. I went into the dentist's room, and he asked me to lie down on a big leather chair. I jumped off as soon as it started reclining. The dentist laughed and said something in English, while pointing to the chair. All I understood was the word "Cindy."

I sat there wondering how Mila felt about the dentist calling me by her daughter's name. The few times Cindy had come to the house, I had noticed how uncomfortable she seemed around Mila. She didn't come very often, and when she did come, it was because Mila had practically forced her to. Mila's older son didn't visit often either. Her second son had never come over, not even once.

Mila said my molar had a huge cavity and would have to come out to let the new tooth grow in. For the rest of the hour, Mila had to translate for me what the dentist said.

"Open your mouth, Cindy.

"That's a good girl, Cindy.

"We're almost done, Cindy."

Mila didn't look at me when she translated. She looked at the wall. While the dentist worked on my mouth, I began to fantasize about what it would be like to be the real Cindy. To be Mila's daughter. Would Mila not have fidgeted the way she was doing now while she stood nearby? Would she have allowed me—just as she allowed the real Cindy when she visited—to go into her and Papi's bedroom without knocking, to lie down on their bed and watch TV? Would she have brushed my hair up in pigtails in the mornings? Let me sit in the kitchen and help her make dinner? Would she have stood by while Papi hit me with his belt?

"We're almost done, Cindy," the dentist said, and maybe it was the grogginess from the anesthesia, but I really liked the sound of that name. I began wishing I could stay in the dentist's office forever, because as soon as we walked out that door, I would once again be Reyna.

"Your daughter was very good," the receptionist said as Mila and I went out the door. Mila held me by the shoulders because I was feeling a bit dizzy and my mouth was numb and my lips felt three times their usual size. My lips throbbed as if they'd been stung by a scorpion.

"Thank you," Mila said. I waved goodbye to the receptionist and gave her a groggy smile.

On the way home, Mila was very quiet. I wondered if she was thinking about her daughter.

"Are you in pain yet?" she asked as we pulled into the driveway.

"No, Mamá Mila," I said. Maybe it was the anesthesia that had made me say that.

Mila took a deep breath and then looked at me. "Just call me Mila. I'm not your mom so you can't call me Mamá. Just Mila, okay?" She said it gently, and yet I felt as if she had yelled at me. The harshness in her voice was very subtle, but I could hear it clearly.

With tears in my eyes, I said, "I'm sorry, Mila. I won't do it again." Then I got out of the car and went into the house, where I saw that my brother and sister were back from school.

"That's what you get for being a traitor," Mago said when I told her what I'd done. "She's right. She's not our mom. Why are you always trying to find mothers everywhere you go?"

"I don't know," I said.

"Besides, she broke up our parents' marriage," Mago continued. "And now you want to call her Mamá?"

I lowered my head in shame.

When we first arrived in the U.S., Mago and I went into Mila and Papi's bedroom to look at her pretty clothes in the closet and to smell her perfumes. I knew Mila had noticed we did because a few days later Papi installed a new doorknob that locked, and from that moment on they would lock their door every time they left the house. But Mago and I were intrigued by Mila, the woman who, in part, was responsible for breaking up my parents' twelve-year marriage. We wanted to know what it was that had made Papi prefer her over Mami. We thought that by looking at her clothes, or going through her toiletries, we would find the answer.

Maybe it was the pretty clothes she wore. During the day she wore her white nurse's uniform because it was required at work, but on the weekends she wore capri pants and pretty blouses, leather sandals with delicate straps. For going out she had nice sets of skirt suits and silk blouses. Her jewelry box had faux pearl necklaces, pearl earrings, gold chains, fancy watches. She had different-colored high heels to match her outfits. Her perfumes were beautiful high-quality scents, not like the perfumes Mami used.

But beside her pretty looks and taste in clothes, Mila had other advantages Mami did not. Mila spoke English, which meant that Papi relied on her for nearly everything because he spoke only Spanish. Mila was a U.S. citizen. She wasn't invisible in this country, as Papi was back then, and as Mami was while she was living here. Also, even though

Mila was born in Mexico, she had been in this country since she was thirteen years old. She was forty years old when we came to live with her and Papi, and by living in the U.S. for most of her life, Mila wasn't the typical Mexican woman. She wasn't afraid of Papi. She didn't cater to his every whim as women in Mexico are taught to do, as Mami had done while living with him. She also had an education and knew her way around this American society in a way Papi did not.

While in Mexico, Mami was so worried Papi would leave her for a gringa. Instead, he found Mila.

I told my sister that she was right. I was being a traitor to my own mother. But how could I make myself stop yearning for a mother when, ever since I was four years old, that is what I had done? And even to this day, I sometimes find myself yearning for her still.

"We have a father," Carlos said. "That's good enough for me."

"You're right," I said, glancing at the kitchen where Mila was chopping vegetables. She didn't like us to be in the kitchen with her. As a matter of fact, she didn't really like us to be in any room with her. It wasn't something that she would say to us, but it was the way she would tense up the moment we walked into the room. It was the way she would look at us, as if wishing it weren't us, but her own children.

Papi came home and asked about my tooth. I took the blood-stained cotton out of my mouth so that he could see the gap where my molar used to be.

"I'm glad everything worked out," Papi said. Then he walked into the kitchen and sat at the table to keep Mila company while she cooked.

"I'm not doing that again, you understand?" I heard Mila say. Papi opened a can of Budweiser and didn't answer.

4

Reyna in fifth grade

One evening, Mila made spaghetti for dinner. The few times Mrs. Giuliano had made it at her house, I claimed not to be hungry so I wouldn't have to eat it while I waited for Mago to pick me up. I loved Mrs. Giuliano's food, except for the spaghetti.

Now Mila was putting a plate full of spaghetti in front of me, and at the sight of those long white strings I felt like running to the bathroom to throw up. I held on tight to my chair and looked away from the plate and tried to think of something beside Pablo and his worms.

In Mexico, most of the children I had known had the same body shape: a big, round belly full of roundworms and really skinny legs and arms. Carlos, Mago, Betty, and I were no exception. But there was one kid, a boy named Pablo, whose abdomen swelled beyond anything we could imagine. He looked as big as a pregnant woman. Abuelita Chinta said Pablo had a serious case of roundworms. I used to have nightmares of his belly exploding and hundreds of white wiggly worms spilling out.

Sometimes Abuelita Chinta would give Mago, Carlos, Betty, and me unripe guavas blended to a pulp. We would drink this concoction unwillingly because sometime later the pains would come. Horrible pains as if our intestines were twisting and twisting like wet clothes being wrung out before going up on the clothesline. We ran to the outhouse and emptied our bowels. No sooner had we come back into the house than we had to run back out again. Once, Carlos started screaming, and when we went to check on him, he was squatting on the ground as a worm wiggled out of him.

Sooner or later the worms would be pooped out. Abuelita Chinta said she was sorry to see us in pain, but we barely had enough to eat as it was, and the parasites were taking away the precious nutrients we ingested.

When we asked her why she wouldn't give this drink to Pablo, Abuelita Chinta said that no amount of her guava drink could help the poor boy. She told Pablo's mother that if he didn't see the doctor soon, he would have serious health issues. When Pablo was nothing but a skeleton with a big belly, his family sold what few possessions they had and took Pablo away to Mexico City. The next time we saw him, his big stomach was gone! He had a scar on his abdomen, and he told us he had to have surgery to get the worms removed. It was a hideous scar. Raised and swollen, the stitches like the legs of a crawling centipede. After that, we hadn't balked at the remedies Abuelita Chinta would give us. But even though Pablo was better, my nightmares took a long time to go away.

Mila went to the living room to watch a telenovela while Mago, Carlos, and I stayed in the kitchen to eat her spaghetti. I strained to hear the theme song playing in the living room. *Mi vida eres tú y solamente tú . . .*

I loved that telenovela. It was called *Cristal* and was from Venezuela, so the characters spoke with a strange Spanish accent. The story was about a girl whose mother had abandoned her as a baby, so she had grown up in an orphanage. Now, as a young woman, she was on her way to becoming a supermodel, and best of all, she and a rich handsome young man were in love! It was a Cinderella story, one of my favorite fairy tales, except I couldn't go watch it with Mila because she didn't like us eating in the living room.

Always, Mila and Papi would eat first, and when they were done, they would call us into the kitchen so that we could eat. I didn't know why they arranged it like that, but it made me feel bad that we couldn't have dinner together, as a family. I thought of that, and the new doorknob Papi had installed on their bedroom door, and I wondered if he was trying to tell us something.

"You're going to have to eat, Nena," Mago said as she slurped down her spaghetti. "Papi will get angry if you don't."

"It's pretty good," Carlos said as he raised a strand of spaghetti over his mouth and then sucked it in really fast, making the strand wiggle as it went into his mouth.

I looked back at the spaghetti and the red sauce. I thought of Pablo again and the surgery he had to get the worms removed. I thought of the scar like a crawling centipede and I just couldn't bring myself to grab my fork and eat.

Papi came out of the bedroom to grab a beer, and noticing my full plate, asked me why I wasn't eating.

"I'm not very hungry, Papi."

"Well, Mila made this meal for you and now you're going to have to eat it. I won't have you being ungrateful."

"I can't eat it, Papi."

Papi started to yell at me, and pretty soon I felt tears sliding down my cheeks because I didn't know how to tell him about Pablo. I kept my eyes on the floor while Papi called me an ingrata, and how could I be so willing to throw away food that he had worked so hard to buy?

Mago said, "The spaghetti reminds her of lombrices, Papi."

"That's ridiculous," he said. "Now, eat it!"

I forced myself to grab my fork, but I knew, as I twirled the spaghetti around, that I wouldn't be able to bring it to my mouth, no matter what. I put the fork down and said, "I can't, Papi. Please, don't make me."

Papi picked up my plate, and I thought he was going to take it away, but the next thing I knew he dumped the spaghetti on my head.

I started screaming as the spaghetti slid down my face and over my eyes. All I saw inside my mind was Pablo's belly exploding, and the worms coming to get me.

Mago and Carlos didn't move. They sat there staring at me with pity, and I wished they would look away. I wished I could get up and run all the way back to Iguala, back to my grandmother's arms. I wished, for the first time, that I were back in Mexico and back to being a little orphan. I wanted to be like Cristal, beautiful and loved by a handsome rich man who would take me away from here.

Papi went back into his room with his beer, and while Mago helped me clean up in the bathroom, Mila made me scrambled eggs, even though I told her I wasn't hungry. Now I would have to eat the eggs because Papi would beat me for sure if I didn't eat Mila's food for the second time that night. As I showered, I cried and thought about my sweet grandmother. She would never have dumped a plate of food on my head. And I wouldn't have had to tell her why I couldn't eat the spaghetti. She would have known why right away. I thought about the Man Behind the Glass. He, too, wouldn't have dumped the spaghetti on my head because he was with me all those years, and he had listened to me tell him about my fears and my dreams. But the father in this house didn't know me. He didn't know me at all.

And I didn't know him.

5

Papi on Christmas

Aᴛᴛᴇʀ ʜᴀᴠɪɴɢ ʟɪᴍɪᴛᴇᴅ access to a television all our lives, Mago, Carlos, and I couldn't get enough of it now. Even though we couldn't understand English very well, we loved to watch *He-Man, ThunderCats, Transformers, Beverly Hills Teens*, and *Jem*. For a minute we'd also owned an Atari. One of Papi's tenants had given it to us after she bought her son a Nintendo, but then Mila took it away and gave it to her own children without even telling us. I missed playing Frogger.

One day, while we were watching *ThunderCats*, Santa Claus appeared on the screen during one of the commercial breaks. Christmas was three weeks away, and we were worried because we didn't have any money to get Papi a present. He would only give us a dollar once in a while. As soon as we got it, we would run down to Barney's

Liquors and Market on Monte Vista Street and buy Now and Laters. Sometimes, when he was in a good mood, Papi would give us a dollar each, and we would pool our money and buy a ham and cheese sandwich from Fidel's Pizza on Avenue 50.

Santa Claus said something I couldn't quite understand. But a telephone number flashed on the screen.

Mago rushed to the rotary phone.

"What are you doing?" Carlos said.

"I'm calling Santa."

"I thought Santa doesn't exist," Carlos said.

"What do you mean he doesn't exist?" I asked. "Don't you see him there on the TV?"

Mago punched Carlos on the arm. "This is the United States, pendejo. Everything exists here."

Mago dialed the number and called Santa. She frowned.

"What's wrong?" Carlos said.

"It's in English," Mago said.

"Doesn't Santa speak Spanish?" I asked.

"Shh," Mago said. She listened intently, her eyebrows pulling together as she concentrated. Then she smiled.

"Is it really Santa?" I asked.

"It must be," Mago said, covering the receiver. "He's talking too fast. All I could make out was 'Ho, ho, ho.' So it must be him, right?" Then she motioned for me to be quiet and got back on the line. "Alo? Santa Clos? I want Barbie. I want bike. Please. Me good girl. Tank you." She gave the phone to Carlos.

"Alo? Alo?" Carlos said, smiling his crooked smile. "A Nintendo. A Nintendo to me. Please."

"My turn, my turn!" I said, jumping excitedly. *Wait, but I don't know how to say "skates" in English!* I turned to Mago and asked her. Carlos gave me the phone, and I clutched it tight in my hands. "Come on, he's going to hang up!"

Mago kept thinking. Finally, she shrugged. "I don't know, Nena."

Frustrated, I put the phone to my ear. "Alo? Santa Clos? Yo quiero patines, por favor. Mándeme unos patines para Navidad. Tank you." Mago took the phone away and hung up. "Do you think he understood what I said?" I asked them.

"He's Santa Claus. I don't see why not," Mago said. "Don't worry, Nena."

We turned back to the TV, but I was no longer interested in *ThunderCats*. I thought about my skates. In Iguala nobody I knew had skates. You can't skate on dirt roads. But here, oh, this was the perfect place to own skates! But now I'd ruined my chance of getting them because I was sure Santa Claus hadn't understood a word I'd said.

"I can't believe you asked for a Barbie," Carlos teased Mago. She punched him in the arm but didn't say anything. Instead, bougainvillea blossomed on her cheeks. I knew why she had done it. When Papi bought me my Barbie, Mago wanted one also, but Papi said she was too old. What my father hadn't understood was that we had never owned a Barbie. So what do you do when all your life you have yearned for such a thing?

"What are we going to do about a present?" Carlos asked. Christmas was the following day, and we still didn't have anything for Papi. I glanced at the Christmas tree Mila bought at Pic 'n' Save. It wasn't real, but it was the most beautiful tree we'd ever owned. I thought about the branch Tío Crece painted back in Mexico. Though we did a good job decorating it, nothing could compare to that six-foot-tall green beauty shining with colorful lights and glittering with silver garlands.

Mila sent us to Barney's to buy a bottle of Mazola oil because she had just run out. As we neared the store, Mago stopped and said, "We're going to do something we have never done before. But at this point, we have no choice."

"What?" Carlos and I asked. Then Mago shared her plan, which involved stealing. Back in Mexico, we had stolen fruit from people's property, but we had never stolen anything from a store. The liquor store had mirrors on the walls, and the Koreans who owned it would never take their eyes off the customers. I'd been there enough times to know that.

"What if we get caught?" I asked, already thinking about the spanking we would get. By then Papi had made it clear what his favorite form of discipline was.

"We won't," Mago said as she pulled us into the store. We split up. Mago said she would distract the owner while Carlos and I took whatever we thought would make good gifts. The thing was that I wished we had discussed what exactly a *good* gift was. The liquor store didn't have much. As I walked around, my stomach churned from fear of getting caught. The Korean lady kept looking at us. Our images were reflected in the mirrors up above. Luckily, her husband wasn't there, and she couldn't keep her eyes on all three of us, could she? Could she tell we were up to no good?

Nothing seemed good enough for Papi. Canned food, laundry items, diapers, sanitary napkins, toilet paper, soda bottles, chips. *What do I take, what do I take?* I glanced at Carlos. He was by the front looking at the bottles of tequila displayed behind the counter. *What does he think he is doing?* I thought. *Those bottles are totally unreachable, and even if he could steal a bottle, why would we want Papi getting more drunk than he already gets?*

Mago picked up the bottle of Mazola oil and took it to the counter. There, she knocked over the newspaper rack and the Korean lady yelled at Mago and hurried to pick up the newspapers. I didn't waste any time. I grabbed an item and hurried out of the store. Carlos came out next, and Mago was last. We rushed up Avenue 50 as fast as we could, our hearts beating faster than when we trespassed into El Cuervo's mango grove. If we got caught, we wouldn't be shot at. We would get deported by Papi.

"So what did you guys get?" Mago asked as we neared the house.

Carlos took a can of Aquanet hairspray from underneath his shirt. "They didn't have much to choose from," he said when Mago laughed.

"And you?" she asked.

I showed her what I grabbed, a bottle of Trés Flores Brilliantine.

"When have you seen Papi use hair polish?" she asked.

"Never," I said. "But Tío Crece uses it. And so does Tía Güera's husband."

Mago groaned.

"It was the only thing for men I could see!" I said, defending myself.

"I can't believe you guys," Mago said as we turned the corner. "We went through all this trouble for those lousy gifts?"

The next day, we ended up giving the bottle of brilliantine to Papi and the hairspray to Mila. Their presents for us were much better, although they weren't what we had asked Santa for. I got a pair of new Pro Wings tennis shoes. Mago got a pretty peach dress, and Carlos a yellow Tonka truck.

Santa never came. I kept waking up at night and glancing at the fireplace by our sofa bed. I was wondering if he was running late. I would tell myself he had many deliveries to make, and that was why he was taking so long. But what if he knew we had stolen things from the store? What if he decided we weren't good kids and didn't deserve his presents?

Two weeks later, there was still no sign of Santa. Papi called us over to the kitchen where he and Mila were going through their mail. "What's this?" Papi said, holding a bill in his hand. "Who in the world did you call? Why is the bill so high?"

Mago, Carlos, and I looked at each other. We never used the phone. We didn't know anyone here, so who would we call?

"We haven't called anyone," Mago said.

"Are you sure?" Mila said.

"Well, a few weeks ago we did call Santa," Mago confessed.

"You did what?" Mila said, taking the bill from Papi to look at the number.

"He was on TV, and he said to call him," Carlos said.

"And we asked him for things, but he didn't bring them," I said.

"I can't believe you kids!" Papi yelled, standing up. We took a step back.

"We didn't know we would get charged for the call," Mago said. "We're sorry, Papi."

"And he didn't bring them," I said again.

"I'm still not done paying my friends back the money they let me borrow for the smuggler," Papi said, one hand on his belt buckle. "Otherwise, I would put you all on the bus back to Mexico this very night!" He took off his belt and gave us a few lashes with it before grabbing his keys and storming out of the house.

"Don't ever do that again," Mila said, writing out a check and putting it inside the return envelope. "Those are just scam artists trying to make money."

"We're sorry, Mila," we said, wiping our teary eyes and massaging the stings on our arms. As we headed back to the living room, I wondered what Mila had meant. *Why would Santa want to make money off of us, when he has so much money he gives away toys to hundreds and thousands of kids?* I wondered.

Papi returned half an hour later and headed straight to the phone. He worked on it for a few minutes, and we didn't know what he was doing until he was done and said, "There, now you can't call anymore." We walked up to the phone and saw the lock on it, so now we couldn't turn the little wheel to dial unless we put in a key.

"What if there's an emergency?" Mago asked. "How are we going to call you?"

But Papi was unmoved.

6

Reyna and Mago

AT ALDAMA, THE girls in fifth and sixth grade were taken to the auditorium and shown a video about puberty. The girls around me kept giggling while watching the video, but I didn't. I couldn't understand the words much, but I could understand the meaning of the images on the screen just fine. Besides, I already knew about menstruation because Mago had told me all about it back in Mexico.

Mago still hadn't become a señorita. Mila said it was because we were so undernourished in Mexico that Mago's body didn't do what it was supposed to do. Now that we'd been in the U.S. for eight months and had better food to eat, Mago prayed her period would come soon. I hoped mine would, too. Even though I was ten and a half, I couldn't wait to become a señorita.

After the assembly, I was given a booklet with a picture of a girl on it. I was also given a sanitary napkin wrapped in cellophane. My very first sanitary napkin! I showed it to Mago as soon as she came home from school.

"Look, look!" I said. "I am going to become a señorita very soon!" I stored my sanitary napkin in my dresser drawer where I kept my underwear.

Every day after Mago picked me up at Mrs. Giuliano's, I would rush home and take my sanitary napkin out to look at it. I had also tried to read the little booklet I was given. There were many words I didn't yet understand, and I had to keep looking them up in the dictionary. My favorite was "rite of passage." It sounded important.

I was confused by this sentence: "Changes take place in a girl pretty fast." For the life of me I couldn't understand why the word "pretty" was there, *after* the word "girl." Mr. López had taught me that an adjective goes before the noun, so it should have read "pretty girl." But if that was so, I wondered if only pretty girls got their periods and not ugly ones. I stood in the mirror and looked at myself, wondering which category I was in. I was not pretty like Mago. Even Betty, as little as she was, was prettier than me. Cindy was way prettier than any of us.

"Am I ugly?" I asked Mago.

"Of course not!" she would say, but she's my sister, so I knew she had to say that.

The following week, Carlos came to pick me up at Mrs. Giuliano's instead of Mago. He said that Mago wasn't feeling well, and she had ended up not going to school. She'd gotten off the bus in front of Burbank, turned around, and come back home.

When we got home, I did what I had always done, open my drawer to look at my sanitary napkin. But it was gone. I took out the drawer and looked behind the dresser wondering if it had fallen out, but it wasn't there. Mago came out of the bathroom looking very pale.

"What's wrong?" I asked her.

She went to lie down on the couch, clutching her stomach.

"I have a fever and really bad cramps," she said.

I felt bad for her, but I wanted to know where my sanitary napkin was. I asked her if she had seen it. "I'm sorry, Nena," she said. "I took it."

"But why?" I yelled. "That was my sanitary napkin. It was mine!"

"It's just that I got my period this morning, Nena. I couldn't find any pads here so I didn't know what else to do."

"I hate you!" I yelled, and then I ran outside into the yard to cry.

When Papi came home, he already knew that Mago had missed school because he got a call from Burbank at work. I had never seen my father so furious. He came barging into the house, and without asking for an explanation, he took off his belt and gave my sister the biggest lashing any of us had gotten thus far, right there on the couch where she had been writhing in pain all day.

"Papi, stop!" Carlos said, but Papi didn't listen and the belt kept whistling through the air. What was worse was that Mago wouldn't tell him what was wrong with her. She just said, "I'm not feeling well, Papi." But those past months we had learned that according to Papi, being sick was no excuse to miss school. *But this isn't a common cold!* I thought. Mago put her arms up to cover her face. Suddenly, I couldn't take it anymore. I forgot I was supposed to be angry at my sister, and I rushed at him and pushed him.

"Don't hit her!" I yelled. "She's menstruating. She's become a se-ñorita. Stop it. Stop it!"

Then Papi steadied his belt and put it down. He looked at the three of us, and for a moment it was as if he had just awakened, as if that person who had just beat up my sister wasn't the one who was now in the room with us. He blinked once, twice, then went into his room and didn't come out.

Mila arrived half an hour later. She'd stopped at her mother's house after work to visit her children. When we told her what Papi had done, she said, "Your father didn't mean to. He doesn't know any bet-ter. It's the way he was raised." She went to the store to buy Mago a package of sanitary napkins.

I clutched my sister's hand and looked at the angry welts. "Why didn't you tell him?" I asked Mago as I sat next to her on the couch.

"I was too embarrassed, Nena. You just don't go telling men you're on your period. Especially a father you haven't seen in eight years!"

"But, but, he wouldn't have hit you."

Mago looked out the window. "It doesn't matter," she said.

"Of course it matters," Carlos said. "And I can't believe he hit *you*. I mean, you're his favorite."

On hearing that, Mago started to cry. I punched Carlos in the arm even though I was thinking the same thing myself. Mago was Papi's "Negra," after all.

When Mila came back with the sanitary napkins, Mago took one from the bag and gave it to me.

"Here, Nena. I know it isn't your special one, I'm sorry."

"It's okay. It was just a napkin," I told her. "This one will be just as special to me." I put it in my drawer to save it for that day when I would become a little woman. I glanced at my father's bedroom door and hoped that my rite of passage wouldn't be as painful as my sister's.

7

Reyna and Papi

Mrs. Anderson announced that the school nurse would be coming in shortly to check the students for hygiene problems. I was surprised at that. Everyone around me looked clean and healthy. All the students had nice clothes on, shoes that were practically new. Nobody was barefoot. No one looked as if they hadn't bathed in days. *Why would we need to be inspected?* I wondered.

When the nurse came, we were asked to form a single file. When it was my turn, I was told to keep my head down while the nurse parted my hair with a wooden stick. When she was done inspecting me, she wrote down something on a paper and told me I couldn't return to school until the lice were gone.

"Lice? What lice? No, you're wrong. I can't have lice!" I told her, shaking my head.

As my eyes began to water, I wanted to tell the nurse I had been in the U.S. long enough to know my hygiene problems were a thing of the past. Back in Mexico, I wanted to say, my head was a nesting ground for lice. My belly was home to worms. Three times a week, Abuelita Chinta would send us to the canal to bathe in its muddy waters, and I often went around barefoot. But here in El Otro Lado, I had tennis shoes. I showered almost every day, and the water that sprinkled down from the showerhead was so clean I could lift up my head and stick out my tongue and catch the water drops that tasted of rain. We no longer had to wash our clothes in the dirty canal water, nor scrape our knuckles raw from scrubbing our dresses on the washing stones. And we didn't have to lay our wet clothes on tops of rocks until they were hard and stiffened by the sun, which left them smelling and feeling like cardboard.

No, here in the U.S. we went to the laundromat down the street, where we didn't have to do anything but load the clothes and then sit on a bench and listen to the machine hum and vibrate as it did the work for us. Then off the clothes went into the dryer, where I then stood and watched them spin around and around in colorful circles. When the dryer beeped, I would open the door, and the clothes would tumble out into my arms, so soft and warm and smelling of flowers, sky, and sunshine. How amazing, I wanted to tell the nurse, that this is how clothes smelled even though they hadn't been touched by a single ray of the sun!

I had never been so clean in my life, and yet here she was telling me I had lice.

How can there be lice in the U.S.? I wanted to ask. *Did they sneak across the border, like me?*

I walked home holding the nurse's note, wondering what to do. *What will Papi do when he finds out I can't return to class until he takes care of the lice problem? What if he finally decides to send me back to Mexico— never mind that he still hasn't finished paying his debt—at learning that I am still the dirty girl he once left behind?*

I spent the afternoon crying. I imagined Papi putting me on a bus to Mexico, me waving goodbye to Mago and Carlos from the window. And how could I ever hope to make Papi proud of me when I came home with news such as this?

When Papi got home, I forced myself to walk up to him and give him the note. I stared at the hand in which he held the note. One of his fingernails had dried blood in it, and I wondered if he had hit himself with a hammer. I wanted to touch his hand, ask him if it hurt. Instead, I wrapped my arms around myself, preparing for the beating I was sure would come. But I was ready to take as many beatings as he wanted to give me, as long as he didn't send me away. "I'm sorry, Papi. I don't know how I got them."

"From other kids at school, I'm sure," he said, hanging up his keys. "It's not your fault."

"You mean, you aren't going to hit me?"

"Just be careful who you're friends with, Chata. Maybe one of them gave you lice." To my surprise, Papi wasn't angry with me. Instead, he spent the rest of the afternoon parting my hair and looking for lice, removing the white nits very carefully so as not to pull out the hair strands. My father, the one who inflicted pain with his belt or his words, the one who had shown little tenderness toward us, who had hands hardened and callused from so many years of hard manual labor, was very gentle when delousing my hair. For the first time since I'd been in this country, Papi devoted a full two hours to me. Only me.

"You probably don't remember this," Papi said as he parted my hair with his fingers. "But when you were little, before I came here, you liked it when I gave you baths. You wouldn't let anyone bathe you except me. When I came home for lunch, you would be standing by the door, and as soon as you saw me, you would come running out to me saying 'Agua. Agua.' Then I would take you to the patio and sit you on the washing stone next to the water tank to bathe you. Sometimes I didn't even have time to eat my lunch. But you wouldn't have it any other way."

I closed my eyes and listened to his story about an event in my life I didn't remember, but that I would treasure from that moment on.

8

Carlos, Mago, and Reyna

EVEN BEFORE BECOMING a señorita, Mago had been changing in many ways. Throughout the past months I had seen the way she looked at boys whenever we accompanied Mila on her errands to the market, the laundromat, or other places. Papi was very clear about that, though. No boyfriends allowed. The month before, Mago had asked him to buy her a makeup set, but Papi was very clear on that also—she could wear only lipstick. He thought she was too old for Barbies but too young for makeup. Mago would say his backward thinking was very frustrating. "This is the United States," she would say, "not Mexico."

On Valentine's Day, I returned to school free of lice—just in time to exchange cards with my classmates. I got lots of good candy. Mago and Carlos didn't really get anything because junior high students don't exchange Valentine Day's cards like they do in elementary school. Mago said, "We're beyond that nonsense," while popping one of my chocolate hearts into her mouth. I told her that was too bad, and I took away my goodies. Then I went to play with my dolls.

It wasn't much fun playing alone. I begged Mago to come play with me. She wasn't as interested in my Barbie as she had been just two months before, which made me sad because that was the only thing Mago had envied me for. Usually, it was me doing the envying. After I pestered her relentlessly, she finally put her notebook down and came over to me.

"Fine, I'll play with you," she said. She picked up Barbie and Ken and took off their clothes. Although I didn't know much about sex, back in Mexico I had seen enough dogs, and sometimes donkeys or pigs, doing what Mago was making Barbie and Ken do.

"What kind of game is that?" I said, grabbing my dolls from her. "You're such a marrana," I said.

She went back to her notebook where she was writing a letter to Mami, Betty, and Abuelita Chinta.

Mago had been writing Mami letters once a month, and she would send them to Abuelita Chinta's shack. In the letter, we always included photographs we would take with Papi's Polaroid camera. There were pictures of us wearing our new clothes from Kmart, of Carlos riding the used bicycle Papi bought him, of us playing baseball in the yard. We would take pictures of us posing on Papi's red Mustang, of us celebrating holidays like Halloween and Christmas. Always in the pictures, we were smiling, as if life was more than we could ever have hoped for in this perfect place.

Through the pictures, we wanted Mami to see we were doing great and that she shouldn't worry. We would never tell her about the dark side of Papi, in part so that she wouldn't worry about us, and also because we didn't want to admit we now understood her fear when he had come after her with a gun. There was something about Papi that could frighten us to the core, gun or no gun. In the white area of the pictures, Mago would always write: *"To our beloved mother, whom we love and adore—despite everything. Your children, Mago, Carlos, and Reyna."*

Mami had never written back. But once in a while we would get a letter from Tía Emperatriz. This is how we learned that our cousin Élida had run off with a man in the neighborhood. Mago was actually quite jealous that Élida had found someone she loved and who loved her back. But half a year later, a letter from Tía Emperatriz said that Élida's lover had brought her back to Abuela Evila's house saying that Élida couldn't have babies and was therefore useless as a woman and wife. It was the talk of the neighborhood, Tía Emperatriz said. In her most recent letter, we had learned that Tía María Félix had kept her promise and had finally brought Élida to the U.S. so that Abuela Evila's neighbors would stop talking about her daughter.

Back then we hadn't known where in Los Angeles Tía María Félix lived, and even if we had known, we probably wouldn't have gone to visit Élida. We just didn't have that kind of relationship with our cousin. My father wasn't close to his sister, either, and he never talked about visiting Tía María Félix, and for years we knew nothing about her. It wasn't until he was in stage four of his cancer that he and Tía María Félix were finally reunited. My aunt would visit him daily, and they would spend hours reminiscing about times gone by and lamenting their broken relationships with their children. While my siblings and I had been struggling to overcome the gap that was created between us and our father when he'd left us behind, Élida had been doing the same thing with her mother. And like us, they had also failed to repair their relationship.

Immigration took a toll on us all.

Mago finished her letter and gave it to Mila so that she could send it off the next time she went to the post office. At night, as we were lying in our sofa bed, Mago said she wanted us to play a game.

"What kind of game?" I asked.

"Mamá y Papá," she said.

"How do you play that?"

"Here, I'll show you." Then she leaned over and started to touch me in a weird way. Her fingers slid down my body. In the darkness, I felt her lips on my neck. Then I felt something wet on my earlobe.

"What are you doing? It's gross!" I said, pushing her off me. I turned my back on her, wiping her saliva off my earlobe. "What's wrong with you?"

"Forget it," she said. She turned her back to me. Then in the darkness, I heard her say, "I'm going on fifteen and I haven't ever been kissed."

"It's not a big deal."

"You're not even eleven. What do you know? I want someone to like me. I want a boyfriend."

"You're not allowed."

"And what if no one ever loves me? What if my scars gross them out?"

"You can hardly see them."

"That's what you think."

"I hope Papi throws you a quinceañera," I said as I wrapped my arms around her. "You'd look like a princess with your pink dress."

Mago didn't say anything for a while. I thought she had fallen asleep, but then she said, "There's a boy."

I turned to face her again. "Don't tell me you have a boyfriend?" I asked, a little too loud. Mago hit me with her elbow to be quiet. Carlos didn't wake up, even though he was sleeping on the floor near our bed. I hoped Papi hadn't heard me, either.

"No. He doesn't even know I exist," she said. She went on to tell me about a guy named Pepe she had a crush on. But he didn't notice her because she was an ESL student, whereas he was a pocho. Even though his parents were Mexican, he had been born in this country and didn't speak a word of Spanish. He hung out with the popular kids, unlike Mago, who, because she was an ESL student, did not.

"Have you tried talking to him?" I asked.

"Are you stupid? He doesn't speak Spanish, didn't you hear me?"

"Speak to him in English then."

"My English isn't good enough. It'll never be good enough," she said.

On Saturday morning, Papi woke us up at eight as he always did, even though it was the weekend and we begged him to let us sleep in. Instead, he put Los Tigres del Norte on the stereo and blasted the volume. No matter how many pillows we put over our ears, nothing could keep the music out. "¡Ya levántense, huevones!" Papi called out over the music. Carlos was up and ready to go help Papi with chores before I could rub the sleep from my eyes.

As we were cleaning the bathroom, Mago stopped scrubbing the toilet and said, "I know what I have to do!" She got up and went to the yard where Papi and Carlos were mowing the lawn. "Papi, can you take us to church tomorrow?"

Papi looked at her as if she were crazy. When we first arrived in the U.S., we missed Abuelita Chinta so much that we asked Papi to take us to church because that was what we had done with her. Papi said he didn't believe in religion. "This is my God," he said as he raised his Budweiser, and then took a drink from it. We had not asked again.

Papi looked at Mago and wiped the sweat off his forehead. "If you kids want to go to church, you can go, but I'm not taking you." Then he started the lawn mower and continued his work.

The following day, Mago and I set out to go to church. She wouldn't tell us why she was going, but I had a pretty good idea. Abuelita Chinta taught us to pray, especially when you want something really badly. There was not a single saint, statue of La Virgen de Guadalupe, or picture of Jesus Christ anywhere at home to pray to. So I knew this was why Mago now wanted to go to church. I wanted to go to church to remember my grandmother and to ask God to give me the chance to make my father proud.

The closest Catholic church was St. Ignatius, which was on Monte Vista Street, but all the way by Avenue 61. Papi wouldn't be bothered with driving us there because he wanted to enjoy his Sunday drinking and watching basketball on the television, and Mila had gone to visit her children. Papi never went with her. Mila's family hated my father and would never welcome him into their home. Carlos wanted to stay with Papi, so just as we had done in Mexico, Mago and I walked to church. It took us forty minutes to get there, and we were out of breath, but we did find what we were looking for.

As soon as we opened the door, I became intoxicated with the smells of incense, melted wax, and flowers. All of a sudden, I was back in Iguala. I was back with my sweet grandmother.

We took a seat in the back pew and listened to mass while surrounded by the saints and Christ, wondering if Abuelita Chinta was at church in Iguala at that very minute, looking up at the face of Jesus, as we were doing now.

Oh, please, tell her we miss her, I said to Jesus. *Tell her how much we love her.*

The next day, I kept wondering if Mago had gotten her prayer answered. When she finally picked me up at Mrs. Giuliano's house, I demanded that she tell me, tell me, tell me.

Mago said, "When Carlos and I were walking down to the bus stop today after school, I noticed that Pepe and his friends were walking right in front of us. Pepe turned around and saw me. He slowed down until I had caught up to him, and he asked me what my name was."

"And? And?" I said, grabbing her arm. I closed my eyes and listened to her story, which was better than the soap operas Mila watched.

"All I managed to say was 'Maggie,'" she said. Maggie? It took me a second to remember she had changed her name at school because even back then she hadn't liked being called Mago by strangers. She also claimed that her teachers had trouble saying her real name, Magloria, and her history teacher had started calling her Maggie. So now she was known as Maggie everywhere but at home. But there was more to the story than that. It was the beginning of her assimilation.

Mago continued her story: "After I told him my name, Pepe started asking me more questions, and very soon he figured out I don't speak English well. He caught up to his friends and didn't look at me again."

"I'm sorry, Mago," I said.

"I could *understand* his questions," Mago told me. "I just couldn't answer them. And I was so nervous." She was close to tears.

"Don't worry, Mago. I'm sure he'll talk to you again, you'll see. You'll get another chance to make a good impression."

But a few days later, Mago told me that as she and Carlos were walking home along the train tracks that run parallel to Figueroa Street, they ran into Pepe and his friends. To Mago's surprise, the boys started throwing gravel at them from the other side of the tracks, yelling, "Wetbacks! Wetbacks!"

Mago told me her heart broke at the sight of Pepe laughing and pointing at her and Carlos. She was so mad she had yelled one of the few cuss words she knew in English, "You maderfockers!"

"Ay, Nena. You don't know how much I wished today that I knew every bad word in English," Mago said between tears. "And there was no point in cussing them out in Spanish. They wouldn't have understood the words anyway. And worse, they would have laughed even harder."

Mago wasn't the only one who was in love with someone at Luther Burbank Junior High School. Not even a week had gone by after the final episode of Mago's love story when she and Carlos came home from school and I found out about a girl named María that Carlos was drooling over on the bus. Now Carlos was very upset, and he and Mago were still arguing about it.

"You didn't have to be so mean to her," Carlos told Mago.

"What happened?" I asked.

Carlos said, "There's a girl named María I like a lot. Her last name is González, so I get to sit behind her in the three classes we share."

"But she doesn't even know he exists," Mago said. Carlos looked away and his cheeks turned red. I knew Carlos didn't have much luck with girls because of his teeth, which was really sad because my brother wasn't ugly. But his upper

Carlos in seventh grade

lip was too thick and once he opened his mouth, and you could see his teeth—the two big front teeth and the tiny, tiny tooth in the middle—well, then that was *all* you would look at. "You should have seen him today on the bus," Mago said as she dropped down onto the couch. "There he is, staring at María from across the aisle, drooling like a cow. It was embarrassing. And finally, this girl comes up to him, really pissed off, and says, 'What are you staring at me for?'"

"And you didn't have to be so mean!" Carlos said again.

"What did you tell her?" I asked Mago as I sat next to her.

"Well, what else? I said, 'You should be grateful my brother is looking at you, since you're so damn ugly.'"

"And she's not!" Carlos said.

"I was trying to defend you, pendejo," Mago said. We all jumped up from the couch when the doorbell rang.

Carlos went and opened the door. Then he turned to look at Mago, his eyes opened wide in surprise.

"Tell your sister to come out," I heard a girl say in Spanish through the screen door.

"It's *her*," Carlos said. "How did she know where we live?"

"How would I know?" Mago said. She went to the door and opened it. "What do you want, girl? You want my brother to stare at you some more?"

"I came to teach you a lesson," the girl said.

"Okay, give me one minute." Mago headed to our dresser and took out a pair of sweatpants and a sweatshirt. She went into the bathroom and changed out of her jeans and blouse.

"Mago, don't go outside," Carlos said. "I don't need you to defend me. I'm not a little kid anymore."

"This is no longer about you," Mago said as she bent down to retie her tennis shoes.

I walked over to the door, and there I saw the girl that had my brother drooling like a cow. Behind her were three other girls. María was very pretty. Her skin was light and she had a few freckles sprinkled on her cheeks. She was wearing white jeans and a black shirt with a hot pink image of Hello Kitty, and white sandals. I instantly envied her Hello Kitty shirt. It had been almost a year since Mila had taken us to Kmart to buy us clothes. She'd been bringing us bags of clothes from the old ladies at Kingsley Manor. Mago said those were dead people's clothes. I didn't know if the old ladies were dead or not, all I knew was that there was no way I would ever find a Hello Kitty shirt in the bags Mila brought us.

"Look, I'm sorry, María. I won't look at you again, but you don't need to fight my sister," Carlos said.

María pushed him aside and called him a sissy. She and her friends followed Mago to the parking lot of the fourplexes.

María didn't know that Carlos wasn't trying to protect Mago. She didn't know that the previous week Mago's heart had gotten broken, and ever since then she had been itching to punch something or someone. She didn't know that only the day before, Mago had hit me because I had taken her rubber band without permission to put my hair up in a ponytail. She didn't know that Mago had punched Carlos in the stomach because he spilled water on her math homework. But she soon found out.

A second after they reached the parking lot, the fight broke out, and Mago had her fingers wrapped in María's long brown hair and was punching her in that way she had perfected after years of hitting me and Carlos. This time, Mago didn't hold her cuss words back. María spoke Spanish and because of that Mago fired off her cuss words faster than a machine gun. Soon, she had María on the ground and María's pretty, white pants were turning gray. But the worst part came when Mago dragged the girl to the space where Papi always parked the old Ford truck he drove to work. Mago rolled María around and around in the puddle of motor oil from Papi's truck and soon María's white pants were completely black and her friends were rushing over to pull Mago off.

"Enough, enough!" the girls said as they formed a barricade to protect María.

Mago wiped the sweat off her forehead and looked at the girl who was still lying in the puddle of motor oil. "When my brother looks at you again, you better be happy about it, pendeja."

Mago walked back to the apartment, and Carlos and I followed behind her. Carlos turned to look one more time at the girl he sat behind in class. She was on her feet now, trying to smooth out her messy hair. Only Hello Kitty had escaped, unscathed.

Carlos said, "You aren't ugly, María. I am." And then with his head hanging down, he went inside.

I stood there in the parking lot feeling terrified. What was going to happen to *me* when I fell in love? I wondered. *Would I have the same rotten luck as my brother and sister?*

9

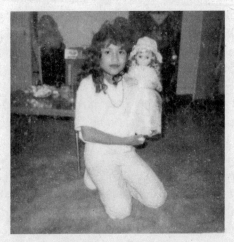

Reyna and her new doll

M RS. ANDERSON ANNOUNCED there was something important
she had to tell us. Through Mr. López, I learned there was
going to be a schoolwide competition. That week, every student in
each class would be writing their very own books, and the teachers
would select the best ones in their classes. From there, the selected
books would be judged and three lucky winners chosen.

I will finally get my chance to make Papi proud!

For the rest of the week we spent a lot of time working on our
projects. Mr. López said we could write our stories in Spanish since
that was the language we knew best. At first, I didn't know what to
write. I'd never written my very own story before. I'd always liked to
read in Mexico, but here in this country, books for kids my age were
very difficult for me to read because of my limited English. The books
Mr. López gave me were those for kindergarteners—books with big

215

letters and lots of pictures. I loved looking at the pictures, but the stories weren't very interesting. *See Spot Run!*

I missed the literature books I left behind in Mexico, the ones I was given at school. I loved the stories in those books. My favorite one was of a little pine tree that wished his needles were made of gold. He got his wish and his needles turned to gold, but a robber came at night and stole them. Then he wished for his leaves to be made of glass, but they broke when a strong wind came. Then he wished his needles to be big glossy leaves, but the next day goats came and ate them. The little pine tree then learned to like himself as he was.

Because I couldn't think of any story of my own to write, I started to write the story of the little tree. But the next day I felt bad about copying someone else's story, so I threw away the pages and started again. I thought and thought, and finally I decided what I was going to write. The story of my birth.

As I wrote, I closed my eyes and saw Mami lying down on the dirt floor over the straw mat. The midwife came into the shack next to Abuela Evila's house and saw Mami bending over in pain. I could perfectly picture the midwife lighting a fire under the comal, the big round griddle where Mami made tortillas, and putting a pot of water there to boil. I could feel the heat of the flames.

"Don't push yet," I heard the midwife say as she sharpened her knife. "You aren't ready yet."

As I wrote, I told about how I couldn't wait to be born and the midwife barely had enough time to catch me before I hit the dirt floor. "It's a girl," the midwife said as she put me into Mami's arms.

Then came the best part of my story, my favorite part. I wrote about how Mami had turned to face the fire so the heat of the flames could warm me. As the midwife cut the umbilical cord, Mami pointed to a spot on the dirt floor and told the midwife to bury it there. I wrote how even though I was now living far away from Mami and my country, I hadn't forgotten where I came from.

Mr. López helped me fix my spelling and gave me suggestions for improving my story. When it was as good as could be, he gave me white paper so I could write it nice and neatly. When I was finished, I started my favorite part, drawing pictures.

Mrs. Anderson showed the class how to bind our books. She gave us two rectangular pieces of cardboard and butcher paper to make the cover. By the end of the week we were all done with our books, and Mrs. Anderson picked them up and put them on her desk. Because it was Friday and we had worked hard all week, she put on a movie for us to watch as a reward. She said she would read our books while we watched our movie.

The movie was about an alien named E.T. who wanted to go home. I felt bad for the alien because life in the U.S. was very difficult for him. I could understand his wanting to go home. I was jealous because he seemed to learn English a lot faster than I had all those months.

I couldn't concentrate on the movie because I kept glancing at Mrs. Anderson. She had put all the books on the right side of her desk. As she read, she began to make two piles. One pile was getting bigger and bigger, and the other pile remained small. I knew the big pile was of the books she hadn't liked.

I froze when she picked up my book. *Here it is. Here is my big chance!* She opened it, flipped through the pages in the blink of an eye, then she closed the book shut and put it in the big pile. My eyes began to burn with tears. My book had been rejected. *But she couldn't have read it. No one reads a book in a second! She doesn't even speak Spanish well, so how can she read it so fast?* I wanted to stand up and say something. I wanted to tell her she had made a mistake, and she should look at it again. But I didn't have the English words to say what I thought, and so I said nothing at all.

E.T. was going home. He was saying bye to his friend and getting into his ship. How I wished I could go home, too, back to Iguala where I could speak to my teacher in my own language. Where I could stand up for what I believed in, not caring if afterward I got hit with the ruler for my rebellion. I didn't want to be in this country if that was how things were always going to be.

At the end of class, Mrs. Anderson held up the books she selected for the competition. Out of the eight books she chose, not even one was written by one of the kids at my table, the non–English speakers.

"You kids did a great job on those books," Mr. López said to us in Spanish. "Just because they weren't chosen doesn't mean they weren't good."

"Just not good enough," I said under my breath. I put my head between my hands, tears threatening to flow as I felt the disappointment come at me like a huge wave. *Don't let go of me, Papi.*

Mr. López looked at me, and then at the other four students at my table. He said, "There is no reason for any of you not to get ahead in life. You will learn English one day. You will find your way. Remember, it doesn't matter where you come from. You're now living in the land of opportunity, where anything is possible."

Mrs. Anderson put all the rejected books around the room to display them. I knew she was doing that so the students wouldn't feel bad for not being chosen. But when we were dismissed, as I was walking by my book, I took it from the shelf where Mrs. Anderson had put it.

One day, I promised myself, thinking about Mr. López's words, *I will write a book that won't be rejected, one that will make my father proud.*

10

Mami at Exposition Park

O NE DAY IN MAY, a year after we'd come to the U.S., Papi fell off a ladder at work and hit his head and injured his knee. He stayed at the hospital overnight for observation, and he had to take a few days off from work until he got better.

Papi wasn't the kind to stay home doing nothing. Early the next morning, he left for downtown to walk around. He took the bus because the doctors told him not to drive. He came home just as Carlos, Mago, and I were sitting down at the kitchen table to do our homework. He took a sip of the beer he had just taken out of a paper bag and said, "Your mother is not in Mexico."

We stared at him, not understanding.

"Didn't you hear me? Your mother is not in Mexico." I'd thought he was joking. Then I realized that he wasn't.

"Where is she, then?" Mago asked, lifting her head from her homework. Carlos and I also stopped what we were doing, and we sat there at the kitchen table and looked at our father.

"She's been in this country for months now, and she hasn't even tried to contact you kids," Papi said.

"But how can she be here?" Carlos asked.

"Are you sure?" I asked.

"Of course I'm sure," Papi said. "I ran into her today." He told us that he'd waited for the bus to come back home. When it arrived, the last passenger to get off was our mother. She lived downtown on a street called San Pedro.

"Your mother never ceases to amaze me," Papi said. He laughed, but it wasn't a happy laugh. It was a laugh of bitter disappointment.

"And Betty?" Mago asked.

"Didn't I just tell you? Your mother never ceases to amaze me. Where do you think your little sister is?"

Mago, Carlos, and I looked at one another. *Where else could Betty be? With Mami of course.*

"Your mother," Papi said, squeezing the empty beer can with his hand, "your mother left your sister in Mexico and came here with her boyfriend." He threw the can against the wall and grabbed another one out of the paper bag.

"Can we go see her?" Carlos asked.

"Did she tell you where exactly she lives?" I asked.

"You want to go *see* her?" Papi said. "Don't you kids have any pride? Your mother doesn't care about you. If she did, she would have called you when she got here. She's been here for months. Months. Why would you want to go see her? Have some pride, pendejos!"

"But she's our mami," I said.

Papi looked at me, and I could tell in his eyes that I had disappointed him with those words. He shook his head. He touched his bump and winced. He got up and said he was going to go lie down. At the door, he turned and said, "Just so you know, your mother has a new child. A boy, not three months old."

He left us there in the kitchen. I felt as if I were the one who had hit her head. I felt an intense pressure building up, and I couldn't breathe, I couldn't think. All I heard in my head were Papi's words: *Your mother doesn't care about you . . . Your mother doesn't care about you . . .*

But even when the dizziness stopped and I could breathe again, I found that I could not stop myself from yearning to see her.

During the weeks following Papi's discovery, we couldn't convince him to allow us to go see Mami. The more we asked, the more he withdrew. He would simply say, "I'm the one who brought you here," and then would lock himself up in his room. With those words, he was asking us to choose between him and her. We didn't know how to tell him that it shouldn't be a matter of choice, that they were both our parents.

It hurt me to think of Betty all alone in Mexico. When Papi and Mami left us there, at least we'd had one another. But Betty, who did Betty have over there? She was like Élida, with no one there to love her except our grandmother. I thought about all those Polaroid pictures we'd sent, of how it must have hurt our little sister to see us here, together, while she was over there all alone.

"Your mother is so selfish, that's why she wouldn't let me bring Betty," Papi said to us. "She used your sister to get back at me."

Mila said to Papi, "We couldn't afford another mouth to feed anyway. It's difficult enough as it is, with the three you already have here, and with the three I have. Even though they aren't with me, I still have to support them."

"Yes, but what if I went back—?"

"We're not going through that again," Mila said. "I will not take responsibility for raising yet another child!"

"Papi is right," Mago said to us. "Why should we go see her after what she did? How many times will she continue to abandon us?"

Carlos and I didn't answer.

But regardless of what Mami had done, the fact remained that Betty was still in Mexico. Mago wrote a letter to Abuelita Chinta to inquire about Betty, and we waited anxiously for a reply. It wasn't until the end of June that a letter arrived from Tía Güera. She told us our little sister was fine and not to worry. She said that in the summer, she would be leaving Iguala to come here to the U.S. Tía

Güera had decided to leave her no-good husband and try her luck in this country. Mami was taking that as an opportunity to bring Betty here. So Tía Güera and Betty would both be making the long journey north together. The only thing was, Tía Güera said, that she would have to leave her own daughter behind with Abuelita Chinta. It made me sad to think of my cousin Lupita, of how now she was the one being abandoned, and I hoped that one day the cycle of leaving children behind would end.

We finally convinced Papi to let us visit Mami when we learned Tía Güera and Betty had safely arrived. We told him—and ourselves—that we really weren't going to see *her*, we were going to see our sister. But of course we knew it was a lie. We were once again following the crumbs back to Mami.

We took the 83 bus to downtown L.A. As we walked east on Seventh Street toward San Pedro Street, we were taken aback by what we saw. This was another side of this country I hadn't seen before. For a moment, I felt as if we had just crossed over into another world.

There were winos everywhere sitting on the ground asking for handouts. Homeless people covered in dirt and dressed in rags pushed shopping carts filled with dirty blankets, old shoes, and plastic bags filled with junk. Women stood on corners dressed in skimpy clothes. Trash littered the sidewalks. Plastic bags whirled up in the air like miniature parachutes. The air was filled with the stench of urine and a rancid smell that was almost overpowering. It made me gag.

We could not believe this was where Mami lived.

"If I didn't know any better, I would think we were back in Mexico," Mago said.

"I didn't think there were places like this in the U.S.," Carlos said.

In Mexico everyone I knew always thought of the U.S. as the most beautiful place in the world, as close to Heaven as you could possibly get.

We found the address Tía Güera had given us and we knocked. Someone came down the stairs and opened the security door. We didn't know who the woman was, but we told her we were there to see our mother.

"What's her name?" she asked.

"Juana."

"Oh, yes, she lives in Room A." She started back up the stairs and we followed behind her. The door to Room A was open. We saw Mami before she saw us. She was sitting on the bed holding a sleeping baby in her arms. Her hair was permed into tight curls and cut short. She had put on a bit more weight, and as always, most of it went straight to her stomach. When she saw us, Mami stood up and came to the door.

"I can't believe you kids are here," she said, smiling. "Look how much you've grown!"

We entered the room and we said hello to Rey, who was sitting at the table. Next to him was Tía Güera. We gave her a hug and told her it was nice to see her. Then my eyes fell on little Betty, who was sitting on the dirty carpet playing with a doll. We rushed to our sister to hug her and cover her in kisses, but Betty pushed us away and rushed to my aunt's side. "A year is a long time for a little kid," Tía Güera said.

"Give her time," Mami said.

"Betty, it's me, Reyna. Don't you remember me?" I said, kneeling down to look at her. Betty hid her face in Tía Güera's chest.

I glanced at Mami, and I thought about Papi, at what he'd said. He was right. It was because of Mami's selfishness that now Betty didn't know us. It was her stupid, stupid pride.

I looked at my five-year-old sister and wondered how long it would take for us to finally feel like a family.

Mami lived in a tiny room big enough for a bed, a dining table, a refrigerator, a TV stand, and boxes of clothes piled against the wall. They had to share the kitchen and bathroom with the rest of the tenants on their floor. I thought about the fourplex Mila and Papi owned. He made three hundred dollars a week. Mila didn't make much more. Between them they had six kids to support, and their many expenses didn't allow them to give up the rent of the larger units. We had to stay in the one-bedroom unit until things got better. But even though we slept in the living room, we at least had the bathroom and kitchen to ourselves, and we didn't have to share them with complete strangers. We also had a backyard to play in. Our carpet wasn't dirty. There weren't roaches scurrying around the walls like here at my mother's.

We crammed into the little room as best we could.

"So how did you end up here?" we asked Mami.

She sat at the table holding her sleeping son in her arms. I tried not to look at him. I didn't want to feel anything for that baby, that brother of mine whose name was Leonardo. Even though he was three months old, I could tell, even then, that he was going to look just like his father. Mago, Carlos, Betty, and I were a mixture of the Grande-Rodríguez genes and anyone who saw us could tell right away we were related. But Leonardo looked nothing like us, and that made it even harder for us to like him.

Mami told us her journey to the U.S. with Rey had happened by chance. A friend of hers had a son who wanted to come here, but he was afraid of making the journey alone. Since Mami had already been here once, her friend asked Mami to accompany her son and to help him once he got here. She even offered to lend Mami the money for her smuggler's fees. Mami didn't think twice about it. She and Rey and the young man set out on their journey, but she couldn't bring Betty, so she left her behind with Abuelita Chinta until she got settled here. In the meantime, though, she started another family with Rey, a boy whose existence we would not have been aware of if Papi had not run into her that day.

Both Rey and Mami worked at a garment factory. Rey operated the steamer, Mami trimmed loose threads. "They pay us miserable wages," Mami said. She must have seen the look on our faces when we'd first walked in because she added, "As you can tell by where we live." She glanced around the room, just as we had done. A roach scurried across the wall, and she hurried to squash it with her sandal. She turned to us and said, "But no poverty here can compare to the poverty we left behind. And at least now I am closer to you, my children."

Mago asked her the question we had all been dying to ask. "Why didn't you tell us you were here?"

Mami took a deep breath and said, "I wanted to give you kids a chance to get to know your father, and for him to know you, without me coming in between you. Do you understand?"

Strangely enough, we did understand, although we didn't believe that was the only reason. Looking back on it now, I think it was at that particular moment in our lives that our relationship with our mother finally hit its lowest point. It was then that I finally understood the kind of person my mother had become. And how little space she was willing to make for us in her life. The only thing I could do was to accept her, although I never—even now—stopped hoping that one day she would change.

We began to visit Mami every other Sunday, and although Papi wasn't happy about it, he knew we needed to see our little sister, so he didn't stop us. One thing we soon came to like about visiting Mami was that she always had soda, chips, and candy at her house. We were jealous that Betty—and later Leonardo—had an unlimited supply of those snacks. With Papi all we drank was water, and we never got junk food unless he gave us a dollar to buy some. He never took us to McDonald's, which was one of Mami's favorite places to eat, or any other fast-food place. It wasn't until years later, when both Betty and Leonardo were extremely overweight, that I realized how lucky Mago, Carlos, and I had been.

Despite the measly salary Mami earned at the factory, she always had enough money to take us out, like to Exposition Park to see the roses, to the Alley to buy us underwear or socks, to Placita Olvera to see the folklórico dances and have a churro.

But whenever we went anywhere with Mami, she would bring along a plastic bag and would pick up cans from the street or rummage through trash bins. Sometimes she would even make us pick up the cans for her, even in public places. It was so embarrassing for Mago, Carlos, and me that we soon started to say no, absolutely not! Betty would end up being the one to run around picking up the cans without Mami even having to ask her to do it. She would run back to Mami with her find, laughing while beer trickled down her bare arm.

"What do you do with those cans?" Carlos asked. We had seen homeless people around her apartment building pushing carts filled with cans on their way to someplace, but we had no idea where they would take them.

"I sell them at the recycling center," Mami said. "I get good money doing this." Good money or not, I couldn't help thinking that Mila wouldn't be caught dead picking up cans. *Why couldn't my mother be a bit like her?* I'd wonder. Mami's apartment always smelled like rotten beer and soda because she only went to the recycling center once a week, so the bags of smashed cans would just sit in a corner of her apartment all week long. I knew then why there were so many roaches.

Eventually, we got used to our double lives. Yet as the months went by, I still wished there were a way we could have our family together, in the same place. I especially wished this when I graduated from Aldama Elementary a year later. Although I was happy to see Papi there—he actually took time off from work to come to my graduation—I wished Mami were there, too. But that was where Papi had drawn the line. He didn't want to see Mami. He said he'd never forgive her for what she did with Betty. Neither he nor my mother were ever willing to accept they had both used Betty as a way to hurt each other, and in the process, had hurt us and my little sister as well.

Mami didn't ask much about him, either. She embraced her new life in this country with Rey and her new baby boy and Betty. The distance between us wasn't two thousand miles anymore. But there was still a gap. I hoped one day we could overcome it.

Carlos, Mago, Reyna, and Betty—finally reunited

11

Papi in the United States

Sometimes Papi would sit us down and talk and talk as if he were try-ing to make up for the eight years he was gone from our lives. But his talks were always about the future, and they always went like this:

"Here in this country, if you aren't educated, you won't go very far.

"School is the key to the future.

"Without an education, you're nothing. So you kids have to study hard. You hear me? Do you hear me?"

He would tell us how important it was to get an education so that one day we could have a good career and not have to ask anyone for anything. "For example, look at your mother," he'd say. "Isn't she ashamed to be on welfare? And what's she doing at a factory? That's a dead-end job. You get paid under the table, don't get benefits. She's not putting money into social security for retirement. That's not the way to live, not here in this country." He didn't mention that he, himself, wasn't getting much out of his job because he was using a social security card he'd bought at MacArthur Park for a hundred bucks.

Papi would tell us that one day we would have great jobs. Be home owners. Have money for retirement. And never be a burden to anyone.

Sometimes, Betty would also be there at the table. She was six years old and had no interest in retirement either. By then, Mami had finally allowed us to bring her over on the weekends because Betty would cry every time we left to go back home. She wanted to come with us. Every time we left her, I felt that we were replaying that day in Mexico. We'd reassured Mami that Papi wouldn't "steal" her back. Not so much because he didn't want to, but because they truly couldn't afford another mouth to feed, as Mila had said. Betty was too little to have any interest in Papi's visions for the future, and since she rarely came over, they would not have any impact on her later in life, as they would me.

"But I'm only eleven and a half, Papi," I would say. "Why do I need to worry about retiring?"

"Chata, one day you will get old," Papi said. "If you think life is hard now, wait until you get old enough that you can't even bathe yourself, then you'll really see how hard life is."

"Like the old people at Kingsley Manor?" I asked.

"Yes, but you wouldn't be able to afford Kingsley Manor if you didn't have a good job before you got too old to work," Papi said. "But see, if you plan ahead, then you'll be better off." I tried to picture myself as an old lady, dressed in a princess dress and walking down the halls of a great mansion, as I imagined Kingsley Manor might look. I decided I really did want to have a good job, as Papi said I should.

"But we don't have papers, Papi," Mago said. "How are we going to have good careers with no papers?"

Papi said, "Just because we're illegal doesn't mean we can't dream. Besides," he said, "our lives are going to change for the better. Soon, that will no longer be an issue."

Papi had been looking at ways to legalize our status. He and Mila got officially married some months before so that she could use her privileges as an American citizen to apply for our green cards. Also, ever since President Reagan approved an amnesty program eight

Reyna and family outside of U.S. Consulate in
Tijuana finalizing green card applications

months earlier, in November, Papi had been going through the process and was hoping to get his green card through that program. Once he did, he could then claim us and legalize our status if our applications through Mila didn't work out. Mami had applied for legal residency as well, but unlike my father, she wasn't concerned about her children's status.

"One way or another," Papi said, "we will stop living in the shadows."

Back then, I hadn't known what exactly he'd meant by that, but when I thought about the way Mrs. Anderson had ignored me, about the fact that I couldn't express myself in class and my lack of English kept me silent, I thought I understood what Papi meant.

In September, Mago became the first person in our family to go to high school. Papi decided to take her shopping for new school clothes, saying that his "Negra" needed to look her best on such an important day because after this his "Negra" was going to go on to college and make us all proud.

"How about me?" I asked. "I need clothes, too. I'm starting junior high."

"But you weren't the first one," Mago said. "I was."

Papi told Carlos and me that he didn't have enough money for us all. Back then, I didn't know that his small paycheck didn't go very far to support his three children. I didn't know that divorcing my mother in order to marry Mila had cost lawyer fees, that the green card applications for the four of us had cost money, and so would the rest of the application process. So when he and Mago left for Fashion 21, I was left behind, angry at my father and thinking him a cheapskate for not taking Carlos and me clothes shopping as well.

I was also angry at my sister. It wasn't my fault that she was the firstborn. It wasn't my fault that she would get to do everything before I did. Papi said he wanted us to stop living in the shadows. Whether we got a green card or not, I promised myself that I *would* stop living in the shadow—of my sister, at least. I would find a way to be the first at something. Something that would make my father proud.

If I thought Aldama Elementary was big, I was overwhelmed when I saw that Luther Burbank Junior High School was even bigger. Thankfully, I would not be alone at school. Carlos was starting ninth grade, and he would be here with me for a year. He took me to my first class, which was Intermediate ESL. Finally, I would no longer be in a corner of my classroom as I learned English. I would be in a room where all the students were English learners.

My teacher's name was Mr. Salazar. His name sounded familiar, and I couldn't remember where I'd heard it until he took roll. When he called out my name, he paused and asked, "Grande? Are you by any chance related to Maggie Grande?"

"Yes, she's my sister," I said, remembering that Mago had mentioned him to me before.

Mr. Salazar had a huge thick mustache, but even his bushy hair couldn't cover up that big smile. "Your sister was a wonderful student. She was one of my best and brightest." He looked at me, as if measuring me up. My stomach churned. I just knew that no matter what I did, he would always compare me to my sister. And even if I did end up being one of his "best and brightest," Mago had done it first.

Luckily, no one knew my sister in my math and science classes, so there was a chance I could prove myself there without being compared to Mago, even if they were my least favorite subjects. In PE, as the teacher took roll, she stopped at my name and once again, my stomach made a flip. "Reyna Grande?" she asked. "Is that really your name, Reyna *Grande*?"

I tried to ignore the students' giggles. *Yeah, yeah, I'm a big queen, but I'm only four feet eight inches tall, so what?*

"Yes, that's me," I said, already thinking she was going to ask me if I was Mago's sister. But I was surprised when she didn't.

"You're too young to be called that, don't you think?" she asked. Her hair was so blond it was almost white under the sunlight. "Do you mind if I call you Princess?" I was so relieved that she didn't know my sister that I almost shouted out a big yes!

But I simply nodded, and just like that, I became a princess.

My last class was something called band. Carlos said it was an elective, but I hadn't chosen it. All the electives, except metal shop and band, were already full, so when the counselor was filling up my schedule, he said, "I'll put you in band," without asking me if that's what I wanted. I knew it had something to do with music, but I didn't really know what to expect. Carlos asked to be put in metal shop.

As I walked into my classroom, I hit my foot on the leg of a chair. I cried out in pain. The teacher asked, "Are you okay?"

I took a deep breath and answered in English as best as I could, "Yes, teacher. I just hurt my big finger." I limped toward an empty chair and sat on it, feeling proud of myself for answering him in his own language.

"Your big finger?" he asked. All the students were looking at me weird. "Oh, you mean your big toe!" he said and laughed. Everyone else laughed with him.

"You don't have fingers on your feet," he gently explained. "You have toes."

I wanted to slap myself because I should have known that. I had learned body parts at Aldama. It was just that sometimes I would still forget things like that. In Spanish there is only one word for finger or toe, and that is "dedo," so you don't have to worry about whether your "dedo" is on your feet or hands. Why did English have to be so complicated?

When the teacher, whose name was Mr. Adams, asked me what

instrument I wanted to play, I didn't know what to say. He pointed to the closets, where I saw rows upon rows of black cases. He opened several cases to reveal beautiful golden and silver instruments whose names I did not know.

"So, which one do you want to play?" he asked again.

"How much it costs?" I asked, wondering if Papi would even have any money to buy me one of those instruments. They looked expensive.

Mr. Adams laughed. "They won't cost you a thing," he said. "They belong to the school, but you can borrow them and take them home with you."

I found that completely unbelievable. In Mexico, nothing was free in school. Not even a pencil. He asked me again what I wanted to play. I didn't know much about instruments. Mr. Adams told me their names as he pointed to them: clarinet, trumpet, trombone, piccolo, flute, saxophone, French horn. So many instruments that I could take home!

"Here, try this," he said. "You need a small instrument." He handed me a clarinet.

Just then, my eyes fell on the shiny golden beauty in one of the cases. I said, "That's the one I want."

Mr. Adams turned to look at where I was pointing. He said, "It's an alto sax. You sure that's the one you want?"

"Yes, I'm sure."

"But you're so small," he said. I put out my hand and he handed me the case.

Once all the students had their instruments, Mr. Adams showed us how to play them and taught us some musical notes. The saxophone was heavy and the neck strap dug into my skin. I got dizzy as I blew through the mouthpiece, and at first I couldn't make any sounds. By the end of class, I had managed to create something that sounded like music. I loved playing an instrument because I knew that it didn't matter whether I spoke perfect English or not. It didn't matter that I had a "wetback" accent. Reading music didn't require me to be fluent in any spoken language. And I didn't need to speak, just play.

I went home with my alto sax, and as soon as Papi got home, I showed it to him. Mago had never come home with an instrument, so finally I had found something I was first at! Papi held the alto sax in his hand and turned it this way and that. "Are you sure you don't have to pay for this?" he asked.

"No, Papi, the school lets students borrow them for free."

Papi was amazed. He asked me to play something. Mago rolled her eyes at me and left us alone. I took the sax from him and played the scale Mr. Adams had taught me, except I didn't remember it that well. But Papi didn't criticize me for messing up. Instead he said, "You know, when I was in third grade, my teacher brought some drums to class and started to teach us how to play them. We couldn't take them home, but still, it was nice coming to school and having the chance to learn to play an instrument. I hoped to join the color guard when I got to sixth grade. But a few weeks later, when I turned nine, your grandfather said I was old enough to join him at the fields, and he pulled me out of school. I never got to play the drum again. And I've been working ever since."

Papi got up and headed to the refrigerator where he took out a Budweiser. Then he went into his room. I sat in the living room to practice my sax, but Mago and Carlos complained about the noise and sent me outside. I went to the yard and continued to practice, and I played with all my heart, for myself and for my papi, who never got another chance to play anything.

Reyna and her sax

12

Papi

JUST LIKE ABUELA Evila, Papi did not allow us to go out into the neighborhood to play. He would say, "I want you here, at home, where I can see what you're doing. I won't have you hanging out with the wrong kids and becoming cholos."

We weren't interested in becoming gang members, but it was hard not to come across them. Highland Park was home to one of the biggest gangs in Los Angeles—the Avenues. There was a family of Avenues living next to us, in fact. Although we tried to stay away from them, they wouldn't stay away from us. One of the boys, Tino, would sneak into our yard every few nights to fill up his buckets with water from the garden hose. Their utilities were always getting shut off when they didn't pay their bills on time. The father was in jail for taking the blame for a crime his oldest son had committed, and the mother was usually doing drugs instead of taking care of her children.

Papi would never say anything to them. He'd say, "I'm not going to put our lives in danger for a bucket of water." But one night, when Papi was coming home from the liquor store with a six-pack of beer, a thug came out from the shadows with a knife and told Papi to hand over his wallet. In the dim light of the streetlamp, Papi caught a glimpse of the cholo's face and said, "I let you take water from me and now you're threatening me with a knife?"

Papi later told us that Tino had actually apologized to him and put his knife away. "Good thing I've never said anything about the water," Papi said. "He would have stabbed me right then and there because I wasn't about to hand over my wallet that easily."

The firing of gunshots was a regular occurrence in our neighborhood. Almost every night we would hear popping noises in the distance. But one night, what we heard was louder than pops. Mago and I were in the living room watching our favorite soap opera, *Quinceañera,* and we were so engrossed in the TV we didn't pay much attention to the noises. But then Papi and Carlos were running into the house and Papi was yelling, "Get down. Get down!" We immediately dropped to the floor.

"What's happening, Natalio?" Mila asked as she came out of her room. It was now quiet outside except for the barking of a dog and a car alarm going off.

Papi had been outside finishing some repairs he was doing on the plumbing, and Carlos had been practicing his soccer moves in the parking lot. Papi said that a car had driven by and the men inside shot at three cholos that were walking by. The bullets shattered the windshields of the car that belonged to one of their tenants. Carlos was playing just a few inches away from that car.

"One of the cholos got hit," Papi said. "He's still out there, but the others took off running."

When we were sure no more gunshots would follow, we went outside and saw the man who was crawling on the sidewalk. "Help me," he said, groaning. "Help me."

Papi stood in front of Mago, Carlos, Mila, and me and put his arms out, keeping us back. The young man's head was shaved close to his scalp and he was wearing a plaid long-sleeve shirt. He grabbed hold of the front gate and tried to pull himself up. "Help me," he said again.

I looked at Papi. *Why isn't he helping him?* "Do something," I said, pulling on his sleeve.

"Let's go inside," Papi said. He grabbed me by my shoulders and turned me around.

"But he'll die," Mago said.

"Go inside," Papi said again. Mila went straight to the phone and called 911.

"We have to help him!" I said.

"We've done all we can for him," Papi said. "If I go out there and help him, tomorrow I will be the one who gets shot. Or you kids. Those stupid cholos will come seeking revenge, believe me. I don't want to come home and find you kids clinging to the gate with a bullet hole in your chest!" I recognized the terror in my father's face. I had seen it once before, at the border, during our third crossing as we were running from the helicopter. It was the look of an animal that can sense danger and is ready to protect its young.

We stood in the kitchen looking at each other. Soon, we heard the sound of sirens approaching the house. Papi went outside and told us to stay inside. Through the window we saw the police and the ambulance arrive. We were too curious to do as we were told, so we went outside just as the paramedics were prying the cholo's fingers from our gate. They lay him on the sidewalk and tore open his shirt. He wasn't moving or breathing. To the right of his chest was a small bullet hole. I stared at the pool of blood beneath our gate. I reached to grab my father's hand, and he squeezed mine tight.

The next day, Papi decided to go to adult school and improve his English once and for all. He was still going through the process of legalizing his status through President Reagan's amnesty program, IRCA. He hoped that soon that green card he so desired would help him become more than just a maintenance worker. But, first, he had to learn the language. "Once I'm a legal resident, and I speak better

English, things are going to change," he said. "I'm going to move us out of this neighborhood." So far, he had depended on Mila for everything. She had to write out the checks to pay the bills. She had to take me, Mago, and Carlos to our doctors' appointments because Papi didn't feel comfortable doing it. Mila went grocery shopping. Mila went to our parent-teacher conferences because Papi made her go in his stead. Mila dealt with their Asian tenants who couldn't speak Spanish. Papi would stay in his room and wouldn't come out, except to go to work or to the liquor store.

Papi bought himself a notebook and borrowed a pencil and a sharpener from me. I even gave him my eraser that smelled of strawberries, for good luck. We watched as he left the house and headed to Franklin High School, where they had night classes for adults. It filled me with pride to see my father go to school. All his talk about education, about the importance of school, seemed to mean so much more when I saw him full of determination to learn. My father's desire for a better life was palpable. It was contagious. It was one of the things I most respected about him. And I hoped with all my heart that he would be granted amnesty and be allowed to step out of the shadows.

Yet a few weeks after he'd started going to school, Papi found out something terrible. Tía Emperatriz had stolen his dream house. My aunt had finally gotten married, but at that point she had been so desperate to do so that she found herself a man who was much older, who had already been married once, but who could not take care of her. The bitterness of her disappointing marriage changed her. Somehow, she managed to get Abuela Evila to sign over to her the deed to her property, which included the land on which Papi's house had been built. My father had been allowing her to stay in the house in his absence, since he wasn't there anyway and he needed someone to take care of it. But he never imagined his sister would outright steal the house from him.

"How could she do that?" Mila asked. "Your own sister. And your mother, why would she hand over your house to Emperatriz, just like that? You've been a good son. Look at all the money you've been sending her all these years. Without you, she would have starved already."

"What are you going to do?" Mago asked Papi. We knew what that house meant to him. We knew it was his backup plan in case things didn't work out for him here in the U.S. It was an investment that had cost us our relationship with our parents, that cost Mami her marriage with my father. The price for that house had been too high to pay, as Mami once said. And now, it had been stolen from him.

"I'm going to go over there and get my house back!" Papi said, slamming his fist on the kitchen table.

"You can't go, Natalio. If you get caught on your way back, your green card application will be denied. Do you really want to jeopardize your chance at becoming legal?" Mila said.

But Papi wasn't listening. "I'm not going to lose that house. I can't lose that house. It's all I have."

"But we don't have money to pay for your plane ticket. We don't have money to pay for a smuggler to bring you back," Mila insisted. "We're barely making it as it is."

But Papi wouldn't listen, and by the next day, he was gone.

While he was in Mexico, it took a lot of effort for me to stay focused in school. I wondered what Papi was doing. I wondered if by now my aunt and my grandmother had realized their mistake and given the house back to its rightful owner. It hurt me to know that Tía Emperatriz had acted in such a dishonest way. She'd been so kind to us, and I had always remembered her fondly. Now, she had not only betrayed Papi but us as well.

I wondered if Papi was already on his way back to us. I prayed that he would cross the border safely. I prayed that he wouldn't get killed or hurt or caught by la migra. My stomach hurt knowing that if he did get caught, he would lose his chance at becoming a legal resident, at finally having that security he desperately desired. And what would become of his dreams, which by then were also becoming my dreams?

Two weeks later, we came home from school to find Papi sitting at the kitchen table, his head hanging low. His face was pale, despite the sunburn he'd gotten while crossing the border. His eyes were red and puffy from lack of sleep. He looked thinner than when he'd left. We rushed to him, happy that he had made it across the border safely. He turned to us and said, "I'm never going back there again."

I thought about all those times Mago, Carlos, and I had helped to carry bricks and buckets of mortar to the bricklayers. I thought about those nights when we couldn't sleep because we had been so sore. I thought about the years that Papi was gone, that Mami was gone, so that they could build that dream house.

"What happened, Papi?" Mago asked.

He told us that Abuela Evila was ill and frail, and somehow my aunt had managed to coerce my grandmother into deeding her the property. While he was there, my aunt had said that what was done was done. She said Papi didn't need a house when he had so much already. Didn't he live there in that beautiful country? What more could he want? He said that neither his father nor his mother stood up for him, that neither parent fought by his side. He said, "I've never felt so alone in my life."

I wished I could go to my father and wrap my arms around him, tell him that I understood his loss, tell him that it hurt me as much as it hurt him, that he wasn't alone—he had us, his children. But I didn't know how to hold him. I didn't know how to say what I felt, so I said nothing at all.

In the evenings at five thirty, I would look at Papi's bedroom door and wonder if that day he would finally come out with his notebook under his arm, ready to go back to school. But the door remained closed. After two weeks of looking at his closed door, I realized that the dream house wasn't the only thing he had lost.

13

Reyna and Papi

By the end of the summer before eighth grade began, I had two things to celebrate: I had become a señorita, and unlike my sister's, my body bled in silence. I had also successfully completed the ESL program and had gotten rid of my status as an ESL student.

When the new school year started, I was enrolled in regular eighth-grade English. Over the last year, I had become addicted to reading, in part because I was not good at making friends. I shied away from kids because there was always something for which they would make fun of me: my ridiculous name, my height, my Payless tennis shoes, my thick accent, the unfashionable clothes I would wear courtesy of the old ladies at Kingsley Manor.

Every Friday before heading home, I would stop at the Arroyo Seco Library for books. The maximum I was allowed to borrow was ten, and I would read them all during the week. At first, I mostly read the fairy-tale collections the library owned, from the Brothers Grimm to *The 1001 Arabian Nights.* Fairy tales reminded me of Iguala, of story time on the radio. When I was done with those books, the librarian then led me to the young adult section and handed me books she recommended. They had titles like *Sweet Valley High* and *The Babysitters Club.* As my reading skills got better, I started to read thicker books. My favorites were by an author named V. C. Andrews.

I enjoyed the Sweet Valley Junior High and Sweet Valley High series, but those books had nothing to do with my own life. The characters were twin sisters who had sun-kissed blond hair, a golden tan, dazzling blue-green eyes, perfect size-six figures—characters whose world was so different from my own. And yet I kept reading those books because I was seduced by the twins' lives. Those books gave me a glimpse into a world I wished to belong to, where there were no alcoholic fathers, no mothers who left you over and over again, no fear of deportation. I wondered what it would be like to live in a place like that. That world was the perfect place I had imagined the U.S. to be.

But with V. C. Andrews's books, I found a connection. Even though she wasn't writing about my Mexican culture, I could relate to her characters and their experiences. I was blown away when I read *Flowers in the Attic,* which was a story about four kids who, when their father died, were taken by their mother to live with their grandparents. The kids were locked up in the attic, and soon the mother started to visit them less and less and began dating other men, leaving them at the mercy of their evil grandmother.

When I read *Heaven,* I immediately related to the poverty the children lived in, although the setting was rural West Virginia, not Guerrero, Mexico. In *My Sweet Audrina,* I knew firsthand the longing Audrina felt for her father, that desperate desire to be loved by him.

Another thing I liked about V. C. Andrews's books was that they made me feel better in a way. True, my life was very difficult, but in no way as bad as her characters' lives. Abuela Evila didn't feed us much, but at least, as far as I know, she never tried to poison us!

I read so much that sometimes I would hide under the covers with a flashlight and not go to sleep until I was finished with my book. When I got my first pair of eyeglasses later that year, Mago said, "Now you look like a librarian," as if to insult me. But it only made me love books even more.

Halfway into the school year, I found out that Burbank was having a short-story competition. My English teacher encouraged all her students to enter. I thought about the story I wrote at Aldama Elementary. I was afraid of my writing once again being rejected. Yet part of me had something to prove. *I am in regular English classes now, aren't I? With the exception of my pronunciation skills, my English is almost as good as the native speakers', isn't it? I might have a chance this time, right?*

And what if by some miracle I did win? Wouldn't Papi finally be proud of me? I didn't allow myself to think that he might not be. So far, making my father proud had turned out to be impossible. He'd never once come to my band concerts. And I wasn't the only one trying to get his attention. Carlos had joined a soccer team, but Papi wouldn't go to his games. Mago had taken an interest in modern dance, performing at basketball games during halftime and at other events, but Papi wouldn't go see for himself how good a dancer she was.

So what chance did I have of making my father finally take notice? Probably none, but I wanted to try.

Because of the influence of *Sweet Valley High,* I wrote a short story about identical twins—Beverly and Kimberly. But in my short story, when the twins were very little, they were separated when their parents divorced. The mother kept Beverly, and the father took Kimberly. One day when they were teenagers, the twins were reunited by chance, and they had to struggle to recoup all that lost time and find a way to overcome the separation. Looking back on it now, I realize that first short story of mine would set the tone for all my other stories—stories of broken families, absent parents, and siblings that were separated—for that was the world I lived in, the world I knew.

I turned in my short story, and, for the following two weeks, I was anxious about the results. By then I was beginning to fall in love with writing. In my writing, you couldn't hear my accent, which is why playing the sax, writing, and drawing were my favorite ways of expressing myself.

When the time came to find out the results, they were given through the PA system during homeroom. "Congratulations to all the students who entered the short-story contest," the principal said over the speaker. I held my breath and put my head between my hands. "Remember, that even if you didn't place, you're still a winner."

She started off with the honorable mentions, but my name wasn't one of them. Then she announced the third-place winner. It wasn't me. Then the second-place winner. It wasn't me, and by now tears were starting to form. "And the first-place winner is—Reyna Grande."

I looked at the speaker. Had I just heard my name? My homeroom teacher clapped and said, "Congratulations, Reyna. I'm so proud of you." All the students looked at me, and for the first time, they weren't looking at me to criticize me, but to congratulate me.

When I went to my English class, my teacher had the competition prize for me. In front of the whole class, she handed me a blue ribbon that read "First Place" and my prize, which was two tickets stapled to a brochure. A picture of a beautiful cruise ship was on the cover of the brochure.

Had I just won two tickets to go on a cruise? My heart started to race. *Won't Papi finally be proud of me when he finds out that I'm taking him on a cruise!*

"These are tickets to go to the *Queen Mary*," my teacher said.

"The *Queen Mary*?" I asked. I glanced at the picture of the cruise ship. What a beautiful name for a ship. But I'd never heard of it before.

"Where is it?" I asked my teacher.

"In Long Beach."

I didn't know where Long Beach was either, but I was so excited just thinking about the adventure I was going to have on that cruise and how much fun it would be to share it with Papi. Maybe we could have a father-daughter moment when we could finally bond, when we could finally overcome the gap our separation had created. I thought of us standing on the deck as the ship pulled away from the harbor. I pictured us holding hands, and not letting go as we became surrounded in azure.

"Um, you do know what the *Queen Mary* is, right?" my teacher asked, interrupting my reverie. When I shook my head, she told me a brief history about the *Queen Mary*, except that I stopped listening when she got to the part that the *Queen Mary* didn't go anywhere. I didn't ask why in the world the school would give me tickets for a cruise ship that didn't go on cruises. I went back to my seat, and for the rest of the day I couldn't stop thinking about the adventure I thought I was going to share with my father.

Despite the disappointment about the cruise, I went home that day feeling proud, and I couldn't wait for Papi to come home to give him the news.

As soon as he opened the door, I ran to him and told him about getting first place in a competition. I showed him the prize and my short story. Papi glanced at the tickets. "What the hell is the *Queen Mary*?"

I told him it was a cruise ship, but I hated admitting that it didn't go anywhere.

"So what's the point of going to see it?"

"Because I won!"

"I don't even know where it is."

"It's in Long Beach."

"Long Beach is a big place," he said. "I don't want to get lost."

"Couldn't we ask for directions?" I asked. But I already knew what his final answer would be. Papi didn't go anywhere unless he knew where he was going.

Without another glance, Papi handed me back the tickets and short story. I put them and the ribbon inside a little box where I stored my keepsakes. I told myself that the prize wasn't important. It was the fact that my writing hadn't been rejected that mattered. I took out my notebook from my backpack, found a clean page, and I started to write another story.

14

Reyna and "RoboCop"

Y FIRST LOVE was a forbidden love.

My first love had velvety eyes the color of the mountains in Iguala. They reminded me of home.

My first love was a boy on a bicycle. From the corner of my eye I saw him riding lazily down Avenue 50 on the opposite side of the street. He didn't pedal but let gravity pull him down the street. In this way, he kept pace with me as I made my way to the liquor store to buy Papi a bottle of charcoal lighter. As I went into the store, I turned to look at him. He waited there at the corner on his bike. I knew he would still be there when I came out.

The boy I loved was named Luis Gómez, and he was from El Salvador. Two weeks before, my friend Phuong, whom I had met in ESL class, had pointed him out to me during lunch. She'd said, "Do you see that boy there, the one with the green eyes?" When I spotted him among the other boys he was with, I nodded at Phuong. She said, "I love him. Go talk to him for me." She pushed me toward him, but I didn't move. How could I go up to a complete stranger to talk to him about my friend? She said that Luis had just started ESL class and didn't speak much English. Phuong didn't speak a lot either, and that was why she hadn't passed to regular English as I had.

Mago had passed, too. Now at Franklin High School, she didn't hang out with any ESL students. She moved in "better circles" now that she'd gotten a good grasp of the English language. Carlos was in regular English, too, but he liked the ESL kids, and those were the friends he had at Franklin. I was following his lead. I was not ashamed, as Mago was, of people knowing where I came from.

Phuong wanted me to act as her messenger, and she would tell me what to tell Luis in Spanish for her. She said, "Reyna, you and me are sisters, you need help me." Phuong said we were like sisters because I looked Asian, just like her. Sometimes teachers and students would think I was Chinese, or Filipino, or Japanese, or Thai. I would tell people, "I'm Mexican, from Mexico," but sometimes they wouldn't believe me.

I finally gathered up the nerve to go talk to Luis during lunch the following day, and I told him my friend Phuong loved him, just as she had told me to tell him. Luis laughed and said she hardly knew him, so how could she love him? I didn't know what to say to him then, because as he looked at me with those green eyes of his, I knew that I—just like Phuong—was a goner.

Every day I would deliver messages to him from Phuong, but that only took a minute or two and after that he asked me questions, not about Phuong but about me. Phuong wasn't stupid. She wasn't able to speak Spanish and couldn't really understand what we were saying to each other from where she waited, but by the end of the week Phuong wasn't talking to me anymore. She said, "You are bad sister, Reyna Grande," and then turned and walked away.

I guess I wasn't meant to be anyone's Cupid.

I came out of Barney's Liquors and Market with the charcoal lighter, and I knew I should hurry home because Papi was making carne asada on the grill and was waiting for me to come back. But Luis waved at me from across the street and motioned for me to come over. The light wasn't even green yet, but my feet were already pointed in that direction, and I took a step onto the street. The light had turned green by the time I was halfway to Luis and his emerald eyes.

He said, "Let's go for a walk," and he got off his bike and walked alongside me. He didn't talk much, and I didn't either. Ours was a silent love. I glanced at him from the corner of my eye. He had curly hair, curlier than mine, and it was the color of crushed brown sugar, like the kind Abuelita Chinta would put on boiled ripe guavas to make them syrupy. Luis said, "Have you ever been kissed?" and I shook my head, feeling the ground turn into mud beneath my feet. I felt a rushing in my head, and I looked into his green eyes. I thought of the vacant lot by Abuela Evila's house, of Carlos, Mago, and me driving the old car toward the Mountain That Has a Headache. Except now it was the mountain that was moving toward me, and I got lost in its velvety beauty.

∽

Papi said, "Where the hell have you been?"

I glanced off into the distance, and in my dreamy haze I handed over the charcoal lighter and walked past Papi. I wondered if Luis was thinking about me and about the kiss we'd just shared. My lips were still throbbing.

Papi whacked me on the head with his hand. "Answer me," he said.

"They didn't have any lighter fluid at the liquor store, so I had to go to the store on Avenue 52," I said.

He said he wasn't stupid. He knew I was lying. He said, "As long as you live under my roof, you aren't going to lie to me, girl. Now where were you?"

I couldn't tell him about my first kiss. He would beat me for sure, ruin the whole memory of it. And why couldn't he just let me be so that I could replay the most important moment of my life again and again without disruption?

"Answer me now!" he said, putting a hand on his belt.

"I don't have to live under your roof if I don't want to," I said defiantly, thinking about the kiss. In my euphoria, all I could think was that he couldn't treat me like a little girl anymore. "Whenever I want, I can go live with my mother."

I turned around and headed to the gate. I walked toward the corner of Avenue 50 as if I were on my way to catch the bus. I didn't really mean to leave, but I was tired of Papi always making me feel as if *he* were our only option. Maybe he was. Mami had never once told us to come live with her. How would we have fit in that tiny room of hers? But Papi didn't need to know that.

Luis and his friends were sitting on the block wall surrounding the house on the corner. He lived on the other side of Granada Street. He was sitting there, and he and his friends whistled at me. Luis shouted something at me, and I didn't hear what he said, but the next thing I knew my hair felt as if it had caught on something and was tearing right out of my scalp.

"Hija de la chingada, you're not going anywhere!" Papi said from behind me. He pulled me back to the house by my hair, and I yelled for him to let me go. Luis and his friends whistled louder, and I thought I heard them laughing. I couldn't see Luis through my tears, but I knew he was there, witnessing my shame. Papi took me into the house, and Mago and Carlos begged him to let me go, but he took off his belt and whipped me with it. I thought about Luis and his green eyes, and soon, I didn't even feel the sting of the belt.

On Monday during lunch, I went in search of Luis. I wondered if he would ask me to be his girlfriend now that we had shared a kiss. But when I came up to him and his friends, Luis glanced at me and then turned around as if I weren't there. His friends pointed at me, and Luis shook his head and didn't turn to look at me. Farther down the hallway, I saw Phuong with her Asian friends. She smirked and then turned away from me, and it hurt me to know I had lost my friend for a boy who was no longer interested in me. Was I a bad kisser? Is that why he didn't want to talk to me? Or was it that Papi had humiliated me in front of him? Did he think I was still a little girl because I got beaten by my father? I touched the right side of my thigh where Papi's belt buckle left a raised tattoo. Maybe Luis thought like my father and like my mother. Maybe, it was just too easy to leave me.

I returned to my favorite spot—the steps that led up to the band room. Mr. Adams wasn't there so I sat on the steps and took out my V. C. Andrews book because she, at least, was still my friend.

15

Mago, Mila, Reyna, and Papi at
Mago's graduation

IN JUNE, FIVE years after we arrived in the U.S., Mago made history. She became the first person in our family—from either side—to get a high school diploma. I became the third person (after Mago and Carlos) to graduate from junior high. My little accomplishment might not have been much to be proud of, but I told myself this was just the beginning. Through all his talks of the future, my father had instilled in me something I could not put a name to in English, but in Spanish it was called "ganas."

When my father beat me, and in his drunken stupor called me a pendeja and an hija de la chingada, I held on to the vision of the future he had given me during his sober moments. I thought about that vision when the blows came, because the father who beat me, the one who preferred to stay home and drink rather than to attend my band concerts or parent-teacher conferences, wasn't the same father who told me that one day I would be somebody in this country. That much I knew.

A second thing to celebrate was that, the month before, our green cards had finally arrived. We had become legal residents of the United States! Finally we could let go of our fear of being deported and look to the future with hope. Papi said, "I've done my part. The rest is up to you." And the three of us clutched our green cards in our hands, imagining the possibilities. The first one to take advantage of our new status was, of course, Mago. It was just in time for her to be able to attend college and be eligible for financial aid. In Mexico, the biggest dream Mago had was to be a lawyer's secretary. Now, Mago didn't want to be a secretary—she wanted to be the lawyer who had a secretary. That is what Papi had taught us—that here in this country we could be anything. Papi took out a $5,000 loan under his name to help her with her college expenses because he said his "Negra" was going to make us proud.

In the summer, I attended band camp at Franklin High School because that was now my new school. I was glad Franklin had a marching band. I liked Burbank's little band, but all we did was have a couple of concerts each year. But here at Franklin, we would be doing parades, football games, pep rallies, and lots of other things we didn't do at Burbank. The best part was that the school provided each student with a marching uniform. It was navy blue and gold, and it had Franklin's mascot—a panther—on the front. The only thing they didn't provide was the marching shoes, which Mago bought me with the money she earned at a collection agency where she now worked part-time.

Every day we did drills and practiced marching around the football field. During our breaks, I would find a quiet spot to eat my lunch, away from the rest of the band members. I hardly knew any of them. There was one boy, Axel, whom I had met in the band at Burbank. He was a year ahead of me, so this was my first time seeing him since he'd graduated from Burbank. He had his own friends now, and I was too shy to say anything to him except hello in the mornings.

After years of being laughed at because of my name and my "wetback" accent, which I still had no matter how good my writing skills had gotten, I was a full-blown introvert. I looked at Axel and his friends, and I wished I had the courage to go sit with them. Instead, I hid behind my eyeglasses and buried my nose in the Stephen King novel I had brought.

Band camp made the summer go by quickly. Next thing I knew August came to an end, and September was upon us. On the seventh, I would be turning fifteen.

I wouldn't be having a quinceañera, as I had always dreamed of.

Papi said those kinds of parties were too expensive. A few months before, we had finally moved into the three-bedroom apartment so that Mago, Carlos, and I could have privacy. Papi said we were too old to be sleeping in the living room. Now with his and Mila's part of the mortgage being much more than before, Papi said there was no money for anything, especially a party. Instead, that Labor Day weekend he was taking me to Raging Waters for the first time. I told him he couldn't fool me. We weren't going there to celebrate my fifteenth birthday. We were going there because Kingsley Manor was having an employee summer picnic. He said he wouldn't be going if it weren't for my birthday. I replied to him in English with a word I'd picked up at school from other kids.

"Whatever."

A few days before our trip to Raging Waters, I came home exhausted after band practice. Mago arrived after I did. Together, we cleaned the apartment and made sure all our chores were done before Papi got home. He didn't like coming home to a dirty house. Carlos wasn't back yet. That whole summer he'd been going to the park to play soccer with his friends. We'd told him to get back before Papi arrived from work. Papi didn't like to have us out in the streets too late.

When Papi and Mila came home from work, there was still no sign of Carlos. "Where's your brother?" he asked. We told him we didn't know. He grabbed a beer from the fridge and went to his room.

Soon, it was seven o'clock, and we still had no idea what was keeping Carlos. He had never stayed that late at the park. Mago and

I asked Papi if we should go look for him, but he shook his head no. "You can't be walking around in the dark by yourselves. Besides, your brother is already in big trouble, with me."

Mago and I went into our room, and, while I practiced my sax, Mago bleached her arm hairs. Now that she had a job, she was always doing things to herself. She bought tons of makeup and was always practicing in front of the mirror, but no matter how much she put on, she couldn't hide the scars on her face to her satisfaction. Then she came home one day with a pair of underwear that had padded buttocks because she said she hated her flat butt. Another time, she bought packets of gum that curbed her appetite because she said she was too fat.

"Come here, Nena. I'll do your arms. They're hairier than mine," she said. "And look, when you bleach the hair it makes your skin look lighter!" she said as she extended her arm for me to see.

What saved me from getting my arm hair bleached was that we heard the door open, and we ran out to the living room to see Carlos being carried in the arms of two men.

"What happened?" Mago said as we rushed to help. Carlos's face was pale and covered in sweat. He groaned with every step the men took. They carried him over to the couch.

"His leg is hurt," one of the men said as he wiped his dirty, sweaty face with his soccer shirt.

"One of the guys from the other team tried to get the ball from him and kicked his shin instead of the ball," the other guy said. "Your brother doesn't have shin guards. We took him to a boneset- ter, but I think that huesero only made things worse. I think his bone is broken."

We thanked the men, and they left. Carlos was trying hard to keep from crying.

"I told you!" Papi yelled as he came out of his room and saw that Carlos was back. "I told you to stop going to the park. I told you to stay out of trouble, but you don't listen to me. Ahora te chingas!" Papi started to walk away, heading to his room. *What does he mean that now Carlos is screwed?*

"Where are you going?" Mago said. "You have to take him to the hospital!"

"Well, I'm not going to," Papi said as he paused at his bedroom door. "That will teach him a lesson." Then he slammed his door shut.

Mago and I looked at each other in horror. *How could he not take him to the hospital? What if his leg really is broken?* We turned to Mila. We were waiting for her to say that *she* would take our brother. Hadn't it been she who had always taken us to the doctor, anyway? Instead, she said, "Let me try to convince him," and went into the bedroom.

We sat on the couch with Carlos. He winced in pain at any little movement. He said, "It really hurts, Mago. I can't stand it anymore." And then he started to cry. I couldn't remember the last time I saw him cry. Even when Papi beat him, he held in his tears, even though this made Papi get madder and hit him harder.

Mago got up and went to knock on Papi's bedroom door. I didn't know why Mila hadn't come back out. "You can't leave him like that! He's in a lot of pain!" Mago said through the door. But there was no answer. She just kept talking to the door, and no matter how much she yelled, Papi never came out.

Mago went to the kitchen to boil water. She came back with a pot of hot water, a container of salt, and clean kitchen towels. She poured the salt into the hot water and said that maybe that would keep the swelling down.

I wished I had the courage to do something. Call 911. Go get the neighbors. *Something.* Mago and I glanced at each other and quickly looked away, shame choking us up inside, for neither of us was courageous enough to defy our father.

All night long we took turns putting hot towels on Carlos's leg. We gave him aspirin and tried to get him to sleep. It was a long, long night for the three of us. I thought about those nights in Mexico, of how Mago had helped us pass the time by telling us stories about our father, by digging out the memories that made her happy, like the one about the Day of the Three Wise Men when he had brought us gifts. But that night, as Carlos and I looked at her for comfort, she could not say anything. What was there to say? I thought about the Man Behind the Glass, of how I wished I hadn't left him behind in Mexico. In his eternal silence, he had been a much better father than the one we lived with now.

Morning came and Papi still refused to take Carlos to the hospital, saying that he wasn't going to miss work because of my brother's stupidity. We looked at Mila, pleading with her, but she simply looked away, not wanting to go against Papi's wishes. They both left for work. Mago left for work, too, promising to come back with help. That day was my last day of band camp and Carlos said I shouldn't miss it. He said, "Go, I'll be fine." But I didn't want to go. I couldn't go and leave my brother like that.

At work, Mago told her coworkers about our situation and they volunteered to help her take Carlos to the hospital. They arrived during their lunch hour. It took five people to get Carlos out of the house. Two were supporting him by his shoulders, and the other three were holding up his legs, being especially careful with the left leg to keep it from moving. Any little movement would make Carlos cry out in pain.

Just as they were about to put him in the car of one of Mago's coworkers, Papi got home. "I came to take him to the hospital," he said as he got out of his truck.

"Well, it's too late now," Mago said. "*I'm* the one who is taking him."

"He's my son. I'll take him."

Mago stared angrily at Papi, and I thought she was going to argue with him about it. But she was smart enough to realize that Carlos had to get to the hospital, and it didn't matter who took him, as long as someone did. She asked her coworkers to put Carlos inside Papi's truck. They ended up putting him in the bed of the truck so that Carlos could keep his leg straight. We watched as they drove away, and poor Carlos kept wincing every time the truck went over a pothole. He came home with his leg in a cast. He had broken both his tibia and fibula.

"That's the only way your father knows how to be," Mila said to us later that evening. "He was abused by his parents so that is all he knows."

We didn't tell Mila we were sick and tired of her justifying Papi's behavior with the same lame excuses. We understood what Papi must have gone through because we knew what Abuela Evila and Abuelo Augurio were like. But that didn't make us feel better. If Papi knew what it felt like to be abused by his parents, then shouldn't he understand how we felt? Shouldn't he try to be a better father? Also, it wasn't our fault that his own family had turned their backs on him, even going as far as stealing the house he worked so hard to build. So why take it out on us? Why take out all his frustrations and disappointments on us?

"I came back for you, didn't I?" he said to us sometimes when we would speak up.

Then we would shut up and lower our heads, and we would continue to take his beatings. Even the time he punched me in the nose so hard it broke, as I watched the drops of blood landing on my tennis shoe, I told myself that maybe he was right. We shouldn't expect anything better from him. He didn't forget us, after all. We were here because of him. *I* was in this country because of him. I *begged* him to bring me. I got what I wanted, after all. How could I complain now, simply because things weren't all that we had hoped for?

On Labor Day weekend, we went to Raging Waters as planned. Mago brought along her boyfriend, Juan, a guy she met at school and who lived down the street from us in the large apartment building by Fidel's Pizza—her first official boyfriend since Papi had finally given her permission to date. They told me I could join them, but I knew I was just going to be in the way. Besides, I didn't like Juan. Not that there was anything wrong with him. It was just that now, instead of spending time with me, Mago spent her free time with him. I wished Papi hadn't allowed her to have a boyfriend. But Mago would be turning nineteen the following month, and even Papi couldn't keep her from growing up. I was afraid of the day when she would no longer be *my* Mago, but someone else's.

Mila and Papi spent the day together, talking to their coworkers. Because Carlos had his leg in a cast, he had no choice but to stay in the same spot, watching over our stuff. I spent the day by myself. I walked from one side of the park to the other, wondering what rides I could go on. Most of the kids had someone to hang out with. I seemed to be the only person at Raging Waters who was alone. I tried to go on the rides, but on the third one, when I went down a waterslide and landed in the pool and couldn't touch the bottom, I freaked out. I didn't know how to swim, and the death of my five-year-old cousin Catalina still haunted me.

I decided to call it quits and went back to hang out with Carlos. "Why don't you go on the rides?" Carlos asked, looking longingly at the blue pools glittering in the sun and the big waterslides all around us. So many years dreaming about swimming in the pools of La Quinta Castrejón, and now that we were in a place a hundred times more beautiful, we couldn't enjoy it.

"It sucks going on them alone," I said.

"Well, it sure sucks being here like this," he said, raising one of his crutches. So he and I sat there, watching dripping wet kids run from ride to ride, laughing and screaming, until finally, it was time to go home.

Carlos at Raging Waters

16

Reyna at Franklin High School

After Carlos broke his leg, things were not the same between Mago and Papi. It wasn't something that one could see right away, but I knew my sister better than I knew myself, and I could tune in to her emotions in the same way I could twist the mouthpiece of my sax until I knew the sound that came out was just right.

Before, she would take pride in coming home on paydays and would happily hand over half of her salary to Papi to help him with the household expenses. Now, her fingers hesitated for a second too long before they released the bills. Papi didn't notice it. He didn't know her the way I did.

She no longer had the feverish desire to be the best in school because it made Papi happy. Even though she was now the first person in our family to attend college, she was no longer concerned about being the "best and brightest" in her classes at Waterson College. Instead, she talked about looking for a full-time job so she could buy herself a car and pretty clothes. She talked about her desire to go out with her coworkers, who spent their weekends dancing at clubs.

"Papi wouldn't want you to be out partying," I would tell her.

She would shrug and say, "I don't give a damn what he wants or doesn't want." And just like that, the father she had longed for while in Mexico, the father she had dreamed would be her hero, vanished in her eyes. Unfortunately, it wasn't the same for me, and I could not so easily dismiss my desire to please him. My father's acceptance of me had become my sole reason for being.

One day in November, as I was walking with Mago down Figueroa Street, where we had gone to make another payment at Fashion 21 for the clothes Mago had put on layaway, we passed by the shops and looked longingly at the shoes and pretty clothes the mannequins in the windows were wearing. As we passed by a dress boutique, Mago stopped abruptly and pulled me over to the display window. A mannequin was wearing the most beautiful quinceañera dress we'd ever seen.

I looked at Mago, wondering if she was feeling bad about not having had a real quinceañera. When she turned sixteen, Papi had actually thrown her a party, perhaps because he had felt bad she didn't have a quinceañera. The party was held in the six-car parking lot at the apartments. Mago wore the long, puffy blue dress she wore at her junior-high graduation and had her hair permed.

Now, as she looked intently at the dress, I wanted to remind her of that party, tell her that a sweet sixteen party in a parking lot was better than no party at all. I thought about those nights in Mexico when we would go sell cigarettes and snacks with our mother at La Quinta Castrejón and watch the young girls with their beautiful quinceañera dresses. I recognized the look of longing in her eyes, and I knew that if I were to see myself in a mirror right then, it would be the same look I would see in my own eyes.

"Come on," she said, turning around and pulling me away from the dress. She was deep in thought, and just as I was about to ask her what she was thinking, she stopped and said to me, "You know what, Nena? I'm going to throw you a quinceañera."

"What are you talking about? You're crazy," I said. "I already turned fifteen two months ago. And besides, where are you going to get the money?"

"I don't know, but I'll get it. I'll ask my friends to be the godparents. But I'll do it."

I thought my sister had gone insane. Quinceañeras were expensive, and there was no way Mago, with her part-time job, could pull it off.

When we got home, Mago got on the phone with her friends and told them what was on her mind. She didn't want to tell Papi about it. "This is *my* gift to you," she said. "I don't want him to have anything to do with this." But I insisted that she tell him. Who knew? He might actually get excited about it. This might be a way for them to repair their relationship. Finally, I managed to convince her, but when she told Papi about it, he was even more skeptical than me. "Estás loca," he said, and he didn't offer to help.

I tried not to get excited about the quinceañera, knowing that pretty soon Mago would come to her senses and realize it wasn't going to happen. To my surprise, on Sunday when we visited Mami and Mago told her about her plans, Mami got onboard with the quinceañera and offered to help get some godparents. Mago said she wasn't very surprised at Mami's response. She said, "Don't you remember those nights at La Quinta Castrejón?" And I suddenly knew what she meant. Those nights at La Quinta, we weren't the only ones watching girls blooming out of limousines like pink peonies. Mami was, too—Mami, who also never had a quinceañera, who was also once a starry-eyed girl with glittery dreams.

Not even a week had gone by before Mami called to tell us that a friend of hers would be the godparent for the cake, another would take care of the catering, and she would pay for the souvenirs. Mago's friends offered to help pay for the hall, the mass, the photographer, the floral arrangements, and the DJ. Mago didn't look for a godparent for the dress. She would be buying my quinceañera dress herself. She set the date for May 2, which left us a little over five months.

Mago's excitement was contagious. Even Carlos wanted to participate. He offered to be one of my escorts and helped me find a chambelán. I gathered up my nerve to ask Axel to be my chambelán, but the next day he told me he couldn't because his family wouldn't let him participate. I also asked my girlfriends to be my maids, and luckily, their families accepted.

Mago hired a professional dressmaker to make me a dress. It cost $350. The bottom part was made of layers and layers of blue tulle. The top part was made of white satin, and the sleeves were decorated with blue satin bows. I looked like a princess, just as I had always dreamed.

I hadn't done my first communion because Papi never took us to church, and after her heart was broken by that boy in junior high, Mago never made another attempt to go back to St. Ignatius. Without Abuelita Chinta to remind us to pray and to keep God in our hearts and minds, we had lost our religion.

But that day, I stood outside the church at Placita Olvera, about to have a mass in my honor. I was officially going to become a little woman in the eyes of God. The problem was that in order to have this mass we had to lie to the priest about having done my first communion. When the priest asked, Mago right away said that I had done my first communion in Mexico but didn't have the certificate to prove it. He believed us, and I felt bad afterward for lying to the priest.

The organ player started to play, and my court, composed of six couples, walked into the church in pairs. I held on to my own escort, who was a friend of my brother's. He was a sweet boy, but there was nothing romantic between us. It was strictly business. He was there to hold my hand, take pictures with me, and dance the waltz with me, but the next day, he could go on with his life and I with mine. I thought about Axel. I wished his family had allowed him to participate. I wished he were there with me instead of a boy I hardly knew.

My heart beat faster as I went into the church. My eyes fell on the statue of Jesus Christ hanging on the wall. *Forgive me for my lie, Jesus.* I held on to my chambelán as we walked down the aisle. People smiled at me and congratulated me. Papi and Mila were sitting to my left. Mago, Mami, Betty, Rey, and my little brother Leonardo were sitting to my right.

Too soon we got to the altar, and I was kneeling before the priest. Jesus looked down on me from his cross, and my eyes were starting to burn because I was about to commit a grave sin. I turned to look at Mago, who was sitting in the front pew. I wanted her to stop this. I wanted her to tell the priest we had lied and that I shouldn't be having this mass. But she was so excited, my sister, so proud of what she had accomplished that day, that I knew I must go through with this no matter what. I could not ruin the party my sister had worked so hard to give me.

The dreaded moment came when the sacred Host was put onto my tongue and it stuck to the roof of my mouth as soon as I closed it. Tears filled my eyes as the Host began to dissolve, and I pictured Jesus bursting down from Heaven in a blinding beam of light and sending me straight to the worst Hell imaginable, a Hell where I would spend all of eternity alone, without my Mago, for even though I wanted to stop being overshadowed by my sister and her bigger-than-life personality, I was terrified of being without her, of being on my own, of making my way in the world without her by my side. *Forgive me, Jesus. Please, don't take my sister away from me.*

After mass, we took pictures outside the church. "Nena, ¿qué te pasa? Smile!" Mago said as the photographer took picture after picture. But I couldn't do it, and in all the pictures I looked as if I were attending a funeral.

As we headed to Los Feliz to take pictures at Mulholland Fountain on the corner of Riverside and Los Feliz Boulevard, I told Mago what was on my mind. "I'm going to go to Hell. I've committed a great sin." I started to cry. She laughed.

"Nena, all that is nonsense. First of all, there is no Hell or the devil. Those are just stories Abuela Evila liked to frighten us with. Come on, when are you going to stop believing in that? Use that imagination of yours for other things. Second of all, if there *is* a Hell, we're already living in it." She wiped away my tears and hugged me. From then on, I started to smile in the pictures, and I didn't think about my fear of being punished for lying to the priest. Mago was right. We were already living in some kind of Hell in this strange place of broken beauty.

The reception was held at the Highland Hall on Figueroa Street. That night was a night when my wishes came true. I had wished to have my father and mother together in the same room. Now, there they were, although on opposite sides of the banquet hall. My mother was running around helping to serve food to the guests. She was wearing a black dress covered in sequins. She'd even had her hair done at a beauty salon. I'd never seen her looking so glamorous. My father was on the opposite side of the room wearing a dress shirt and tie, sitting next to Mila. She took sips of her soda while my father drank beer after beer as if afraid it would run out. The photographer called them over and took pictures of us. First, I took one with my mother. Then I took one with my father. And just as he was walking away, I pulled his arm back and I took one with both, my father and mother on either side of me.

Finally, it was time for the waltz I would dance with my father. The DJ didn't have "El Vals de las Mariposas" so my father and I danced to a classical song. But I didn't feel those overpowering emotions I

Reyna at her quinceañera

thought I would feel when I would finally dance with my father. My heart wasn't racing, my palms weren't sweating, my head wasn't spinning. I didn't feel a thing. I smelled the alcohol on his breath and I kept turning my face away from his. Always, my eyes returned to my sister, who was standing by the door looking at me proudly.

And I knew, I *knew*, that I should have been dancing this waltz with her.

17

Reyna as a member of
All City Honor Marching Band

IN NOVEMBER OF my junior year at Franklin, I received the good news that I had been accepted into the All City Honor Marching Band, which was composed of students from sixty high schools in the Los Angeles Unified School District. In order to get in, I had to switch from the sax to bells. The All City Honor Marching Band only accepted brass and percussion players. I was glad I had taken a piano class at Burbank, but it was with great sadness that, at the beginning of my junior year, I gave up my saxophone and switched to the beautiful—but extremely heavy—marching band bells. The tinkling sound was so sweet that even after practice was over, I could still hear it in my head. It was like having a fairy in my ears, although it didn't occur to me that one day that sweet, but very high-pitched tinkling sound would be the cause of my partial hearing loss.

I was not the only one who switched instruments. Axel temporarily gave up his clarinet to play the trumpet so that he could also get into the All City Band. Soon after, we found ourselves riding on the school bus on Saturday mornings. I was happy to know that he and I would be marching in the Rose Parade together.

As usual, my father hadn't said anything about me getting accepted into the All City Band. But since he didn't say I couldn't be in it, even though it would require me to be out of the house every Saturday, I told myself that inside he really was proud. I hadn't had the chance of being a flag bearer back in Mexico, like Mago, but marching in the Rose Parade in front of millions of people was even better!

Every Saturday, we were taken over to Dodger Stadium where we practiced the songs we would be performing in the Rose Parade. My favorite was "La Malagueña." Later in the day, all one hundred–plus band members lined up to practice marching around Dodger Stadium. It was a six-mile march. By the end of each practice, everyone's feet were hurting and our bodies were sore.

Axel and I started sitting on the back of the bus together. I knew he liked me and I definitely liked him, but he didn't want anyone to know about our romance. Even after we shared our first kiss in the bus, he didn't want anyone to know. He was ashamed to be with me, that I knew.

Ever since I started at Franklin, I had earned a bad reputation. Perhaps "earned" is not the right word. Earned implies something added, like a bonus, a plus. "Cursed" was a better word. Yes, cursed with a bad reputation. Since summer practice of the previous year, the girls in the marching band started whispering things about me, saying that I was conceited just because I didn't hang out with them and kept my head buried in a book. Later, when the school year started, and we began to attend football games and parades, I was still too shy to make friends. I didn't know how to. This led to even more talking until it got to the point where I couldn't look at any girl without feeling despised. Even to this day, people still misinterpret my shyness for arrogance.

One day something snapped inside of me, and I began to rebel.

I was getting enough hassle at home, to also be getting it at school from complete strangers. An anger I had never felt bubbled up inside of me, and I lashed out. I pretended I didn't care what anyone said or thought. I began to answer back to my drum major—who was a girl quick to say bad things about me. Once, as we were practicing our formations at the field, she asked everyone to bring their instruments even though we weren't going to be playing them. I decided to leave my bells in the band room because my back was hurting, and they were too heavy to be carrying around if I wasn't going to be using them. When the drum major saw me without my instrument she said, "Reyna, go get your instrument. Now!"

The field was on the opposite side of the band room, on the other side of the bridge that connected one side of the school to the other, and I tried to tell her that it made no sense for me to have the bells on if we weren't going to play that day. She kept insisting, so I ended up yelling at her, "If you want the bells, then you go get them yourself!" After that, she hated me even more for being defiant in front of the whole band.

The only ones who weren't mean to me were the guys, but that was because they only wanted one thing from me, and that was something kids at school called "a scam." It meant making out with someone, but when I looked it up in the dictionary the definition was different, more appropriate to what was really happening—I was being swindled, cheated, tricked. When the kissing was over, the boys would go on their merry way without another glance. I was left feeling the same way I felt when my father would glance at me without really *seeing* me. I was left feeling as if I didn't exist. As if I didn't matter.

And what if I don't matter? What if that is the reason why I can't have a boy like me for longer than a day? For more than just a scam? I would ask myself many times. I didn't know then just how much my relationship with my father would affect my relationship with other men. I didn't know that my need to be loved by him—and his inability to show affection—would make me desperate to find it elsewhere. The more he denied me his love, the more I would seek it in the boys I would meet.

Yet, I thought Axel was different from the other boys at school. Even though he was from Guatemala, and not Mexico like me, I had a connection with him that I hadn't had with any other boy. His parents had left him to be raised by his grandmother, just as I had been raised by my grandmothers a lifetime before. I understood Axel and the pain he felt at his parents' absence. But he, too, just wanted to kiss me in the school bus on our way to and from Dodger Stadium, yet when the bus pulled over in front of Franklin, our romance was put on hold until the next weekend.

∞

Finally, the day of the Rose Parade arrived, and Mago was the one who got up with me at five in the morning to help me get ready. She walked me over to Franklin and waited with me for the school bus to pick me up. Later, she hitched a ride from a friend and met up with me in Pasadena, where she walked the parade route alongside me with a borrowed video camera. I would glance at her from the corner of my eye, and once in a while I would lose her in the crowd, and I would think she had gotten tired of the walk, but later she would reappear up Colorado Boulevard with the video camera aimed at me. My father and mother were not there. But Mago was. And her presence, as always, filled the void of my parents' absence.

When the Rose Parade was over and there were no more weekend bus rides to Dodger Stadium, Axel and I would only see each other after school and hang out in places where we wouldn't be seen.

"Why can't we just be like a normal couple?" I would ask him.

"I'm just not ready yet," he would say. I wished he weren't so afraid of what people might say.

One day after school, while we stood outside the band room waiting for Mr. Quan to arrive and start practice, I overheard the clarinet players say that Axel had asked a cheerleader to the prom.

"And what did she say?" one of the girls asked. I leaned closer to listen, but just then Mr. Quan arrived and we went inside the band room. I glanced at Axel from across the room, and I wanted to go ask him about what I'd heard. I wanted him to tell me it wasn't true.

"Hey, Axel, I heard Marlene said yes," one of the trumpet players said. Axel nodded and then looked at me. I looked down at my sax, pretended that I was busy putting it together. I felt my throat tighten and my teeth clench in my mouth. I didn't know how I was going to be able to get enough air to blow into the sax and play.

"I'm sorry," Axel said after practice. I shrugged my shoulders and pretended that I didn't care.

I went home and told Mago about it. She said, "Forget him, Reyna. He's not worth it."

I wanted to tell her that she was wrong. It was me who wasn't worth anything. *Why else would Papi treat me the way he does? Why else would the guys at school treat me the way they do?*

The day of the prom, I spent the better part of the day listening to music from *Les Misérables,* especially "On My Own." I would close my eyes and imagine myself walking by myself on a rainy night, thinking of Axel, wishing he was with me.

"Come on, Nena, let's go," Mago said, turning off the music.

She was taking me dancing to distract me. Carlos didn't want to come because he didn't like the same music as Mago. He preferred dancing to Mexican music like quebraditas and norteñas, whereas Mago liked house and techno. I didn't care either way. Since I was a band geek, I was into marching and concert music because that was what we played in band.

We headed over to the Riviera Club in Eagle Rock in Mago's Toyota Tercel. The car smelled of new plastic and coconut, and for a second I felt a pang of sadness to know what this car had cost my sister. Three months earlier, Mago and Papi had gone to the dealership on Figueroa Street so that she could buy herself a brand-new car. Papi cosigned for her, but he regretted it soon after. A brand-new car comes with a big monthly bill. Not long after buying herself this car, Mago felt the burden of her debt and found a full-time job in the classified department at *La Opinión,* a Spanish-language newspaper. It was a good thing she had found that job. Mago had accrued too much debt from all the pretty clothes and shoes she was buying. It was as if she were trying to make up for all those years in Mexico when we had only rags to wear. I would go with her to May Co., Robinsons, and the Broadway to make payments on her credit cards, but she would never manage to pay them down. She said she was sick of the old ladies' clothes Mila would bring home to us from Kingsley Manor. She said she wanted to dress her own way, develop her own style. She'd flick her hair, which was now dyed a dark brown with golden highlights, and tell me that never again would she wear hand-me-downs. Her friends in Mexico would never recognize her now.

Sometimes, I hardly recognized her myself. My sister was becoming a classy young woman, that was for sure. But between the credit card debt and the car loan, Mago had dropped out of college to work full time. I ran a finger along the dashboard as Mago sped up Figueroa Street, wondering if she would ever find her way back to college, if she would ever again care about our father's dreams for her. I tried not to judge my sister too harshly. Hadn't she given up so much of herself for Carlos and me? Really, it was only fair for her to have the pretty things she wanted, I would tell myself. And she wasn't selfish. Even then Mago had still continued to look out for us, give us the things our parents could not or would not provide, like the year before when Carlos had had his heart set on a graduation ring to commemorate his accomplishment of being the second in the Grande-Rodríguez family to graduate from high school. Papi hadn't had the money, so Mago had bought Carlos the ring. She had also paid for his ticket so that he could go to Senior Grad Night at Magic Mountain. And that wasn't all she did. She continued to provide the emotional support we needed. Like at that moment, when I was feeling—as Anne of Green Gables would have said—"in the depths of despair," because of a boy who could only love me when no one was looking.

Mago went into the club first and then her friend came out to give me Mago's ID so I could use it to get in. Whenever I wore Mago's makeup and her clothes, I would almost look like her—almost, if you didn't pay attention to the fact that I was an uglier, unrefined version of her. I danced with her friends, but I couldn't seem to lose myself in the music, the way they did. I ended up sitting at the table most of the time looking at Mago glide across the floor, the colorful disco lights flashing all around her. I thought about Axel. *Is he dancing with the cheerleader now? Or are they sitting at a table together, holding hands? Maybe they have gone somewhere else by now, maybe to the beach where she can lean against him while the wind whips her hair around her face.* One thing I knew for sure was this: He wasn't feeling ashamed at being seen with her.

18

*Mago and Reyna with
Carlos at his wedding*

A MONTH LATER, my father came home with an old yellow Datsun he'd bought from a friend. He told Carlos the car was for him. Carlos had just finished his first year at Los Angeles City College. "My Carnal is going to make me proud," Papi said while looking at Mago in disappointment. The car was old, but Carlos didn't care. He smiled and rushed to grab the keys from Papi. They went for a drive, and I watched as they drove away. I turned to glance at Mago's Toyota Tercel. I was glad Papi had thought about getting Carlos a car so he wouldn't be tempted to buy one himself and get into debt. Mago's Tercel was beautiful, the color of a calm ocean, but when I thought about what it had really cost her, I would find myself hating it, as if it were the car's fault my sister had given up her education.

"We'll see how long that piece of junk lasts," Mago said.

I hoped that when I started college, Papi would buy me a car, too. Even if it was an old rickety one like the one he'd bought Carlos. As long as it came from my father, I knew I would treasure it, the way I treasured anything positive he said to me during his rare sober moments.

What my father hadn't been counting on when he got Carlos the car was that now it would also be easier for Carlos to see his girlfriend. Her name was Griselda, and he'd met her at Franklin. She was his first official girlfriend, and Carlos was crazy about her. Mago and I thought it was because Griselda didn't seem to care about Carlos's crooked teeth, which were the bane of his existence. Even though he would beg our father to help him get his teeth fixed, Papi would keep telling him no, that it was expensive and he couldn't afford it. Just like Mago and her scars, Carlos couldn't see past the ugliness of his teeth.

Between school and his girlfriend, Carlos stayed busy. The summer passed, and the fall semester began with Carlos doing very well in school. His dream was to major in criminal justice and catch bad guys. Like Papi, he had no tolerance for gang members. He swore to clean up the streets of Los Angeles and get rid of them. But one day, he came home and told Papi that he was very much in love.

"You mean you think you're in love," Papi said. "At your age, what do you know about being in love?" Carlos would be turning twenty in February.

"I love Griselda, and I'm going to marry her," Carlos said. "I'm asking you to please go with me to ask for her hand in marriage."

"You're crazy," Papi said. "I will do no such thing. I don't know what you're thinking. You're going to school. Do you know what's going to happen if you get married? You will have to drop out of school and get a job so that you can support your wife. Why would you want to throw away your chance at getting an education to marry some girl you just met?"

"I love her," Carlos said.

"I don't know why I even brought you kids to this country, just so you could throw it all away. It was an opportunity of a lifetime, do you realize that?" Papi said. This time, he didn't just look at Carlos, but at Mago and me. "Do you know how many people would die to be in your shoes? To have the opportunities you have here?"

Back then, I hadn't really been aware of the many young people who, like us, had been brought to the U.S. as children, but who, unlike us, had not been lucky enough to get their legal residency. My father was right. There were many people who would have died to have the chance that my siblings and I had of going to college. But it wouldn't be until later that I would finally understand.

"I don't care," Carlos said, standing up. "I'm going to marry her."

Mago and I tried to talk Carlos out of this marriage, but he refused to listen. Next thing I knew, he had asked my mother to go with him to Griselda's house to ask for her hand in marriage. My mother went along with his plans and just like that, a month and a half after his twentieth birthday, Carlos became a married man, the head of his own household. Just as Papi had feared, Carlos dropped out of college, found a small apartment for himself and his new wife, and got himself two jobs.

Eighteen months—and a son—later, he got divorced, but he never finished college.

19

Cousin Lupita washing dishes in Abuelita Chinta's backyard

D URING MY SENIOR year at Franklin, Mago decided to accompany
our mother on her upcoming trip to Mexico. Like my father,
my mother was also one of the 2.9 million people who'd gotten their
legal residency through the Immigration Reform and Control Act of
1986. Ever since she had become a legal resident of the United States,
my mother had been going to Mexico every year, sometimes even
twice a year. By then, she had quit her factory job and once again had
turned to selling Avon, although now she sold those cosmetics at the
Starlite Swapmeet, where she rented a booth. Even though we had
suggested she learn English and find herself a better job, my mother
insisted on living the way she had lived in Mexico or the way she had
lived when she was still undocumented. She refused to learn English
and how to drive a car. She refused to look for a job that could offer
her benefits—such as medical insurance and a pension plan, and
where she could finally get off welfare.

Whenever she found herself missing her country, she would pull

Leonardo and Betty out of Ninth Street Elementary and take them with her. Rey would remain to tend the booth at the swapmeet, because even though he was now a legal resident, he, just like my mother, didn't take advantage of the opportunities available to him.

Unlike my father, who was a tyrant when it came to school and who had demanded nothing but perfect attendance from us, my mother didn't really care that her youngest children were losing out on their education. Even though both Leonardo and Betty had been born in this country, they hardly spoke a word of English. Their education at Ninth Street Elementary was in Spanish, and they were put in classes along with the rest of the immigrant children. Their lack of a good early education—because of both the bad school and my mother's unwillingness to value education—would put my younger siblings at a disadvantage. So it would come as no surprise when later Betty and Leonardo would both drop out of high school, and Betty would get involved in gangs and end up a teenage mother.

Back then, Mago, Carlos, and I had yet to visit Iguala. When Tía Emperatriz stole my father's house, he said he would no longer return to the place of his birth. "What for?" he'd said. "I have nothing there." He did return once, when his mother died four years later in 1997, but he never went back after that. And years later, on his deathbed, he would still mourn the loss of his house and continue to beg Tía Emperatriz to give it back.

I soon found out that the reason Mago wanted to go to Mexico was because her best friend Gaby (whom she met at *La Opinión*) wanted to go to Acapulco, which is a three-hour bus ride from Iguala. "I'll just go with you to Iguala for a few days," Mago told Mami as we drove over to the travel agency. "Then I'll join my friend in Acapulco." I'd thought she wanted to go to Mexico because she missed our family and the place that we had once called home. I know I did.

As we were sitting with the travel agent and going over the details of the airfare, Mago surprised me when she asked me if I wanted to go. "I don't have any money," I said.

"When do you ever?" Mago said, rolling her eyes. "I'm offering to buy you the plane ticket. Do you want to go or not?"

I touched my belly button, something I hadn't done in a long time, and I once again felt that yearning for my home country, although it shamed me to realize that the yearning wasn't as strong as it used to be. I thought about all those credit-card bills Mago had, her car payments, the bills for the telephone line she'd installed in our bedroom, the money she had to give our father for household expenses. I thought about the student loans she still had to repay for a college education she had given up on.

"I don't know," I said, ashamed of myself for not being able to tell her that no, I didn't want her to spend any more money because I would rather she used it to return to school.

"I know you want to go," she said. She handed her credit card to the travel agent and purchased our tickets.

Mago, Mami, Leonardo, Betty, and I went to Mexico a few weeks later. Carlos couldn't come because of his new responsibilities as head of his own household. Papi was furious when he found out I would be missing a week and a half of school to go on the trip, but Mago told him he was going to have to let me go because our tickets were nonrefundable. I felt awful about having to miss school. I could count the times I had missed on one hand: in fifth grade when I had lice, seventh grade when I had the chicken pox, eighth grade when we had to go to the U.S. Consulate in Tijuana to process our paperwork for our legal residency, and now, a visit home in my senior year. In the end, Papi gave in when I came home with the assignments my teachers gave me so that I wouldn't fall behind while I was gone. As much as I hated missing school and not getting that perfect attendance certificate I loved to get at the end of a semester, I was desperate to return to the country of my birth.

I didn't know what to expect when I returned to Mexico. Two months from then, I would be celebrating my eighth anniversary in the United States. I was seventeen years old. I thought I was no longer that little girl who had once lived there, although now I realize that little girl will always be inside me.

As we made our way to Abuelita Chinta's house, we drove over the bridge above the river in which my cousin Catalina drowned. It was no longer much of a river but a dumping ground for trash.

"That's gross!" Mago said as we got hit with the smell of stagnant, putrid water.

We passed by the train station, and I was shocked to see it completely empty.

"Where are the vendors? Where are the travelers?" I asked the taxi driver.

He told us that a year before, the Mexican government had privatized the railroad system, and the service to Iguala was suspended. There were no more passengers coming through every day. There were no more vendors who sold their wares and food. There were no more people from neighboring towns who would go there to catch the train. Men like my uncles, who had unloaded the freight trains to make a living, had found it even harder to survive.

As we sped down the road, I turned to look at the train station, feeling my eyes burn with tears. It was no longer one of the most important places in Iguala. Now, it was just a relic, an open wound that would never let the community forget that there once had been such a thing as progress.

Since we had too many suitcases, the taxi driver had no choice but to leave us at Abuelita Chinta's doorstep, instead of dropping us off at the main road. But that meant he now had to drive over the unpaved road that was full of holes and jutting rocks. I felt as if we were on a ship being tossed around by a storm.

"Jesus Christ," Mago said. "I can't believe these roads. They would ruin my Tercel for sure!"

As soon as we got to the tamarind tree by Doña Chefa's house, I knew we were almost there. My heart started to beat faster. We pulled up in front of my grandmother's little shack. I knew that I had been in the U.S. for too long when the sight of my grandmother's shack, with its bamboo sticks, corrugated metal roof, and tar-soaked cardboard, shocked me. *Had I really lived in this place?*

A few feet away from the house was an abandoned freight car left to rust on the tracks. There were five children playing in it, and I felt a pang of sadness that they would never know the Iguala I had known, the lively place travelers would visit. They would never hear the whistle of the evening train or taste the wonderful chicken quesadillas that Mago had once sold at the train station. Seeing those kids' dusty bare feet, dirty hair, and torn clothing, I knew how my father

Freight cars left to rust on the tracks by Abuelita Chinta's house

had seen us those many years ago when he'd returned. I wondered if he had also felt his heart break.

Tía Güera and Abuelita Chinta came out to greet us. My aunt had built herself a shack next to my grandmother's. She had returned to her no-good husband even though he would drink his wages away, beat her, and cheat on her. She held a baby girl in her arms. Then she called out the names Lupita and Angel and two of the kids who had been playing in the abandoned freight car came running.

"Say hello to your cousins and your aunt," Tía Güera instructed them. I hadn't recognized Lupita. She was a year younger than Betty, so that put her at eleven. Angel was seven, Leonardo's age. But both my cousins were so skinny and tiny, whereas by then both Betty and Leonardo were overweight from all that junk my mother fed them. Here, next to my cousins, who barely had enough to eat, that extra weight was even more shameful to look at.

My grandmother's face was mapped with more wrinkles, her hair was mostly gray now, and a few more teeth had fallen out. But when she hugged me, I breathed in her scent of almond oil and epazote, and I couldn't believe I was back in my grandmother's arms. Her scent was all I needed to feel that I was home.

"I have prayed for this moment for so long," Abuelita Chinta said, squeezing me tight. "God has finally answered my prayers." By then

I had grown to my full height—five feet, zero inches. I was so used to looking up at everyone that I felt awkward having to look down at my tiny grandmother, who was three inches shorter than me. How tiny and fragile she seemed to me now.

We went into the shack with her, and not long after we had sat down to eat the meal Abuelita Chinta had prepared for us, Mago began to complain. "Look at my shoes," she said. "They're covered in dust. Ugh."

"Get over it," I said, thinking about Abuelita Chinta's feet. Hadn't Mago seen the layer of dust on our grandmother's feet, the dirt caked under her toenails? Abuelita Chinta gave her a rag, and Mago went to the washing stone to wipe her shoes and wash her feet.

After our meal, Tío Gary arrived with his children in tow. I was shocked to see how skinny my uncle was. He had a rope tied around his waist because he didn't have a belt to hold up his pants. After my cousin Catalina's death, he and his wife had divorced, and now he had remarried and fathered more children. At that time he had four boys; the youngest would eventually die from leukemia because my uncle did not have the resources to help his child.

While we sat outside the shack, we heard the familiar sound of Don Lino's truck. We turned to see it bumping and jerking its way down the dirt road. All the neighbors' kids, including my cousins,

Don Lino's truck

ran out to meet the truck, just as I had done while living there. For a moment, I felt like running to climb on it. As the truck passed by us, I smiled at hearing the laughter of the children on top of the truck. I waved at them, and they waved back.

Mago scrambled out of the way when Don Lino's truck sent a cloud of dust toward us. "Ugh!" she said, and went into the shack.

"Why don't you go to El Otro Lado, Gary?" my mother asked my uncle. "You can give your children a better life if you do." I watched the kids get off Don Lino's truck. My uncle turned to look at his own children who were making their way back to us. He shook his head.

"I'd rather be poor, but together," was my uncle's reply. I didn't know then that my mother encouraged my uncle to go north every time she visited. I didn't know that his reply had never changed. I thought about my father, the choice that he had made to go north, and the price we had paid for that decision. But I also knew that something good had come from that decision. As Papi often said, my siblings and I had been given the opportunity of a lifetime. How could we let it go to waste? As I looked at my cousins walking down the dirt road, I thought of my father, of what he wanted our future to be like, and I understood.

I took advantage of being there and quickly set out to look for the friends I'd left behind. Some of them were already married and had children! Others were still living at home and working as maids, or at the U.S.-owned garment factory nearby, or whatever else they could find. But things had changed. When you come from the U.S., people look at you differently. They treat you differently.

The boys looked at me as if they wanted to marry me there on the spot so that I could take them back with me to El Otro Lado. My girlfriends didn't invite me into their houses like they used to. Instead, they stood outside with me and blocked the entrance to their houses with their bodies, and I knew it was because they didn't want me to see the poverty they lived in. They didn't offer me anything to eat or drink because they couldn't afford to feed themselves, let alone a guest. They didn't tell me much about their lives because I knew that they thought it could never compare to *my* life, now that I was living in that beautiful place they all yearned for.

Instead, I awkwardly stood with my seventeen-year-old friend Meche in front of her shack. I didn't know what to say to her as she held her baby in her arms and tried to wipe the dirt and mucus off his face with the corner of her blouse. She didn't look at me. She looked past me, at the huizache trees behind me, her cheeks reddened with the shame of knowing that no matter how hard she wiped, the layer of dirt would never come off.

I was determined to make her see that I was still the same Reyna, but I didn't know how to do that. In the U.S., the only people I spoke Spanish with were my mother and father. With everyone else I communicated in English, with Mago, Carlos, Mila, and my teachers and friends at school. And as I stood there trying to have a talk with Meche, I kept stumbling on my Spanish words. She laughed and said I spoke like a pocha.

It was an awkward conversation. I tried to think of something else to talk about beside school, marching band, my writing, books, and the colleges I had applied to the semester before. I was afraid to admit that perhaps I might not be the same little girl who used to make mud tortillas and whose only dream of the future was to one day have her parents back.

As I walked away from Meche's house, I realized there was something else I had lost the day I left my hometown. Even though my umbilical cord was buried in Iguala, I was no longer considered Mexican enough. To the people there, who had seen me grow up, I was no longer one of them.

When I returned to Abuelita Chinta's house after visiting my friends, Mago was angry at me. "Where have you been?" she asked. "I'm the one who brought you here, remember? You can't just do what you want. I wanted to leave for Acapulco today. I'm so sick of this place. Now look at what time it is."

"I wanted to spend time with my friends before we left," I said.

She pointed to the shacks on the other side of the canal where Meche lived and said, "I don't know why you want to be over there with that trash."

"What do you mean 'trash'? Have you forgotten this is where you come from?" I was so furious, and before I could stop myself, I pushed her.

"Just because I used to live here, it doesn't mean that I still need to be friends with these people," she said, pushing me back. "Let them dare call me a little orphan now."

"You conceited brat," I said, pushing her even harder.

Next thing I knew, Mago and I were pulling at each other's hair and tumbling to the ground.

"Reyna, Reyna, leave your sister alone!" Mami yelled. But I couldn't stop. I didn't know why I was so angry at my sister. *How could she just sever the ties that bind us to this place, to these childhood friends of ours who weren't able to escape this poverty like we did?* I was so angry at her for quitting college and ruining her chances for a successful life. Now I realized that we owed it to *them*, our cousins, our friends, to do something with our lives. If not for us, then for them, because they would never be able to. I understood so clearly now why Papi said there were so many people who would die to have the opportunities we had, who would kill to get their hands on a green card. Mago's and Carlos's refusal to see that angered me more than anything.

"Stop! Stop!" Mami said. And finally I did. Mago looked at me as if she didn't know me. I ran into my grandmother's house crying and feeling ashamed. For the first time in my life, I had raised a hand to my sister.

How could I stop myself from feeling sad that Mago no longer cared about Mexico, that she didn't think of this place as special because it was once our home? Her home was now the United States. Unlike me, she had no accent when she spoke English. Now I knew why that was. Even in her speech, she was trying to erase Mexico completely.

I didn't know if I ever could. Or would want to.

20

Mago, Reyna, and Betty

A COUPLE OF WEEKS after we'd gotten back from Mexico, Mago said, "Gaby and I are looking into renting an apartment together."

"Really?" I asked, looking away from the TV where I had been watching *Anne of Green Gables* on the Disney Channel. "You aren't leaving me, are you?"

She shook her head and threw a pillow at me. "How can you think that? Of course I'll take you with me. We can leave here and finally be in a place where we can be happy."

I threw the pillow back at her so that she wouldn't see how relieved I was. I knew she had forgiven me for the fight we'd had in Mexico.

She said she understood, but for a second there, I thought she was going to tell me she was leaving without me.

I turned back to the TV and continued to follow Anne Shirley on her adventures. I wanted to be like Anne, strong, adventurous, pretty, and smart. I wanted to have her imagination and her way with words. But most of all, I wanted to live in a beautiful place like she did. Like me, Anne had lost her parents when she was little, and as a little orphan, her childhood had been very difficult. But Anne got lucky when she was adopted by a brother and sister who let Anne be who she wanted to be, who learned to love her and praise her for her talents, and who were not afraid to tell her that they were proud of her.

Sometimes, I would imagine getting adopted by Marilla and Matthew, too. I knew they would have been proud of my accomplishments. Like my latest one—where I had been chosen to be the assistant drum major of Franklin's marching band now that I was in my senior year. Since the drum major was a Jehovah's Witness, and his religion didn't allow him to participate in most of our events, it was me who designed the field formations to the music Mr. Quan had chosen for us to learn. It was me who led the band to second place in a competition held at Wilson High School. It was me who led the band at the 1992 Highland Park Christmas Parade on Figueroa Street. Even though the parade route was only a ten-minute walk from my house, my father had not come to see me march.

This is why I was jealous of Anne. Because, unlike me, she had people who noticed even the smallest of her accomplishments.

The weeks passed with no news about an apartment. That spring semester, I enrolled in track and field. I didn't really like running, but Mago did. On the weekends we would go to Franklin to jog around the football field, and she always left me in the dust. I thought that if I practiced every day at school, I would get faster so that I could keep up with my sister. So far, track and field hadn't made me faster, but it had gotten me a boyfriend!

His name was Steve, and he was two years younger than me. He was fifteen, and I was seventeen. But he was so cute I didn't care what anyone said about me dating a freshman. Even though he was younger, Steve tried to act older than me. He would tell me he wanted us to make love, to be each other's firsts. I would tell him no, absolutely not! I wanted to be a virgin when I got married, as Mago wanted to. Besides, I told him that soon he and I might not be together anymore. If Mago rented an apartment too far from Franklin, I knew I would have to transfer, never mind that I was in my last semester of high school. I would follow my Mago to the ends of the earth if I had to.

A week later, while we were getting ready for bed, Mago said that she and Gaby had found an apartment in La Habra. I didn't know where that was, and how far from school it would be, but before I could tell her that anywhere was fine with me she said, "Nena, I won't be able to take you with me."

I sat down on my bed and looked at my feet, not knowing what to say. I thought about my quinceañera, about receiving communion when I wasn't supposed to. *Here it is*, I thought. *Judgment Day. Please, don't take away my Mago, God. Punish me in another way, if you must. But don't take her from me.*

"Why?" was all I managed to say.

"The manager doesn't allow extra people in the apartment. Gaby already has her son, and her aunt is also going to be living with us so that she can babysit. With me that makes four."

"But I could share a room with you, just like we've always done."

"I know, but they won't allow more than four people in the apartment." She stood up from her bed and came to sit with me. "Besides, Nena, you have two and a half months to go before you finish high school. It wouldn't be right to pull you out now and transfer you to another school. I'm sorry, Nena. I really wanted to take you with me."

"Then stay," I said, clutching her hand. "Like you said, I'm almost done with school. In June I could start looking for a job, and we can rent a place together. We can even take Betty with us. Be a family."

She stared at the floor and shook her head. "I can't stand being here anymore. I feel that I'm going to go crazy. I want to live my life in peace, do what I want without having to explain anything to anyone."

I thought about her new boyfriend, Victor, whom she had met at

La Opinión. I knew she hated it that Papi didn't let her go out much. Now that Carlos had married and left home, Papi had been even more vigilant with us girls. I knew Victor was one of the reasons why Mago was so desperate to get out. Like Carlos, she was also in love, too in love to put up with our father's restrictions and house rules. But how could she not wait for me to graduate so that we could leave together? She put her arm around me, and we stayed like that for a long time. She didn't say when she was leaving and I didn't ask. I kept hoping that maybe, just maybe, things would change.

A few days later, I knew that it was for real when Mago broke the news to Papi. "You're such an ungrateful daughter. After everything I have done for you, ¿así es cómo me pagas?" He said that she just wanted to be able to go out with as many men as she wanted without anyone telling her what was right or wrong. He banged his fists on the table and stood up. "If you leave this house," he told Mago, "you will be dead to me. I won't ever want to see you again."

Mago didn't say anything. We stayed at the kitchen table long after Papi had left.

"Stay with us, Mago," I said, grabbing her hand. "Stay with *me*."

Every day I would come home from school, wondering if that was the day she would leave. But in the evening, Mago would come home as she always had. Papi didn't talk to her, but by the second week it was as if nothing had happened. Mago didn't bring up the subject anymore and Papi ended the silent treatment. All of us even went out to dinner at Papi's favorite restaurant—La Perla in East L.A.—when I received my acceptance letter from the University of California, Irvine, which I would be attending in the fall. Although I knew that a university was much more expensive than a community college, my guidance counselor had encouraged me to apply to universities. He'd said that I couldn't waste my good grades. All the extracurricular activities I had done, like marching band, creative writing, art, and track and field, would only help me to get in. He'd been right.

Mago told me how proud she was of me. Papi didn't say anything like that, but the fact that he took us to his favorite restaurant said a lot, especially because he hardly ever took us anywhere. I loved the murals at La Perla. My favorite was one of a little fishing village. I didn't know what magic the artist had used to make his murals change from day to night as the lights hanging on the ceiling changed color from red to blue. We sat there and listened to the mariachi, and I sang along with them. Papi sang along to "Volver, Volver." I looked at his smile and I smiled, too. Nothing made him happier than to listen to the songs of Vicente Fernández. Mago and I sang along and I got lost in the beauty of the murals at La Perla. I imagined living in the perfect little village with all my family. Always together.

Two days later, I came home to an empty bedroom.

If I had known she was leaving that day, I would have stayed home, convinced her not to go. But she had not said a word when I left for school. Instead, after hanging out with Steve after school, listening to him harass me yet again to have sex with him, I came home at four thirty, an hour before Papi got back from work, enough time to tidy up the house and pretend I had come home a lot earlier.

But when I opened the door of the bedroom, the first thing I saw was the empty closet. All of my sister's clothes were gone, all except for a pair of overall shorts I often borrowed from her. A farewell present? I dropped onto her bed. I looked up at all the posters she had taped on the wall, photos she had torn from magazines, many of which were of Adela Noriega and Thalía, her favorite actresses ever since she had watched the soap opera *Quinceañera*. I couldn't believe she would leave like that, without telling me goodbye. I thought about when my mother left with the wrestler without saying goodbye. Perhaps, like my mother, Mago didn't want to see my tears. Maybe she thought it was better this way. But I didn't think coming home to an empty closet was better than saying goodbye and watching her go out the door.

I heard the front door open and close. My father was home, and I hadn't done my chores. I rushed out to the kitchen to wash the dishes. My hands shook as I picked them up to lather them. My eyes burned from crying.

He came into the kitchen and grabbed a beer, not saying anything to me. I'd gotten used to him ignoring me. And honestly, I preferred that to the times when he did pay attention, because when he did, it was only to insult me or reprimand me for something or other. But that day I knew I had to break the silence. I just didn't know how to tell him that Mago was gone. I waited until he took a drink from his beer, and before he disappeared into his bedroom, I blurted out the news.

"Mago se fue," I said.

He turned around to look at me. I shut off the faucet and dried my hands with a towel.

"What?"

"She's gone."

He turned around and headed to my bedroom. He stood there in the middle, just as I had done earlier, and looked at the empty closet, the empty dresser drawers. He glanced at Mago's posters on the wall, the only reminder that she had lived there.

"You're not allowed to see your sister anymore. If she wants to leave, que se vaya. But you," he said as he pointed a finger at me, "will have nothing to do with her." I stood in the room, listening to him say that my sister was an ungrateful daughter. "After everything I've done for her, this is how she repays me? If she wants to go and live a corrupted life, then I'll start thinking of her as being dead to me," he said. He talked about Carlos, about how disappointed he was in him, and now, in Mago. He looked at me and shook his head. He looked at me as if I had disappointed him, too, even though I was still there, with him.

I wanted to tell him that I would be different, that I had seen with my own eyes the poverty he had helped us escape. I had seen with my own eyes the reason he had been such a tyrant about school. I wanted to tell him that I would do what Mago and Carlos hadn't done. I would go to UC Irvine, and get my degree. I would be somebody he could be proud of.

But he said to me, "You can forget all about going to that university. You're going to be a failure, too, just like them, so don't even bother." Then he walked away.

"No, Papi, please!" I begged. But he slammed his bedroom door shut.

I went back to my room. A room which was now only mine. *He isn't serious*, I told myself. *He's just angry with Mago. He'll change his mind tomorrow. He will. He knows how important this is for me, for the family. He will let me go.* I got under the covers of my sister's bed and buried my nose in the pillow, trying to drown myself in her favorite scent—Beautiful by Estée Lauder. I thought about Abuelita Chinta, my mother, and now my sister. The void inside me became bigger and bigger, as I realized that the women I loved most in my life were far away.

My graduation came and went, and true to his word, Papi wouldn't allow me to send in my paperwork to UC Irvine. Since I was still underage, it required his personal and financial information, and his signature, which he refused to give me. I was too much of a coward to falsify his signature. I was too much of a coward to fight him on it. I fought him instead about Mago. I couldn't win two fights, but maybe, I might win the one that mattered to me more. Papi threatened to beat me if I dared to step out of the house to go see her. I hoped with time he would change his mind about that, too.

Then the news broke that Carlos's wife was pregnant, and a month later, Mago confessed that she, too, was expecting. This pushed my father over the edge. And it terrified me to the core. Now that Mago was going to have her own baby to hold and cherish, there would be no room for me in her life.

"You'll always be my Nena," Mago said to me over the phone. When I didn't say anything she said, "I'm going to go pick you up and take you somewhere. You tell your father that I'm going to go visit you, and he can't do anything about it."

"You know he'll get angry," I said.

"Who gives a damn?" she said.

Several times during the week I approached my father to tell him Mago was coming to pick me up on Sunday, and that I was going out with her whether he liked it or not. But just as I was about to say it, I would get choked up with fear, and I would turn around and go back to my room.

That summer was when my father's drinking worsened. Following my mother's suggestion, I'd been selling my father's empty beer cans at the recycling center. I could always tell how much he'd drunk that week by the money I would get. The previous week, I had gotten thirty dollars. That was the most I'd ever gotten. Lately, in the morning, I would wake to the sound of a beer can being opened. My father had now started to drink before he left for work, and when he returned, he would drink all evening before going to bed. He argued with Mila over everything, even about her weekly visits to her children. He would tell her that her place was here, at home. Mila's older son was legally blind, and Mila had to make sure he got the help he needed. Her second son and Cindy had troubles of their own. I couldn't blame Mila for always wanting to be over there, by their side. My father didn't see it that way. He hated her family because they had never accepted him. They had always blamed him for breaking up Mila's first marriage. Although I had never seen him hit Mila, there were times when I could almost see the urge inside him. He would hit me instead.

True to her word, Mago came over on Sunday. I told Mila that Mago was downstairs, and she didn't think it was a good idea. "Your dad's going to get mad," she said as she watched me head toward their bedroom.

When he didn't open the door, I mustered the nerve to open it myself. He was sitting on a chair looking out the window with a beer in his hand. I went in with hesitant steps. This was foreign territory to me, having never been allowed to spend much time in their bedroom. He was listening to his favorite song by Los Tigres del Norte, "La Jaula de Oro."

Even though the music wasn't too loud, he acted as if he hadn't heard me coming in.

"¿Qué quieres?" he said when I came to stand right next to him.

"Mago is downstairs. She wants to take me out."

"Tell her to leave. I already told you that I don't want her coming here. I don't want her seeing you."

"But she's my sister!"

"She chose to leave, didn't she? If she really cared about you, she wouldn't have left."

I started to cry then, like I always did with him. He always knew how to say things that would hurt me to the core. I hated crying. I hated letting him see how much power he had over me. To make me cry just like that, without even laying a finger on me. "She's my sister and I want to see her," I said.

"¡Ya te dije que no!"

I started walking away, determined to disobey him. "Well, I'm going anyway. She's all I have, and you can't keep me away from her!"

Just as I got to the door, he called my name. I stopped and turned around. "If you go out with her," he said, "don't you ever come back here."

"Fine!"

I rushed out of the room, past the dining room, the kitchen, out the back door. *This is what I needed! Now that he's kicked me out, Mago will be forced to take me with her. I can finally be with her!* I was halfway down the stairs, and I could see Mago's green Tercel parked in front of the apartments. Suddenly, I felt as if my hair was tearing right out of my scalp. "You aren't going anywhere!" Papi yelled, yanking my hair so hard I fell over backward. I reached up to hold on to my hair. He tightened his grip on it and dragged me up the stairs. I screamed for Mago. The last thing I saw before he dragged me into the apartment was Mago getting out of the car.

"Mago! Mago!" I yelled over and over again. My father slammed me against the kitchen wall and began to beat me with his fists. Mila stood by the door of the living room. "Get my sister," I yelled to her. "Get my sister!" She turned and ran out of the house.

The beating continued and his fist connected with my nose. I covered my face, trying to protect myself. I looked down at my shirt and saw drops of blood landing on it. *Where is she? Why won't she come and stop him? Take me away from him?* "Mago! Mago!" I yelled. There was a rushing in my ear as his fists fell on me, hard as rocks.

"¡Ya déjala!" a voice said. Suddenly, the blows stopped.

I opened my eyes. I was on the floor, crying. My father stood above me. Mila walked back into the kitchen, and I asked her where Mago was. It wasn't her voice that I had heard. "Why won't she come?" I said.

"She left," Mila said.

I shook my head, unable to believe what Mila had said. It couldn't be true. *How could Mago have left when she knew he was hitting me? No, no. There has to be a mistake.* "Mago!" I yelled at the top of my lungs. "Mago!"

But no one answered.

"¿Ya ves?" Papi said. "That's how much she cares." I glanced at the door, waiting for my sister to come, but she didn't. I looked up at my father, at his fists, and at that moment I just wanted him to keep going, to keep beating me and beating me with those hands that were the same shape as my own. Beat me until I could no longer think anymore, until they made me disappear, cease to exist. *She left. She left. She left.*

He went back to his room with another beer in his hand. Mila helped me to stand up.

"You should understand," Mila said to me as I headed to my bedroom. "Your sister is pregnant. If she had come up here to defend you, who knows what he would have done to her. He could have hurt the baby."

I left her in the kitchen and made my way to my room to lock myself in.

21

Reyna in her senior year

M Y BEDROOM WAS my prison.

No, my bedroom was my haven. From the door in, I was safe. From the door out, the demons would come with their mocking faces. I stayed in my room and suffered from hunger, picturing Mila cooking, she and Papi eating dinner, watching TV in the living room. I waited and waited, trying not to think of the way my stomach seemed to chew on itself to appease its hunger. I peed in a bucket I had taken from my father's shed and kept in the corner of the room. I lay in bed and waited. I was afraid that if I came out of the room to eat or go to the bathroom, he'd come down on me like a vulture. Little by little he pecked away at my soul. I was afraid, sometimes, that one day there would be nothing left.

Finally, the television would get shut off. Finally, I would hear their footsteps fading into their bedroom. Finally, they would fall asleep. I tiptoed out of the room and dumped the pee in the bucket into the toilet. Then I rushed to the kitchen and grabbed whatever Mila had made for dinner. I didn't bother heating it up. He might come out, and I didn't want to see him. I gobbled down the food in my room and hid the dirty plate under the bed. I breathed in relief, my stomach finally pacified.

I tossed and turned in bed. I knew sleep wouldn't come. It was yet another thing I had lost. I couldn't remember the last time I'd had a good night's sleep. I lay awake, wondering what my sister and brother were doing, what my mother was doing, what the whole world was doing while I was there, a prisoner in my own room.

I turned on the TV and kept the volume as low as possible. I stuffed the cracks in the door with my underwear so that he wouldn't see the light from the TV. This was as close as I could come to making myself disappear from his sight.

Then I discovered my hero, there on the TV. Dr. Sam Beckett. He was a physicist who traveled in time to fix the lives of other people in a show called *Quantum Leap*. Oh, how I wished Dr. Sam Beckett could jump into my life! Come and live it for me. Make things right in a way I could not, in a way I might never be able to.

During the day I would move my furniture around. One day the bed was in the north corner of the room. The next day it would be in the south or east or west corner. I called Steve and asked him to come over. He helped me move the TV and the dresser to the other side of the room. "Why are you always moving your furniture?" he asked as he sat down on my bed.

I shrugged, not knowing how to tell him that it helped me feel as if I had just moved elsewhere. As if I lived anywhere but here.

I was jealous of him. Franklin was back in session, so he had somewhere to go, something to do. I didn't have a job, and since Papi had not allowed me to go to UC Irvine, or to a community college, as I had asked, what was there for me to do but to move my furniture around? I sat next to Steve on my bed, and I let him pull me down with him.

He wasn't supposed to be there. My cousin Lola and her family had moved to the unit downstairs, and if she saw him, or if the neighbors saw him and told my father, there would be hell to pay. But I held him tight as I remembered there wasn't anything else my father could do to me anymore. Besides, Steve was all I had left.

He tugged on my pants, as he always did. I put my hand over his to keep him from pulling down my zipper, as I always did. I knew what he wanted from me. I thought about Mago. She had a life of her own now. She was going to be a mother. She was making a family of her own. What did I have except for this horny Italian boy with hazel eyes who only wanted one thing from me? And what if I lost him, too?

"Okay," I sighed, letting go of his hand.

"Okay? You mean—? Really?" he asked.

I heard the sound of the zipper. I felt my pants being clumsily pulled down. I felt his weight on me, and for a moment I felt as if I was not as meaningless as I had thought. For a second, I felt that I still mattered.

I lost my virginity in my bedroom, in my father's house. *Right under your nose.* I felt the pain between my legs, and I bit my lips to keep from crying out. *I don't need to leave this house to be a loose woman,* I thought, as I held on to Steve with all my might. *No, I'll do it here, in your house, and see if I care.*

A few weeks later, as I was waiting for the bus to go see my mother, I saw an ad taped to the bus stop. It read "Do You Want to Be in the Movies?" I put the flyer in my purse. *Maybe I could be a movie extra and make money so that I could rent my own place. What kind of skills does one need to just walk around or sit around and blend in with the background? I'm excellent at that.*

When I got to my mom's apartment on San Pedro Street, I asked her to take me to the Alley and buy me a dress to wear to the talent agency. She bought me a canary-yellow dress with bell-shaped sleeves and big golden buttons. She said it was so bright, for sure I would stand out in a crowd and get hired.

The next day I took the bus to the agency, which was on Wilshire

Boulevard, not too far from Beverly Hills. I felt so good in my bright yellow dress that my mother had bought for me. It was one of the few things I owned purchased by her. There were other people waiting in the lobby, and they all had leather folders or manila envelopes with them. I wondered what was inside. Nobody but me was wearing glasses, so I took them off, even though everything looked blurry. They were cheap, thick-rimmed glasses that made me look like a nerd, and I didn't want to look like a band geek today. I wanted to look glamorous. I thought of Mago. If she were still living at home, she would have done my hair up really nicely. She would have made me look like a movie star with her magic makeup brush. Then I realized that I probably wouldn't be sitting there if Mago were still at home. She would have protected me, instead of me now trying to fend for myself.

When I was called in, the first thing the woman said was, "Do you have your portfolio?"

"What's that?" I asked.

"Your pictures. We need professional photos of you."

"I—ah—no, I don't have any photos."

She went on to explain that I needed to bring eight-by-ten-inch photos, in color and black and white. She also said the agency charged a fee in order to put me in their system.

I had barely managed to get the money I needed to pay for the bus fare, let alone to pay the agency to get me a job. I walked out of there feeling disappointed. I didn't even put my glasses back on. I wanted to hide in my blindness a little longer and not face the real world that awaited me. How could I leave my father's house if I had no job? I wondered.

While I sat at the bus stop to go back home—still jobless—a car pulled over. The two guys in the car looked like Italian mobsters, wearing black suits and ties. The one in the passenger seat called out to me.

"Hey, are you a model?"

"Me? No," I said, feeling my cheeks get hot from embarrassment. *Me? A model? I wish . . .*

"Well, you should be. Do you want to be a model?"

I wanted to tell them that they were the ones who needed glasses, more than me. Surely they could see that I was not pretty enough to be a model. Nowhere near that. And couldn't they see my body? Couldn't they see how short I was?

But I needed a job, and when they asked me again if I wanted to be a model, I thought about my favorite telenovela *Cristal,* of how she had met her handsome rich love at the modeling place where she worked. I said, "Yeah, I guess."

"Well, get in the car and we'll take you to our office. We're agents, and we can help you."

I hesitated as I took a step toward their car. They were complete strangers. I shouldn't trust anything they said. What if they were lying and did something to me? But I needed money. I got in the backseat.

They drove me to a building farther up Wilshire, which was similar to the six-story building where the other agency was. When they pulled over, I breathed a sigh of relief. If their office was in that fancy place, then maybe they were who they said they were.

They took me to a huge office with a large desk and two leather sofas and offered me some water. They didn't tell me to sit, so I stood there in the middle of the office, looking at them without squinting, so that they wouldn't notice that I needed glasses. They sat on the leather couch and one of them said, "Okay, take off your dress."

"Excuse me?" I said.

"Take off your dress," the other one said. "If you want to be a model, we have to see what you've got."

"But, but . . ."

"Hey, what do you think models do all day? They take off their clothes and have their picture taken."

I put my water glass down and started to unbutton my dress. Suddenly, I hated that dress. They stared at me as I began to take it off. I slid the top of my dress off my shoulders, down to my waist. Then, I couldn't go any further.

"Come on, you can do it," they said. Even though the men were blurry, I knew that they were staring at my exposed breasts.

What the hell are you doing? a voice inside me said. I didn't recognize that voice. *Get out of there, now!* the voice said again. And I knew who it was. It was the other me—the other Reyna, the one who still believed in that bright future my father had once said I could have.

"I'm sorry, I've made a mistake," I said. I rushed out the door as I struggled to put my dress back on.

"Hey, come back here!" the men yelled. I ran out of the building, down Wilshire Boulevard, my heart beating hard against my chest. I didn't look back. I was afraid to look back. I pictured them running after me, dragging me back to their office, forcing me to do things I didn't want to do, forcing me into a path where there would be no turning back. Finally, I couldn't run any longer and stopped, my side hurting me, my lungs screaming for air. I turned around, and the street was empty. No one was chasing me. *Forget the job, Reyna. Forget the horny boyfriend. Focus on school,* I heard the other me say. As I sat at the bus stop waiting to go home, I took my glasses out of my purse and everything came back into focus.

I called Steve to come over, and when he arrived, I told him I wanted to break up. He agreed it was for the best. We were playing with fire. We were having unprotected sex, and we knew that there would be consequences if we didn't stop. I didn't think things would go as smoothly with my father. When he came home, I didn't hide in my bedroom. Instead, I went out to the kitchen and said, "Tomorrow I'm going to Pasadena City College to enroll." I waited for him to say no. I was ready for a fight. But my father looked at me, and whatever he saw in my eyes made him keep quiet. I turned around, and as I headed back to my room, he started to talk.

"You know, Chata, when my father took me to the fields to work, my job was to guide the oxen in a straight line. My father gave me a rod and said that if the oxen didn't listen to me, to hit them as hard as I could. I was nine years old, Chata. Do you understand?"

I took a deep breath, unable to say anything. I wanted to say something. I was still too angry to forgive all that he had done to me, but I wanted to understand what he was trying to tell me. But too soon, he had turned away from me. Too soon, he was opening the refrigerator door, taking out a Budweiser, and I knew that the father who had spoken just a minute ago was gone.

22

Reyna and Diana at a scholarship dinner

I N THE SUMMER, I enrolled in an English class at Pasadena City College that was part of the requirements to transfer to a four-year college. My teacher's name was Diana Savas. When I walked into the classroom, my first thought was that she was Latina. She had short black hair and brown eyes framed by glasses. She was not too tall nor too short, and full-figured—"llenita," as we say in Spanish. It turned out that she was a Greek-American who, to my surprise, spoke excellent Spanish. The thought that a non-Latina took the time to learn my native tongue pleased me and impressed me.

A couple of weeks into the summer semester, Dr. Savas assigned us an expository essay about the groups to which we belonged (racial, economic, religious, and so on). I went home to work on my essay, but it was difficult for me to do it. What group did I belong to? I had no idea. I'd never thought of myself belonging anywhere outside of my family. So that is what I wrote, about my family and the place I had come from.

A few days after turning in my essay, Dr. Savas asked me to come to her office. "You wrote an autobiographical essay," she said. "I need you to do the essay again, but," she added, "I think you're a very good writer."

When she handed me back my paper, I felt different. With those words, it was as if she had opened my eyes to something I could not yet see. When the summer ended, I passed the class with an A, but I was sad that I would no longer have Dr. Savas as a teacher.

When the fall semester began, I stopped by her office to say hello. It was my nineteenth birthday, and I shyly mentioned it to her because there was no one to celebrate my birthday with. She picked up a book she had on her desk and said, "I went to see a panel of Latino writers this weekend and bought this book. I think you'll like it." She handed it to me, and I looked down at the cover to read the title. *The Moths and Other Stories*, by Helena María Viramontes. I'd never heard of it before. Latino literature wasn't something I was familiar with.

"I want you to have it," she said with a smile. That was another thing I liked about her, her honest smile. She took it from me and wrote *Happy Birthday, Reynita*, on the title page and handed it back to me. No one had ever called me Reynita. Not even my mother.

I thanked her for the book. She was shocked to find out that it was the very first book I'd ever been given, one that I could keep and not have to return to the library.

I went home and read *The Moths*. For the first time since I'd become an avid reader, I found myself reading about characters that lived in a world similar to my own, characters with the same color skin as mine. With the same heartaches and dreams.

As the weeks went by, I visited Dr. Savas—or Diana, as she said I should call her—at her office between classes. I never told her about life at home. We talked instead about books and writing. She was always asking me about my latest story, my latest poem. Sometimes I wanted to tell her about all the problems at home, about the increasing arguments between Mila and my father. Lately, they'd been fighting over a woman. Mila had discovered my father was having an affair with someone at work. He denied it. I could hear them yelling in their bedroom. When I got home from school, sometimes they would be in the living room screaming at each other. I would walk by them and head to my bedroom. It was better if I stayed out of their way and didn't take sides, but I couldn't help thinking that now Mila knew how my mother had felt when my father was cheating on her with Mila.

One evening, I heard Mila screaming my name. I had brought Betty over for the weekend because by then she had gotten into gangs. She was in the habit of stealing my mother's rent money and was driving her crazy. I wanted to help my thirteen-year-old sister, but I would bring her over for another reason, too. I was lonely.

Mila screamed again, and Betty and I went running into the living room. My father had shoved Mila onto the couch and was on top of her, punching her. Mila had her arms up to her face, trying to block his fists. Then, with his right hand on her face, he pushed her head into the couch. Mila squirmed beneath him, but she wasn't able to get him off. Betty glanced at me, as if waiting to see what I would do. I put my arm around her and pulled her close. I wished she wasn't seeing this. I wished I hadn't brought her over that weekend. I couldn't believe he was hitting Mila. All those years I had been on the receiving end of his fists. Not her. Never her.

I got over my shock and ran to help my stepmother. I pushed Papi hard, but he wouldn't budge. "Leave her alone!" I said again, pushing against him, but he was like a boulder.

Finally, I managed to get him off Mila. She stood up from the couch and ran out the door, down the stairs. He followed behind her, cursing at her. I heard the sounds of metal falling, and my stepmother crying out: "Natalio. Stop it! Stop it!" Then I heard my cousin Lola and her husband yelling at my father to leave Mila alone.

When Betty and I rushed downstairs, Mila was sobbing in Lola's arms, and my father was being restrained by Lola's husband, Chente. My father broke loose from Chente's grasp, and for a second it seemed as if he was going to pounce on Mila again. Instead, he rushed toward the stairs. It took me a second to realize he was heading my way, and I quickly moved myself and Betty out of the way to let him pass. I was so relieved when he didn't notice us. He just went into the apartment without a word.

Mila was bleeding from her leg. My father had pushed her onto the gardening tools he had beneath the stairwell, and she had cut herself on the spikes of the rake when it fell on top of her.

"Come on, Mila, you need to go to the hospital," Lola said. Her husband helped Mila to the car, and I stood there not knowing what to do. *Should I go with her? Should I stay with him?*

"Stay with your father," Lola said, making the choice for me. "Go keep an eye on him."

I stood there on the first step, and I couldn't get myself to take the next step up, and the next step up, to go back to the apartment. Betty and I looked at each other, not knowing what to do. Her eyebrows were plucked thin, like a typical chola, and her eyes were rimmed with too much black liner. But at the moment, she wasn't putting on her tough-girl chola mask. She was a frightened teenage girl. I wished I were like Mago. She would have known how to protect us. I didn't know how to be a little mother to my sister.

"Jesus," Betty said, shaking her head at what had just happened.

Eventually, I found the courage to take Betty and myself back upstairs. We went through the back door, tiptoed across the kitchen, and I poked my head into the living room. Papi had turned off the light and was sitting there on the couch, motionless. I wondered if he had fallen asleep. We went into my room and stayed there.

Sometime later, someone was shaking me to wake me up. I opened my eyes and saw a female police officer standing over me. She shined a flashlight into my eyes. "What's going on?" I said.

She took me and Betty into the living room, and there I saw two other police officers putting handcuffs on my father. Then they walked him out the door. I stood there while they made their way down the stairs. I couldn't take my eyes off the handcuffs. I couldn't believe my father was being arrested. I glanced at Betty, and I wished she weren't here to see him like that. Since our mother was always telling Betty bad things about him, she didn't like him very much to begin with. What would she think of him now, to see her father turned into a criminal?

When they put him in the car, he looked up at us for a brief moment before the car door closed and the police took him away.

The female cop told us to go back inside, and we sat in the living room. She wanted to know everything that had happened between him and Mila. I found that I couldn't speak. How could I tell her about all the abuse? How could I tell her that I was ashamed of what he had done, as if I were just as guilty because of the fact that I was his daughter? How could I say that even though I knew he'd gotten what he deserved, I was still afraid for him? I didn't want anything to happen to him. I didn't want him to be in jail. *What's going to happen to him?* I wanted to ask her. *To me? To all of us?*

To my surprise, when I went to drop off Betty, my mother offered to take me in. She said, "He's gotten what he deserved. I'll never forget all the beatings he gave me when we were married." That was the first time my mother and I had ever talked about the abuse we had both suffered at the hands of my father. It made me feel closer to her than I had in years. I decided to take her up on her offer because I knew that I couldn't live with Mila and my father anymore. Mila had returned from the hospital black and blue from head to toe. It shamed me to look at her.

I took my few belongings to my mother's tiny apartment. That night, I slept on the floor, wedged against the dining table. My mother, Betty, and Leonardo slept sideways on the bed, with their feet hanging over the edge. Rey slept on the floor, right against the entertainment center. If I reached out, I could touch him. That's how small the room was.

By the second night, I knew I could not stay there. My last class at PCC ended at 7:00 PM. It took me nearly three hours on the bus to get from Pasadena to downtown L.A. It was almost ten when I found myself walking alone down Seventh Street. Homeless people, reeking of pee, littered the sidewalks, and I had to step over them. Drunks pushed their shopping carts. Prostitutes stood on corners. Men drove by and whistled at me. I walked so fast my side was hurting, my legs were burning. When a group of men turned the corner and started to head toward me, I took off running and didn't look back.

"Why don't you drop that last class?" my mother said when I got to her house. I tried to catch my breath, but it was coming in gasps. I shook my head, horrified at her suggestion. *That's how it starts*, I wanted to tell her. *Once you drop one class, it makes it easier to drop them all.*

I went to see Diana during her office hours. I needed someone to talk to and the only person I could trust was her. I knocked on Diana's office door, and for a moment I thought about turning around and leaving. *Why should I burden someone else with my worries?* As soon as she opened the door and said "Reynita!" in that high-pitched voice of hers, I felt that I had made the right decision to come and see her.

I told Diana about what had happened over the weekend and the past three days I'd been at my mother's. I couldn't stop the tears from coming even though I had told myself not to cry, that Diana didn't need my drama. I didn't want to burden her with my problems. Diana grabbed my hand and said, "Reynita, you can't be in that situation any longer. You have to think about school, that's all you should worry about." We were quiet after that, and I wiped the tears from my eyes. How could I not worry? How could I escape all of this? I had nowhere to go.

"Would you like to come stay at my house?" Diana asked.

"What?" I asked, rubbing my eyes.

"I live across the street in a house owned by PCC, and it's got three bedrooms."

"But Diana, I don't want to trouble you. I just couldn't—" Then I stopped myself, took a deep breath and mustered up the nerve to say what I really wanted to say. "Yes, I'll come live with you, Diana."

"From now on, Reynita, my home will be your home," she said.

Diana was originally from the Midwest. She'd come out to Los Angeles to teach at UCLA. Later, she had left her job to get a PhD and became a self-supporting student. She had no family in Los Angeles and she had forged her way alone. She was thirty-nine when I came to live with her. I didn't know then that Diana had seen in me a resemblance to herself, a young woman trying to find her way in this big city, all alone, but with a huge desire to accomplish her goals. It was that, and especially the thought of me walking the dark, dangerous streets of Skid Row if I stayed at my mother's, that had made Diana want to take me in.

At first, it was awkward for me to be in Diana's house. My instinct was to lock myself up in the guest room, and keep out of her way, giving her as little trouble as possible. At my father's house, I had learned to be invisible.

But a few days later Diana knocked on the door. She poked her head into the room and asked me if I wanted to join her in the living room. Since I didn't want her to mistake my survival skills for ungratefulness, I accepted her invitation.

By then, Mila had dropped the charges, and my father had come home. They told me I could return, but I knew that I could not. Something told me things were only going to get worse between them. I left them to fight their own battles. I was glad my father was not in trouble with the law, but at the same time, I was disappointed in Mila for dropping the charges and staying. I thought she was a different kind of woman.

So I found myself sitting in the living room in the safety of Diana's house, and it was a rare feeling to be out in the living room and not be afraid that someone would yell at me, beat me, or put me down. Diana graded papers, and I did my homework while we listened to melancholy Greek music. I didn't understand the words, but the rhythm reminded me of the songs Tía Emperatriz liked to listen to.

Diana wasn't married and didn't have children, but she had four small dogs who kept her company. The third bedroom had been converted into a library, and she had cases and cases full of books, so many books that some of them spilled into the living room. I had never been in a house that had books. I thought I was in Heaven. During a break from grading she went into that room and came back with a book. She handed it to me and said, "Here, have you read this?"

I took the book from her and read the title, *The House on Mango Street*. I shook my head. I had never even heard of Sandra Cisneros.

"Reynita, you have to read this book. It's wonderful."

I grabbed the book and found a comfortable spot on the couch, where I read *The House on Mango Street* while Diana kept grading papers. It's difficult to describe the impact the book had on me. It was absolutely beautiful, the poetic language, the beautiful images, the way the words flowed together. But there was more to the book than Cisneros's writing talent that made me love it. When I got to the chapter titled "Sally," I broke down. I shook with an intense sadness and helplessness, and tears burned my eyes. That chapter was about a young girl who lived with an abusive father. Every day she rushed home after school and then she wasn't allowed to go out. *Sally, do you sometimes wish you didn't have to go home? Do you wish your feet would one day keep walking and take you far away from Mango Street, far away* . . . How did Cisneros know that was exactly how I had felt for many years? Just wishing my feet could keep walking, keep walking to another place, to a beautiful home where I was loved and wanted. I re-read the chapter and with every word I felt that Cisneros was reaching out and talking to me. I felt a connection to this author, this person, whom I had never met. Suddenly, I wanted to meet her and ask her, *How did you know? How did you know this is how I felt?*

Diana began to encourage me to write more. She also gave me other books written by Latina authors such as Isabel Allende, Julia Alvarez, and Laura Esquivel, Latina writers who were writing about the things I liked to write about. I began to understand why Diana said I should be a writer. I hadn't been exposed to Chicano/Latino literature before. I had spent too many years reading the wrong kind of books, like *Sweet Valley High* and the Harlequin romance novels I got addicted to in high school, which Mila brought home in paper bags from Kingsley Manor because she knew I liked to read. It was a kind gesture for Mila to bring me those books the old ladies had discarded, but now I wished I hadn't wasted all those years reading Harlequin romances when I could have been reading something more powerful, more meaningful. But I hadn't even known, until then, that Chicano/Latino literature existed.

Those books, like *The House on Mango Street,* proved a revelation. There were people out there who understood, who experienced the things I was going through. Diana planted a seed inside me, and through those books, the seed soon began to grow.

She exposed me to things I had never been exposed to before. She took me to Greek restaurants, teaching me about other cultures besides my own. She showed me foreign films that she liked, and sometimes in the evening we would sit in her backyard and plan my future while throwing balls for her dogs to catch.

One day, I heard about a writing competition from the Townsend Press Scholarship Program, and at Diana's encouragement, I decided to enter. I rewrote the personal essay I had written in her class, and with her help, I polished it and made it as good as it could be. Out of a thousand entries, my essay was a winner. This time, the prize was money, one hundred dollars.

"You have to be a writer, Reynita," Diana would say to me. "You have to transfer to a good school, Reynita." Over and over she repeated this like a chant. "If Alvarez, Cisneros, and Viramontes can publish their stories, so can you, Reynita."

Neither Diana nor I could have known that seventeen years later, I would find myself sitting in Sandra Cisneros's dining room drinking champagne and eating carrot cake. That I would share a car ride with Julia Alvarez. That I would share the stage with Helena María Viramontes at a book reading.

I couldn't have known what the future held for me. All I could do back then was to allow myself to dream.

Reyna at Pasadena City College

23

*Reyna's graduation from
Pasadena City College*

A YEAR AND a half later, when Mila finally decided to leave my father, it came as a surprise. I was beginning to think she was one of those women who stays with a man despite the abuse. She changed in my eyes, and I found myself respecting her for her decision. However, a day after she left my father, she walked into the bank and withdrew a large portion of their savings from their bank account, leaving him with hardly anything. Then, to make matters worse, when my father went to look for her at her mother's house, my father was advised that Mila had called the police and had also filed a restraining order against him.

Carlos said, "Reyna, you have to go back home. He needs you."

"He's never needed anyone," I said. The thought that my father actually needed me was preposterous to me. The thought of going back there made me ill.

A few days later, Carlos called me again. "He tried to kill himself," he said.

"I don't believe you," I said. I didn't believe for a second that my father would hurt himself just because a woman had left him. Besides, did he even love Mila? *A man doesn't hurt and beat the woman he loves, does he?*

Carlos told me that the day before, he had gone to see our father at his new house. While I was away, he and Mila had sold the fourplex and bought the house next door, the one that belonged to the family of gang members. Carlos found him holding his gun. "He says he was cleaning it, but I don't believe it," Carlos said. He told me that our father insisted that he was cleaning the gun, but then Carlos noticed the bullet hole on the wall right behind where he'd been sitting. "You can't be cleaning a gun when it's loaded. What were you thinking?" he asked. My father didn't say anything.

"He needs someone there to keep an eye on him," he told me. "I can't do it. Mago can't do it either. We both work. You have to go back."

By then, Carlos had divorced Griselda and was in a relationship with another woman, the mother of his second son. Mago was living with Victor and their two-year-old son in West Covina. I hung up the phone, and for the rest of the day I couldn't stop thinking about my father. In my mind I saw him on the floor with a bullet hole in his head. What if Carlos was right? What if he was trying to hurt himself? What if, for the first time, he really did need me?

I returned to my father's side because I felt obligated to do so. The spring semester at PCC had ended, graduation had passed, and at the end of that summer, I would be heading north to study at UC Santa Cruz, the school I had chosen based on Diana's recommendation. I didn't want to go up north with a guilty conscience. I wanted to go up there and not have to take any baggage with me except for the things I had packed in my suitcase. I wanted a fresh start.

When I got there, my father was sitting at the dining table by himself. It was dinnertime now, but he was sitting at the table in the dark as if waiting for his meal, as if he'd forgotten that Mila was no longer there to cook for him as she had always done. He played with his empty beer can and looked up when I came in. I was shocked at seeing him so thin, so haggard, although nothing like what he would look like later when he was dying of liver cancer.

"Ya llegué," I said. He looked surprised, and I wondered if Carlos had even told him I was coming back. I asked him if he was hungry, if he wanted me to cook something. He didn't answer me. I opened the refrigerator, but it was almost empty, and my heart started to race because I didn't know how to cook. All those years, Mila had ruled the kitchen and would not allow Mago or me to help her, the way daughters are supposed to help their mothers. It was another way she kept us at a distance. While I lived with Diana, it was she who did most of the cooking. She was a wonderful cook, and although I did help her in the kitchen, I didn't learn enough to feel confident about cooking a meal for my father now, for the first time. Besides, my favorite dish that Diana made was sliced tomatoes sprinkled with olive oil, balsamic vinegar, and dried oregano. Not the typical Mexican dish. What was I going to do? There was no way I could feed sliced tomatoes to my father.

I turned to look at him and found him staring at me. I didn't know if he could see how scared I was of cooking, but he said, "Come on, Chata, let's get out of here." He pulled his chair back and stood up.

"Where to?" I asked.

"El Pollo Loco," he said. I didn't know what to say. He hated eating out. I loved El Pollo Loco, especially the BRC Burrito, so I followed him out the door without complaining. I breathed a sigh of relief knowing that I wouldn't have to cook for him. When we got to his car, he held up the keys to me.

"Here, you drive."

"I don't think that's a good idea," I said. I had recently been learning to drive. Carlos sometimes would take me to practice on weekends. Mago had tried, but she wasn't patient with me, and one time I had bumped her Tercel on a fence and left a dent. She gave me no more lessons after that. I didn't think I was yet good enough to drive my father's car. He would criticize my every move. I just knew it. He would probably yell at me and call me a good-for-nothing. "No, you should drive."

"Here, take the keys. I want you to drive," he said.

I reluctantly took the keys and opened the door. I sat at the wheel, started the car, and then we headed down Granada Street and turned right on Avenue 52. I drove slowly, carefully, but at the intersection of Avenue 52 and Figueroa, I turned too late and ran the red light. Cars honked at me. Tires screeched. I glanced at my father from the corner of my eye. He was staring straight ahead but said nothing. Thankfully, we got to El Pollo Loco with the car still in one piece.

"I'm sorry," I told him as I gave him back the keys.

"That wasn't bad, Chata," he said.

I didn't know what it was that Mila's departure had done to my father, but he wasn't the same man he was before. Edwin, my boyfriend of three months whom I had met at PCC, started to come over in the evenings. Sometimes the three of us would sit in the backyard where my father showed us the zucchini, corn, and carrots he had planted. This was one of the ties he still had to his country—the love for planting and harvesting. Later, I would learn to love gardening as well. During my visits to the hospital, this would be the safest thing to talk about—our vegetable gardens.

Sometimes, we would sit in the living room watching the Lakers game. Edwin was a psychology major, and he was transferring to Cal State, Monterey Bay, which was about an hour south of Santa Cruz. We were going up there together. He had chosen the right field to study. Edwin was a great listener. My father discovered this soon enough, and there were nights when the two of them would stay up talking after I had gone to bed. Edwin had given my father something that neither I nor my siblings could give him—an unbiased ear.

Mago reconciled with my father, too, and she started coming by on the weekends with her little boy, Aidan. Even Betty would sometimes come over when one of us picked her up, which was not as often as we should have. Betty was now having unprotected sex, and not too long before, she'd asked me to drive her to a clinic to take a pregnancy test. Luckily, it had been negative. But I didn't know how long that would be the case. My fourteen-year-old sister was heading down the wrong path, and my mother didn't seem to care.

Mago, Carlos, and I would tell our father to forget Mila. Betty stayed out of it. When he wanted to talk about Mila, we would immediately interrupt him and tell him to move on, that things were better this way. For all those years of having to play tug-of-war with Mila over our father's attention, what else could we do but celebrate their separation? Finally, we had access to our father in a way we had never had. Finally, the wall had come down.

Also, their separation had forced us to take sides, and of course we had to side with our father. When Mila came over to the house to pick up her belongings, she brought along the police, who forced my father to lie down on the floor with his hands behind his back, while Mila went into their bedroom to gather her things. Carlos said, "You can't do that to my father. He isn't a criminal." But the police didn't listen and so my father had to stay on the floor until Mila was done. Carlos and Mila got into an argument over the money she had taken out of their bank account. Carlos said, "How can you leave him with nothing?"

"That's none of your business," Mila said. "This is between me and your father."

I was glad the police were there to keep the peace. Carlos was so angry that he started to cuss at her, and the police had to warn him to calm down. I just stood near my father, and as soon as the police left, I helped him to his feet.

At a court hearing, another argument erupted between us and Mila. Mago and Carlos cussed and insulted her. Like a child caught in a messy divorce, my allegiances were torn. We had never disrespected Mila in any way. We were taught as children to be respectful of adults, no matter what they did to us. Also, my father had always told us that we needed to be grateful to Mila for everything she had done for us, especially about the fact that it was through her that we'd gotten our legal residency, although even if she hadn't helped us, eventually we would have gotten it once my father was given amnesty.

"You guys are leeches," Mila said to us. "If it weren't for me, you would still be wetbacks."

I didn't know how to tell her that we cared about her, but we loved our father more than anything. I didn't know how to make her see that our place was with him. We had wanted to have a father ever since I could remember, and now without her in the picture, we would finally have him back. I wanted to tell her that I thought her children were probably glad to finally have their mother back, as well. But she was like my mother when my father had cheated on her— angry, bitter, hurt. She was blind to everything but her pain.

Despite all the altercations with Mila, my father was no longer as depressed as he had been when I'd first arrived. He was a different father than the one I had come to know. He didn't criticize me. He didn't yell at me. He didn't hit me. He didn't look at me as if I didn't exist. For the first time, my father liked having me around. We continued our trips to El Pollo Loco, although sometimes I would cook for him, and he would eat my food without complaining. I would drive him around the city after work. We would go hiking by the Observatory. We would go to Sycamore Park and jog around the park until dark. I was so hungry to share with him all the things I had done since I'd moved out of his house. I told him about the English tutoring job I'd gotten at the PCC Learning Center. I told him about joining the Lancer Marching Band and marching in the Rose Parade for the third time. I told him about my stint as a staff writer for the PCC newspaper, *The Courier,* and about the time they had published my article "PCC in the Making," which had taken up the whole page, and how after it had been published, the PCC president had even sent me a note to congratulate me on it. I told him about the Townsend Press essay competition, and also the time I had placed in a journalism competition. I told him about the scholarships I had gotten to help me pay for UCSC, like the Hispanic Scholarship Fund, the La Raza Scholarship, the Minority Talent Scholarship, the Huang Future Teachers Scholarship, and the Phi Delta Kappa Scholarship Grant. I wanted him to know that even though I had been apart from him, I still valued what he had taught me.

"Tell me about your new school," he asked me one day as we were jogging side by side.

So I told him about Santa Cruz, about the redwood trees, about the ocean, about the literature and writing classes I was going to take there. "Diana said UCSC is a special place. It's a great school for students who are into the arts. She thinks it will help me grow as a writer."

"Six hours is a long drive," he said.

"I'll come visit you every chance I get," I said. "And you can come visit me."

We didn't speak for the remainder of our jog. But my feet felt heavy as I began to wonder if I should stay. How could I leave now when things were starting to turn around at home, when finally my father was beginning to change? What if I stayed? I had gotten accepted to UCLA, and even though I had turned them down for UCSC, couldn't I tell them I had changed my mind? Wouldn't they take me back?

Diana had said that everyone and their brother want to go to UCLA. There I would be just one of thousands. She'd said that at UCSC things would be different, and that I had to get out of my comfort zone. I couldn't become my own person until I learned to live on my own. When I graduated from PCC, Diana was my guest at the La Raza Scholarship Breakfast. Out of the twenty Latino students who had received scholarships, I was the only one transferring out of the L.A. area.

I wondered if those students found it difficult to leave their families, and if that was why they'd decided to stay close to home. Before I returned to my father's house, I had no family to cling to, so it had been an easy choice to leave. But now, now that I had that father I'd longed for, how could I give him up?

One night, while we were eating the chiles rellenos I'd made for him, he put his fork down and looked at me. He said, "I've been talking to Mila."

"About what?"

He told me he'd been visiting Mila at her mother's house, and they were going to work things out. "I called the lawyer yesterday," he said. "Told him to hold off on the divorce."

"What does that mean?"

"It means she's coming back," he said. I forced myself to swallow my food and I put my fork down. "But there's one condition to her coming back."

"And what's that?" I asked.

"She doesn't want you, Mago, or Carlos around."

"And you've agreed?" I asked, feeling the chile relleno burn a hole in my stomach.

My father looked at his plate, not at me. He didn't look at me, not even once. I stood up and went to pack my bags.

I went to stay at Diana's house for the remaining days before my departure.

Carlos and Mago were furious about what our father had done. Carlos said, "I spent all that time helping him with the lawyer, defending him from Mila and her restraining orders, for what? So that he could just betray us like this?"

"I'm never speaking to him again," Mago said. "He used us. He just wanted us around because he was lonely and depressed, and now that he has her back, he doesn't need us!"

Once again, we were orphans.

I thought about the border that separates the United States and Mexico. I wondered if during their crossing, both my father and mother had lost themselves in that no-man's-land. I wondered if my real parents were still there, caught between two worlds. I imagined them trying to make their way back to us. I truly hoped that one day they would.

24

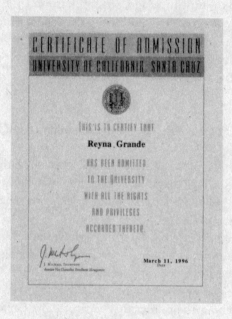

D IANA WAS THE last person I saw before I left for Santa Cruz. Edwin picked me up at her house, and there in her front yard, I said goodbye to her. I waved to her from the car window. As we drove down Colorado Boulevard, I promised myself that one day I would tell everyone about Diana, about this woman who had come into my life when I had most needed someone, and how she had changed it for the better.

On our drive up to Santa Cruz, Edwin said, "Your father is very proud of you, you know. He told me so."

I didn't say anything. I looked out the window, saw the fields stretch out before us as we drove up the 5 North. I thought about my father, about how eighteen years before he had been working in the fields near here, sleeping in an abandoned car in order to save money to build us a house.

"Try to understand him," Edwin said. "He knew you were leaving at the end of the summer. He didn't want to be alone once you left."

"I could have stayed with him," I said.

"For how long? One day, you'll grow up and get married. Have your own family. You wouldn't stay with him forever. He knew that. Besides, he didn't want to hold you back."

When Edwin and I got to UCSC, many students were already there moving in. Because I was transferring as a junior, I got to stay at the student apartments at Kresge East, not the dorms. I sat in the car with Edwin while I watched students and their parents, grandparents, brothers, and sisters carrying boxes. I saw fathers patting their sons on the back, mothers crying while clinging to their daughters. "Do you need anything else?" I heard them ask their children. "We'll miss you," they said.

I thought about my father. I thought about my mother. I thought about Mago, Carlos, and Betty. I wished they were here now, sharing this special day with me. But we were three hundred miles apart, and this time, it was I who had left.

Edwin helped me take my few belongings to my apartment. It only took a couple of trips. "Are you going to be okay?"

"Yeah," I said, although I wasn't sure.

He pulled out of the parking lot and waved goodbye, promising to come back every weekend to visit me. It made me feel good that he wouldn't be too far. I watched him drive away, and as soon as he was out of sight, I began to walk. It was late afternoon, the sun would be going down, and I wanted to see as much of the campus as I could before it got too dark. I walked and immersed myself in the redwood trees, smelling the pungent scent of their needles. The sky here was the bluest I'd ever seen. The air the purest I'd ever inhaled. I felt all the tension in my body begin to fade. There was a beauty here I had never imagined. I heard the wind rustling the trees. I spotted a family of deer, and I stopped and looked at them as they foraged for food.

I couldn't believe there were deer here! At the sight of them, I knew I'd made a good choice to leave Los Angeles and come here. I felt like Anne of Green Gables and her Avonlea. Like her, I had found my place of beauty.

I continued my walk and ended up by Porter College, at the meadow where I could see the ocean shining blue and streaked with orange. I thought about the first time I had seen the ocean in Santa Monica. I thought about my father holding my hand, about how afraid I had been that he would let go of me.

I looked at the ocean, and I realized there was no need to be afraid. I had gotten this far, despite everything. Now, all I had to do was focus on why I was there—to make my dreams a reality. I closed my eyes, and I saw myself at the water's edge, holding tightly to my father's callused hand.

And I let it go.

Epilogue

Reyna at UCSC graduation

I N JUNE OF 1999, I became the first person in my family to graduate from college. At UCSC I earned my BA in creative writing and in film and video and graduated with college honors, honors in the major, and Phi Beta Kappa. My family was there to celebrate that accomplishment with me: Mago, Victor, and their two children; Carlos, his wife, and their daughter; my mother and my brother Leonardo; Betty, her boyfriend Omar, and their son—and my father.

UCSC has a tradition that seniors are asked to write about a teacher who most inspired them. I wrote about Diana. My essay was chosen as the winner, and Diana was flown up to Santa Cruz so that she could be at my graduation. I gave a speech about her at the ceremony, and that was the first time I ever thanked her publicly for what she had done for me. I haven't stopped talking about her since.

In 2000, I became an ESL teacher for the Los Angeles Unified School District, where I hoped to be like Diana, an inspirational teacher. I taught immigrant children in grades six through eight for four years, and that was when I learned that my story wasn't unique. Like me, all the children who walked into my classroom had spent time apart from their parents. In fact, studies show that 80 percent of Latin American children in U.S. schools have been separated from a parent in the process of migration. I've also gotten to see the other side of that experience. In 2003, I taught adult school for the LAUSD, where many of my students were mothers and fathers who had left their children behind. In them, I saw my parents.

The cycle of leaving children behind has not ended. Nor will it end, as long as there is poverty, as long as parents feel that the only way to provide something better for their children is by leaving.

In 2002, I became a citizen of the United States. I have now been in this country for twenty-seven years. The United States is my home; it is the place that allowed me to dream, and later, to make those dreams into realities. But my umbilical cord was buried in Iguala, and I have never forgotten where I came from. I consider myself Mexican American because I am from both places. Both countries are within me. They coexist within me. And my writing is the bridge that connects them both.

In 2006, my first novel, *Across a Hundred Mountains,* was published. The following year it received an American Book Award. In 2009, *Dancing with Butterflies,* my second novel, followed.

In 2008, I received my MFA in creative writing, and I am no longer the only college graduate in the family!

Diana and I are still close. I have known her for half my life. She has seen me become the woman I am today—a wife, mother, and writer.

Carlos, Mago, Betty, and Leonardo are doing well, doing the best they can to fulfill their dreams and live a good life. Ultimately, that is all we can do.

Mila remained by my father's side until the day he died. She also managed to repair her relationship with her children.

Our relationship with our mother has gotten slightly better, although I have come to accept that there will always be a distance between us. My siblings and I have done our best to forgive her, and accept her for who she is.

As for my father, when he was diagnosed with liver cancer in 2010, there were times when I had to stop outside the door of his house—and sometimes, the threshold of his hospital room—to tell myself that the father I was about to see was not the same father I had come to live with twenty-five years ago. I had to leave my emotions at the door—anger, resentment, bitterness, sadness, frustration, regret—before I could step inside the room and be able to look him in the eye and feel nothing but concern for his well-being.

There were times when my emotions got the better of me, and I would not go to the hospital on those days. It was the same for my siblings. "He's gotten what he deserved," we would tell ourselves sometimes. "He chose to drink, and now he has to pay the consequences." Or we would talk about the way he treated us when we came to the U.S. to live with him. "He's reaping what he sowed," we would tell each other on the days we couldn't bring ourselves to go see him. "Now he wants us around, and when we wanted to be there with him, he pushed us away."

But there were also days when I would think of the other father—not the violent, alcoholic one, but the one who left for the U.S. because he wanted to give me something better, the one who did not abandon me in Mexico, the one who would tell me about the importance of an education, the one who taught me to dream big. Whenever I thought about that father, I would spend hours researching liver cancer on the Internet and at the public library hoping to keep him alive as long as possible. I would read books about alternative medicine. I would take him to my neighborhood supermarket which sells organic fruits and vegetables, hormone-free meat, and health products such as milk thistle and stevia. I would cook dandelion soup for him, put it in containers, and then drive over to his house to drop them off.

Then, when he had been in the hospital for two months, when I weighed more than he did, when he needed dialysis every other day and his stomach fluids drained, when his only hope of getting out was by receiving not only a new liver but new kidneys as well, my research and my soup were no longer needed. What was needed was my presence. What was needed was my conversation to help him pass the time.

What was needed was something I was struggling to give—my forgiveness.

The day before my thirty-sixth birthday, I found myself at my father's hospital bed as his life support was turned off. As I held my father's hand, and my life with him flashed through my mind, I thought about that question I had often asked myself: If I had known what life with my father would be like, would I have still followed him to El Otro Lado?

You made me who I am, I thought as he took his last breath. And I knew then that the answer to my question was yes.

Acknowledgments

First and foremost, I would like to thank my editor at Atria, Malaika Adero, for her unwavering support and her belief in this work even before it was finished, and my agent at Full Circle Literary, Adriana Dominguez, for her invaluable guidance and friendship. For the 10th anniversary edition, I would like to thank my editor Michelle Herrera-Mulligan and my agent, Johanna Castillo, for making it possible. I am eternally grateful to Sandra Cisneros for her generosity, and for doing me the honor of writing the foreword for this edition.

Writing this book was particularly challenging for me in many ways, and I might not have completed it had it not been for the generous support of the following people:

Cory Rayala, my wonderful, supportive husband whose keen insights I could not have done without; my mother-in-law, Carol Ruxton. I thank my lucky stars that I have you in my life. My siblings Mago, Carlos, and Betty, because this is your story as much as it is mine. Thank you for your memories, and for filling in the blanks when I couldn't remember. My parents, Natalio Grande and Juana Rodriguez, for giving me something to write about. Diana Savas, my mentor, my teacher, my friend, my hero.

My most sincere gratitude to all the people who critiqued the manuscript, in part or in whole. Thank you all for your contributions:

The Macondo Writers Workshop 2011 participants—Ruth Behar, Emmy Pérez, Estela Gonzalez, Marcela Fuentes, Jessica Viada, Rachel Jennings, Nancy Agabian; my Macondo teachers—Manuel Muñoz and Helena María Viramontes; my former writing teachers—Micah Perks, Leonard Chang, and Leslie Schwartz. My writer friends—Laila Lalami, Nicole Mones, Michele Serros, Thelma Reyna, Patricia Santana, Melinda

Palacio, Sarah Cortez, Zulmara Cline, Lara Rios, Margo Candela, Jamie Martinez, Stella Pope Duarte. My friend Janet Johns. And finally, the lovely ladies in my writing group—Jessica Garrison, Sonia Nazario, Ann Marsh, Lara Bazelon, Lisa Richardson, Toni Ann Johnson, and Tsan Abrahamson.

I am deeply grateful to you all.

Photography Credits

Courtesy of Reyna Grande: pages 14, 30, 75, 103, 118, 119, 274, 278, 279, 316

Courtesy of the Grande Family: pages 3, 5, 18, 23, 32, 39, 42, 47, 55, 58, 61, 69, 77, 84, 89, 94, 112, 129, 134, 141, 143, 146, 165, 168, 176, 182, 188, 192, 198, 202, 205, 211, 215, 219, 226, 227, 229, 233, 234, 240, 245, 250, 257, 258, 263, 265, 271, 283, 293, 299, 307, 308

Courtesy of Grad Images: page 319

© istockphoto: page 153

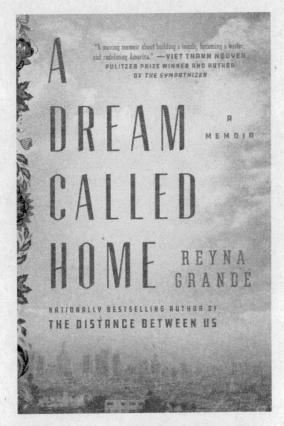

I HAD BEEN SO wrapped up in surviving my first quarter at UCSC, I hadn't yearned for my family as much as I had when I first arrived two months earlier. I had talked to Mago and Carlos a few times, and my father and mother not at all. Once, in a moment of weakness, I had walked over to the pay phone and picked up the receiver to call my father. I was desperate to hear his voice. To hear him call me "Chata," my special nickname. But I didn't dial. Clutching the coins in my fist, I listened to the dial tone until the phone started screeching like a dying rooster and then I hung up.

I knew I should call my mother. Right before I left for Santa Cruz, she had sent my fifteen-year-old sister to Mexico as punishment for her behavior. For a few years now, Betty had been going down the wrong path: getting into gangs, having unprotected sex, stealing the rent money, ditching class, and the last straw—dropping out of high school.

My mother said that she sent Betty to Mexico because if she no longer wanted a high school education, then she would get a different kind of education—she would learn how to be a woman. My aunt would teach my little sister how to cook, clean, and obey the men in her life, especially her future husband, whoever he might be—just the kind of upbringing my grandmother, mother, and aunts had had in our hometown.

I hadn't known what my mother was planning until it was too late. My sister was already on a plane to Mexico by the time I found out what was happening. "I can't deal with her anymore," my mother said when I told her it was the most irresponsible thing she had ever done. Her decision reinforced my idea that my mother had been born without a maternal gene. Or at least when it came to her four oldest children, because she indulged my little half brother and gave him everything.

It shamed me to realize that I hadn't given Betty much thought since I arrived in Santa Cruz, and I should have. Just as my father had banned me from his life, so had Betty been banned from my mother's, though for opposite reasons. I had done nothing but try to make my father proud and help him during his hour of need. Betty had done nothing but make life difficult for herself and my mother, but she had her reasons. She was reacting to my mother's physical and emotional abuse in the only way she knew how—by rebelling. But by hurting my mother, she was also hurting herself in the process.

I picked up the phone and called my mother to see how Betty was doing in exile. My family in Mexico didn't have a phone, which meant I would have to go through my grandmother's neighbor to reach my sister. Besides, I didn't have money for international phone calls.

"She's driving your aunt crazy" was the first thing my mother said. "She's running wild, and your aunt can't control her anymore."

"Well, you shouldn't have sent her down there in the first place," I said. "She's your responsibility, not my aunt's. Why are you always making other people raise your children?" It was a low blow and I knew it, but every time I spoke to my mother, it brought out the pain of the many times she left me, and I retaliated.

As usual, she ignored my comment and said, "Your sister is having an affair with a married man. ¿Me escuchas? She's fifteen years old and already her reputation is ruined!"

I didn't have anything to say to my mother then. The year before, Betty had asked me to take her to the clinic for a pregnancy test. She was fourteen, and as we sat there waiting for the results, I had prayed so hard for it to be negative, which to our relief it was. A pregnancy would have ruined her life. And now here she was again, jeopardizing her future. I couldn't let that happen.

"I'll go check on her," I said. "I'll go to Iguala."

As I walked back to my apartment, I realized there was a big problem with what I had just committed to—I didn't have money for a trip to Mexico. But something told me I needed to make it happen. I was worried about my little sister, so I wracked my brain wondering how I could come up with the cash. I paused halfway across the footbridge, looked up at the redwoods, and said a silent prayer, though I was no longer religious. When my siblings and I arrived in the U.S., it didn't take long for us to lose our religion and forget the teachings of our sweet maternal grandmother, Abuelita Chinta. When we asked our father to take us to church, he refused, raising his can of Budweiser and proclaiming, "This is my God." That quickly put an end to our Catholic faith.

Now I was an atheist, yet when surrounded by such natural splendor here in Santa Cruz, by trees that seemed to nearly reach the heavens, I couldn't help but want to believe in a higher being. God? Goddess? Mother Earth? Tonantzin, Aztec mother goddess?

One of them heard my prayer. The next day, when I stopped at the main office after picking up my mail, I spotted a flyer announcing a $500 research grant Kresge was offering to students. That was the perfect solution! I hurried back to my apartment and filled out the application and letter of intent, explaining that I needed to go to Mexico for a short-story collection I was working on. It wasn't true. I wasn't working on a collection, and I felt ashamed about lying, but it was the only thing I could think of. On the application, I stated that I needed the funds to do research on the town and the people I was writing about.

A few weeks later, I knew that I was meant to go see my sister when I received a letter from Kresge informing me I had received the grant.

This trip would be my second time visiting the country of my birth since I had left at nine. The first visit had been three years before, when I was in high school and I had gone with Mago and my mother. It was on that visit that I realized I was no longer Mexican enough. Everyone treated me like an outsider, as if I was no longer one of them, as if I had lost my right to call Mexico my home.

As soon as winter break arrived, I headed south. My plane landed in Mexico City at 7:00 a.m. and I began the three-hour journey to my hometown. As I rode in the taxi from the airport to the bus station, I lowered the window and breathed in the smell of the city, a mix of diesel fumes, urine, and corn tortillas.

"You aren't from here, are you?" the cabdriver asked me. I held my breath, feeling the floor sinking under me as I imagined the worst. He thought I was American. I was going to get kidnapped!

"Chale, claro que sí," I said, trying to speak Spanish like a real Mexican. But the man shook his head.

"I can hear America in your voice," he said.

Thankfully, I arrived at the bus station safely, where I waited until it was time to board. As my bus traveled south, I thought about my mother. Every time I talked to her, I couldn't control the anger that raged inside me.

Even after all these years, I still felt the devastating blow of her abandonment.

The first time my mother left, I was four years old. She walked away from me, Mago, and Carlos to join my father in El Otro Lado. For many years, I hadn't been able to understand why she had made the choice to leave her children behind to go to my father's side simply because he wanted her to join him. Why did she have to obey him? Why couldn't she have said no and stayed with her children? Later I understood that my mother hadn't wanted to be an abandoned woman. In Iguala, there were women whose husbands had gone north long ago and had completely forgotten about them. How happy and proud my mother had been when my father telephoned and said, "I need you. I want you to come."

And just like that, she packed her bags and, complying with my father's request, dropped off her children at his mother's house. We had to watch her walk away from us, wondering if we would ever see her again. Then we went inside Abuela Evila's house to endure two-and-a-half years of hell.

The irony was that even though my mother left for the U.S. to save her marriage, my father still left her for another woman. Mila was a nurse's assistant, a naturalized U.S. citizen, and a fluent English speaker—a woman who was everything my mother wasn't. When my mother returned to Mexico with my little sister, Betty, it was one of the happiest days of my life. But soon after, she ran off to Acapulco with a wrestler and abandoned us once again. My maternal grandmother did her best to make up for the pain of my mother's absence. But no matter how much Abuelita Chinta loved us—it wasn't enough.

When my father returned to Mexico to get us, my mother refused to let Betty come with us, so we left without her to reunite with our father and find something better in El Otro Lado. I had never gotten over the guilt of leaving Betty behind.

Though my mother, and then Betty, moved to Los Angeles a few years later, and we were then all on the same side of the border, my family had completely disintegrated by then.

I slept during the three-hour bus ride and woke up when the bus was making its way around the mountains cradling my hometown like cupped hands. I looked out the window, holding my breath in anticipation of the first glimpse of my city in the valley below.

Iguala de la Independencia is a city of about 110,000 people. The first Mexican flag was made in Iguala in 1824. The treaty that ended the Mexican War of Independence was written in Iguala, and the Mexican national anthem was sung for the first time there. Despite its richness in history, Iguala is a poor city, with 70 percent of the population living in poverty. Through the years to come, things would get much worse—the mountain on which my bus was traveling would one day be covered in poppy fields to supply the heroin trade with the U.S.

Iguala would become a distribution center where buses would leave the station loaded with drugs destined for cities like Chicago and Los Angeles. It would become a place of infamy when, in 2014, forty-three college students were attacked and forcibly disappeared by the police working with the cartel. During the search for the missing students, numerous mass graves would be found not far from where I grew up.

But those things hadn't happened yet, and when I arrived in Iguala in December of 1996, all I saw were the shacks, the dirt roads, the crumbling houses, the trash—the grinding poverty my father had rescued me from. When I was a child, I had been able to see past the imperfections and find the beauty of my hometown, but now, after all my years of living in the U.S., I no longer could.

I hailed a cab at the bus station. Immediately, the driver said, "You aren't from here, are you?" And I wanted to say that I hadn't even opened my mouth to speak yet, so why the hell would he be asking me that already?

"You put on your seat belt," he said with a smile, anticipating my question.

And I laughed.

The road where my grandmother lived wasn't paved, so taxicabs and buses didn't venture there. I got off at the main road and walked to my grandmother's house, dragging my suitcase behind me. I inhaled the smoke from the burning trash heaps along the nearby railroad tracks. City sanitation services didn't exist in Iguala, so people had to burn their trash every day. I passed the canal in which my siblings and I swam when we were kids, and was shocked at seeing the canal full of trash—old car tires covered in mud, broken pieces of furniture, the skeletal remains of an old mattress. The stagnant water smelled worse than a dead animal, and I held my breath as I hurried past it. Abuelita Chinta lived in a shack made of sticks and cardboard. When I lived here, it had been the only shack on the street, but now there were two of them. My aunt, Tía Güera, had built her own shack next to my grandmother's.

I stood there in front of my grandmother's home, scanning the dirt road, the abandoned freight car left to rust on the train tracks, the piles of burned trash, the children walking barefoot, their feet and legs covered in dust.

I was a long way from Santa Cruz, California.

Abuelita Chinta

MY GRANDMOTHER'S DOOR was open, so I poked my head in and saw her sitting at the dining table with a cutting board on her lap, on which she was slicing a tomato, an onion, and a green jalapeño pepper. I hadn't seen her in three years, but she looked the same to me. As usual, she wore her gray, curly hair tied back, a flowery dress that reached below her knee, and black sandals.

"Abuelita, ya llegué," I said as I came in.

When she smiled at me, I could see that another tooth had fallen out since I had last seen her. I hugged my tiny grandmother and inhaled her scent of almond oil and herbs.

"Gracias a Dios que llegaste bien," she said, squeezing me tight.

She looked at her altar, where a candle was burning next to the statue of La Virgen de Guadalupe, and she crossed herself to thank God I had arrived safely. "The journey can be dangerous for a young girl traveling alone."

"Sí, Abuelita. But I was careful." I sat at the small table with her and watched her finish cutting her vegetables. "What are you making, Abuelita?"

"A taco. Would you like one?" She got up to heat the tortillas on her stove, and I looked around to see where the meat was. There was no pot on the stove, and I could see no food except for the vegetables she had cut up. There were no beans or rice either.

The shack looked exactly as it had when I lived here with my grandmother and my siblings. It was one big room, with no interior walls. My grandmother's bed, the stove, and her altar were near the front door; in the middle was the dining table and in the back a hammock where my uncle slept. The bed that had belonged to my parents was still there, tucked into a corner. Hanging from the rafter on the ceiling was a cage with two sleeping white doves in it. Shafts of sunlight filtered through the bamboo outer walls. The heat of the sun radiating from the corrugated tin metal roof made me sleepy, and I yawned.

My grandmother put the hot tortillas on two plates and filled them up with the tomato, onion, and jalapeño slices. She handed me a plate and apologized for the modest meal.

"Your uncle hasn't been working much lately," she said. "And the little money your mother sent me is gone now."

I took the plate from my grandmother and looked at the taco. In Santa Cruz, I had met my first vegetarians and vegans, and I had been shocked that such things even existed. What would my grandmother say if I told her that in the U.S., people chose to eat the way she was eating now, especially the rich kids who thought being vegan was cool and who shopped at the thrift store, like I did, because they wanted to and not because they had to? Over there, I wanted to tell her, eating a tomato taco was a personal preference and not an act of survival forced on you by poverty and a system of corruption and oppression.

As if reading my thoughts, she said, "Let us be grateful for what God has provided, m'ija."

God wasn't providing all that much, I wanted to say. Or maybe He was a vegan and was trying to get my grandmother to be one, too. Yes, I was being cynical, and I knew full well what my grandmother was saying to me—sometimes even vegetables are hard to come by and you should be grateful when you have them. When I lived here with my grandmother, there were times when we would have nothing to eat except tortillas sprinkled with salt. As a university student, I was struggling to get by, and I wasn't in a position yet to help support my grandmother. But I made a promise to myself that one day, when I was making the kind of dollars that would come from my college degree, I would take care of her, just like she had once taken care of me.

She took a bite of her taco, and I did the same, the tomato juice spilling down my hand, and I licked it because there were no napkins.

"How's it going in El Otro Lado?" my grandmother asked, licking her own fingers. "Your mom tells me you are at a university now."

I nodded and excitedly told my grandmother about Santa Cruz, about the redwood trees, the deer, the bay, the boardwalk, the way the air smelled—a mixture of leaves, soil, salty ocean breeze, and esperanza. What I wouldn't give to be able to take her there! I pictured myself walking around that gorgeous place with my tiny grandmother, pointing out a banana slug crawling on the cinnamon-colored bark of a redwood, plucking a needle from a branch so that she could smell its scent. I reached out to hold her hands, as if by magic I could transport her there with me. I wished I had thought to buy a UCSC Grandma T-shirt for her.

"There are trees near the library that bloom with flowers so white they look as if they are covered in snow," I said, and then, remembering that she had never seen snow, I added, "Or as if a thousand white palomas have landed on them." Doves, she knew well.

Abuelita Chinta smiled and had a faraway look in her eyes, as if she were trying hard to imagine this magical city. When you live in a place like Iguala, it's hard to believe that the world can look any different. My guilt brought me back to reality, and I could feel the calluses in her wrinkled hands, see the layer of dust on her feet, feel the heat radiating from her tin metal roof. Why did I get to enjoy such a beautiful place, but not my grandmother who from a young age had had to work to feed her family? My grandmother never went to school, lived only three hours from Acapulco and yet had never seen the ocean with her own eyes.

"I'm glad you're living in a beautiful place, m'ija," she said, smiling her gap-toothed smile. "After everything you kids went through, you deserve it."

You do, too, Abuelita, I wanted to say.

Just then, Tía Güera came home, trailed by my little cousins, Diana and Ángel. "You're here," she said. "Good."

"Where's Betty?" I asked, standing up to give her a hug. "Is she with Lupe?" I had arrived in the afternoon, and had been surprised no one was home except for my grandmother. My cousin Lupe was fourteen, a year younger than Betty. In Mexico, the schools had two shifts—morning and afternoon. Usually, especially in junior and high school, the poor kids got stuck in the afternoon shift and would have to travel through the dark city at night to get home. It was a dangerous journey, especially for the girls.

"Lupe is in school," my aunt said. "But not your sister. She didn't want to enroll, and I didn't want to force her."

"So where is she now?"

"I don't know," Tía Güera said. "She goes to see her friends, sometimes without telling me." She took a seat on the opposite side of the table and said, "Look, Reyna, I love your sister, and I don't want anything bad to happen to her, but the whole neighborhood is gossiping about her improper relationships with the boys here. I don't want the responsibility anymore. If she ends up pregnant, or worse, I don't want it to be on my watch. Maybe she'll listen to you."

I sighed. I didn't tell my aunt that I might not be able to help much. If the adults around her couldn't get through to my sister, what made them think I could? Betty and I had a good relationship, but not the kind I had once had with Mago.

Finally, my cousin Lupe came, but there was still no sign of Betty. "She's probably over there, by the train station. That's where Chon lives."

"Who?"

"He's the guy Betty has been hanging out with," Lupe said. "But he's already married."

I gave Lupe money and sent her to the nearest food stand to buy us quesadillas. While we sat there and continued waiting, I wondered why both Betty and I had an unhealthy need to be loved and wanted by men. Since our parents rarely showed any tenderness toward us, we had to look outside of home to find it. No matter what anyone said about Betty, I wasn't going to judge her.

When Lupe returned, she wasn't alone.

"Look who I found," Lupe said.

Betty came over to hug me, and everything anyone had said about my little sister faded away as I held her in my arms. This was my Betty. When I first heard that my mother was going to have a baby in the U.S., I hated that baby. I was jealous of the little girl who had come to take my place as the youngest in the family. But when I met her, I thought she was the cutest little girl I had ever seen, with thick, curly black hair and the longest eyelashes. When my mother ran away with a wrestler, leaving us behind—including her American baby—I realized that Betty was like me, nothing special to our mother and just as easy to abandon. I had tried to protect her like Mago had protected me.

But once Mago, Carlos, and I had taken off to the U.S. with our father, and we were forced to leave Betty behind, we drifted apart once again. Through the years, even when Betty ended up in L.A. with our mother, we hardly saw her. We tried to bring her to our father's house on some weekends, but the visits were brief and infrequent. Mago and I had a wonderful bond that did not include Betty. The distance had kept her on the periphery of our sisterhood.

It wasn't until Mago left me to start her own life and make a home for herself that I understood what it was like to have no one, just the way Betty had felt for many years.

This was why I had come to Mexico. It wasn't because I thought I could help her, but because I knew what it was like to be alone.

"I'm here," I said holding her even tighter. "I'm here."

Later that night, Betty and I shared the bed that had once belonged to our parents. My uncle, Tío Crece, slept on a hammock hanging from the rafters and my grandmother slept on her bed near the front door. Between the snoring of my uncle and grandmother, the barking of the dogs outside, and the chirping of crickets, it was hard to fall asleep. Not that I was trying very hard. Betty and I had too much to share.

"I didn't want to be in L.A. anyway," Betty said to me after I told her how sorry I was that my mother had sent her away. "Here, at least, I can get away from her. From *them*."

She meant our stepfather, of course. Even though we had lived apart, in a way our lives hadn't been much different. Living with my father, Mago, Carlos, and I had suffered from my stepmother's indifference. Mila had kept us at arm's length and didn't want much to do with us. She never yelled at us or hit us, but that didn't mean we didn't suffer because of her. Whatever complaints she had, she would give them to our father, who would barge out of the bedroom with belt in hand to give us a whipping. Most of the time we didn't even know what we were being punished for, since Mila never told us directly how we had displeased her.

Rey, our stepfather, was the opposite of Mila. He was quick to beat Betty and yell at her, and he didn't have to go through my mother to show or act on his disapproval. Though we had both grown up in households where beatings and verbal insults were the norm, I had received them only from our father, whereas Betty got them from both our mother and stepfather.

"I'm sorry, Betty," I said. And I meant I was sorry about everything, how immigration and separation had taken a toll on all of us, how even though our parents had emigrated from this very city to go to the U.S. to build us a house, they ended up destroying our home.

As if reading my thoughts, Betty turned to me and said, "Do you think things would have been different if they had never left? Do you think we would all be together as a family?"

The silver moonlight streamed through the gaps in the wall made of bamboo sticks tied together with rope and wire. Her moonlit eyes looked at me with so much hope and innocence, I knew she wanted me to paint a different picture—a different reality—than the one we were living. But there was no point in what-ifs. There was no point in wishing our family's past away.

"There's nothing we can do to change it, Betty. But you know what

I want? I want to one day look back and say that it was worth it. All the pain, all the heartache."

"That's why you're going to college?"

"Yes," I said. "We've already paid a high price for the opportunity. We might as well take advantage of it. We have it in our power to make our future better than our past, Betty, even though at times it doesn't feel like we can ever escape it."

Betty didn't say anything. She turned her back to me and faced the wall. "I don't want to go back there," she said before she fell asleep. "I hope you aren't here to take me back to her."

THE DISTANCE BETWEEN US

REYNA GRANDE

This reading group guide for The Distance Between Us *includes an introduction, discussion questions, and a Q&A with author Reyna Grande. The suggested questions are intended to help your reading group find new and interesting angles and topics for your discussion. We hope that these ideas will enrich your conversation and increase your enjoyment of the book.*

INTRODUCTION

Reyna is two when her father leaves the family in Mexico and crosses the border into the United States, hoping to earn enough money to build a home in Mexico when he returns. When he sends for their mother but leaves Reyna, Mago, and Carlos behind, the siblings suffer great hardship and poverty under the unforgiving hands of their father's mother, Abuela Evila. Abandoned by both parents, the three endure but long for the return of their mother and a father of whom they have little memory. Their mother returns with a baby sister, Elizabeth, setting off a chain of on-again and off-again contact with her children. When their father returns after an eight-year absence and takes Reyna, Mago, and Carlos with him across the border, a new window of opportunity presents itself; however, Reyna, Mago, and Carlos must also deal with their father's alcoholic rages. Recounted in astonishing detail, this memoir narrates one girl's journey out of poverty and her infinite capacity to forgive and love.

TOPICS AND QUESTIONS FOR DISCUSSION

PREREADING QUESTION

Describe a time in which you felt abandoned or separated from a loved one. How did you resolve your feelings?

QUESTIONS FOR DISCUSSION

1. Reyna is two years old when her father leaves Iguala for El Otro Lado (the other side). Why does he leave? Why do Reyna, her mother, and her two siblings—Mago and Carlos—stay behind?

2. When Reyna turns four, her father sends for her mother. Reyna, Mago, and Carlos are left to live with their father's mother (Abuela Evila). Describe Reyna's feelings regarding her mother's leaving and her mother's absence during these early years.

3. Who is "The Man Behind the Glass"? What does he symbolize?

4. Reyna wishes to stay with Abuelita Chinta instead of Abuela Evila. Compare and contrast the two grandmothers and their attitudes and behaviors toward their grandchildren. Are Reyna, Mago, and Carlos better off once they begin living with Abuelita Chinta? Why or why not? Use evidence from the text to support your answer.

5. Who is Élida and why is she favored by Abuela Evila? Is her behavior toward Reyna, Mago, and Carlos justified? Why or why not?

6. In what way does Tía Emperatriz come to the aid of Reyna, Mago, and Carlos? Could she have done more for the three siblings? Why or why not?

7. Describe Reyna's relationship with her sister Mago. Why does Mago feel responsible for Reyna?

8. Describe the hardships Reyna, Mago, and Carlos face growing up in Iguala.

9. What reactions do the three siblings have when they learn they have a younger sister, Elizabeth? Who seems the most impacted by this news and why?

10. Why does Reyna's mother, Juana, return alone from the United States? How does life change for Reyna, Mago, and Carlos when she returns?

11. Who is Rey, and why do Reyna, Mago, and Carlos not like him? What happens when he visits the family during the holidays?

12. Compare and contrast Mago's and Reyna's feelings toward their mother as time after time she chooses her own needs over those of her children. Does she love her children? Use evidence from the text to support your response.

13. As Carlos matures, he has a need for a father figure. Identify the male role models in his life and explain the influences they have on his development.

14. When Reyna's father returns from the United States after an eight-year absence, Reyna is almost ten. How does she feel about his return? Why does he return, and why does he offer to take Mago back to the United States with him? Why does he want to leave Reyna and Carlos behind?

15. How does Reyna feel about the possible separation from Mago? Why does their father decide to take all three children back with him? De-

scribe their harrowing journey. Is life better for them once they reach the United States? Support your answer with evidence from the text.

16. Mila is Natalio's second wife. What are Reyna's earliest perceptions of her? What influence does Mila have on Reyna, Mago, and Carlos?

17. Reyna attends school in both Mexico and the United States. Compare and contrast her experiences in both places. What can readers learn about the challenges poor children have in negotiating school?

18. Reyna does not speak English when she enters school in the United States. How does she overcome this challenge? How is she received by her teachers? By her classmates? What accounts for her ability to succeed?

19. Reyna's father believes in education and supports Mago and Carlos when they enroll in college. Why does he not help Reyna? How does his refusal impact Reyna?

20. To whom does Reyna owe thanks for her success? Why? Do you agree or disagree and why?

QUESTIONS FOR FURTHER DISCUSSION

1. What does Grande's memoir tell us about the struggles of second-language acquisition students in American schools?

2. *The Distance Between Us* is a memoir. What characteristics of a memoir can you identify in the story?

3. Compare and contrast Mago's experiences as a student in Mexico and the United States. What drives her to succeed despite her challenges?

4. Despite her on-again, off-again relationship with her father, Reyna yearns to make her father proud. In what ways did this desire serve

her well? In what ways did it not? How is she able to release her guilt and anger toward her father? Identify and discuss a passage or scene in which she grows the most in her understanding of his capabilities.

5. How do Reyna's perceptions of her mother evolve with time? Use examples from the text to support your response.

6. How might this story be different if it were written from another character's point of view (e.g., Mayo, Carlos, either parent, or either grandparent)?

7. When Reyna returns to Iguala to visit her family, how does she reflect on her youth living in Mexico? How do her attitudes differ from those of her sister Mago? What accounts for their differences?

8. Compare and contrast the ways in which Reyna, Mago, and Carlos deal with the on-again, off-again relationships with their parents? What accounts for their different responses?

9. As Reyna matures into a young woman, how does she resolve her feelings of being abandoned by both her mother and father? Does she view one parent as having been better than the other? Why or why not?

10. How does *The Distance Between Us* contribute to a growing body of literature about immigration to the United States? About the challenges facing children for whom English is a second language?

Guide written by Pam B. Cole, Professor of English Education & Literacy

Kennesaw State University, Kennesaw, GA

This guide has been provided by Simon & Schuster for classroom, library, and reading club use. It may be reproduced in its entirety or excerpted for these purposes.

This guide was written to align with the Common Core State Standards (www.corestandards.org).

A CONVERSATION WITH REYNA GRANDE

Can you tell us about how you came to the decision to write your memoir after working with fiction on your first two novels?

When I was an undergraduate at UC Santa Cruz, as part of my senior thesis I had to write a portion of a book-length manuscript. At first, I wanted to write an autobiographical story of my migration to the U.S., but when I began to write it, I felt I wasn't ready, on an emotional level but also craft-wise. I didn't feel confident enough with my writing skills to be able to write a memoir. So instead, I wrote a novel because I'd been reading and writing fiction for a while and felt more comfortable with that genre. Writing fiction allowed me to explore my fears as a child—of being abandoned, that my father wouldn't come back. That story became *Across a Hundred Mountains*, my very first published novel, where I wrote the life I might have had if circumstances had been different. After that novel, I wrote *Dancing with Butterflies* because I still didn't feel confident enough to write a memoir. In hindsight, I think I was afraid of confronting my own story and telling my own truth. There is something frightening about being the protagonist of the story. Fiction allowed me to write about my personal experiences in a way that I wasn't the subject of the story. But what I discovered, once I was brave enough to write *The Distance Between Us*, is that my fiction wasn't going to heal me from those traumatic moments. Only my memoirs would.

In *The Distance Between Us*, you write about the difficulties of starting fifth grade in California in a school that didn't meet your needs as an immigrant student. What do you wish had been different?

When I came to the U.S. as an undocumented child immigrant, I walked into my fifth-grade classroom with trauma from all the difficult things

I'd just gone through. Unfortunately, my school didn't have resources or services for immigrant kids and my teacher hadn't been properly trained to meet the needs of students like me, so she was unprepared for the task. My school environment added to my trauma and made me feel ashamed to be an immigrant, a border-crosser, and a Spanish speaker. Today, there is more data available to schools about immigrant trauma and how toxic stress impacts student learning and behavior. Understanding the psychological effects of family separation and the trauma of migration can help schools create a safe space for these children. Also, and this to me is really important, providing services for immigrant families is crucial. The best way to help immigrant children is to help their parents as well.

Your migration to the U.S. gave you access to books via the public library and teachers who gifted you books. In *The Distance Between Us*, you mention a couple of titles you treasure, but can you say more about what kinds of writing or authors have inspired you? And what do you tend to read nowadays?

When I was a teenager, the books I read at my public library were fairy tale collections, popular titles by young adult authors such as V.C. Andrews, Francine Pascal, and Christopher Pike, then I moved on to Stephen King and Agatha Christie, and when I discovered the romance section, well, I read every book that had Fabio on the cover! So admittedly, my reading selection left much to be desired. But I didn't have anyone curating my reading list and helping me find culturally relevant books or books that would encourage more critical thinking. Luckily, that came later when I got to college. As I mention in *The Distance Between Us*, my English professor introduced me to Latina writers and gave me *The House on Mango Street* by Sandra Cisneros, *The Moths and Other Stories* by Helena María Viramontes, *The Stories of Eva Luna* by Isabel Allende, and *How the García Girls Lost Their Accents* by Julia Álvarez. My education on Chicano/Latino literature continued at UC Santa Cruz, where my professor, Marta Navarro, introduced me to more Chicana writers such as Gloria Anzaldúa and Ana Castillo. But the author that I most connected with was Juan Rulfo because he was a Mexican writing about poverty in Mexico. His book, *El llano en llamas / The Burning Plain*, spoke to me because I saw my own experiences with poverty reflected in his book. Most importantly, it gave me permission to write about my own Mexican poverty. Before that, I didn't know those experiences were worth writing about.

I still appreciate a good book written by a Chicano / Latino author, and many titles have found a home on my bookshelves, but here are some favorites: Justin Torres's *We, the Animals*, Daisy Hernandez's *A Cup of Water Under My Bed*, Silvia Moreno-Garcia's *Mexican Gothic*, and Maceo Montoya's *Letters to the Poet from His Brother*.

You said in your memoir that your discovery of Chicano literature shifted your perspective. How? In what ways do you hope that *The Distance Between Us* shifts your readers' perspectives?

Discovering Chicano literature was empowering. Even though I was an avid reader, I was never exposed to books where I could actually *see* myself. Books can either be windows or mirrors. Ideally, you should have both. But what happens when all you do is look through windows? You feel like an outsider. You are always on the outside, looking in. You feel invisible. And you begin to think that maybe your story doesn't matter, and that's why it isn't in any literature you read. Then, you begin to think that it is *you* who doesn't matter. In *The Distance Between Us*, I hope to offer a mirror to everyone who has had to cross borders—geographical or otherwise—and to those who have felt like outsiders or not enough. I also hope to offer a window to people who want to learn more about migration and have more empathy and compassion for our immigrant community.

The Spanish language occupies a center-stage place in your memoir. How has your relationship with Spanish and with bilingualism changed over your lifetime?

I wrote an essay about this called "Losing My Mother Tongue" published in *Nepantla Familias: An Anthology of Mexican American Literature on Families in Between Worlds*. In this essay, I explore my very complicated relationship with Spanish which began the day I set foot in my fifth-grade classroom. When my teacher sent me to the corner and ignored me the whole year, it made me think that I spoke the *wrong* language. I learned English at the expense of my Spanish. Because I was shamed into learning English, it replaced my mother tongue. It took me years to learn the right term for what had happened to me—subtractive bilingualism—which leads to a negative self-image.

Losing my mother tongue led to feelings of disdain for the Spanish language, but also for my parents, especially my mother. She never learned English, never assimilated, and so for a long time I had disdain for what she represented—she was the "wrong" kind of immigrant. My language trauma also led me to not teach my children Spanish. Luckily, when we moved to northern California and my daughter was in second grade, the local school had a dual language immersion program in Spanish and English. I enrolled my daughter, and within six months, she was becoming bilingual without the trauma I had experienced in school. Hers is additive bilingualism. She was never asked to sacrifice a part of her being to learn a language.

Immigration is often immediately associated with Latinos, but place, placelessness, and journeys to begin anew in an unfamiliar home transcend culture and nationality. What connection have you found between your own story and those from immigrants of other nationalities?

Immigrants have similar longings and dreams and face similar challenges. Many immigrants, and especially immigrants of color, are affected by trauma. I recently co-edited an anthology by and about undocumented or formerly undocumented immigrants called *Somewhere We Are Human: Authentic Voices on Migration, Survival, and New Beginnings*. In this collection, we featured migrants from all over Latin America, but also countries such as Nigeria, Korea, Iran, Brazil, Bangladesh, Taiwan, Indonesia, Vietnam, the Philippines, among others. It was incredible to see the commonalities, regardless of where we are from.

Of course, I will say again what I said before: your experience as an immigrant, and the level of trauma you are subjected to, are greatly increased because of the color of your skin and where you are from. Regardless of what politicians say, race greatly affects immigration policy and how we guard our borders—who we welcome, and who we keep out.

Did you do research in any form in writing *The Distance Between Us*? **If so, how was the experience of doing research for your memoir different from doing research for your novels?**

My process for writing *The Distance Between Us* was to begin with what I could remember. I visited the places I grew up to generate more memories. Once I ran out of memories, I interviewed my siblings and other family members. I didn't do much research beyond reading a bit about the decades I write about to add a few details about the politics that impacted me.

It wasn't until I wrote *A Ballad of Love and Glory* that researching became a huge part of my writing process. It was daunting, and now I have even more respect for historical fiction writers. I easily read over one hundred books about the Mexican–American War and everything else related to the story. With this book, I did have to double-check my dates and facts. I wanted to be as accurate as possible in writing this story about the U.S. invasion of Mexico in the 1840s because I knew many of my readers were never taught this history in school. I know I wasn't! Getting the facts right was important to me because this moment in history has been either forgotten or distorted to fit into the rosy narrative of the U.S. national mythology.

Do you find writing, and more specifically writing about your lived experiences, cathartic? If so, how do you recover after the catharsis of writing emotionally draining scenes?

Absolutely. The reason I started writing in the first place was that I discovered that writing could be a wonderful way to heal from trauma. It is my favorite form of self-expression. Writing memoir has led me to a place of understanding and forgiveness. It has helped me reframe how I see my experiences and to take pride in everything that makes me who I am. It forces you to confront some difficult truths about yourself. It's emotionally challenging to write memoir, but it is also the most rewarding. As Kahlil Gibran writes, "Is not the cup that holds your wine the very cup that was burned in the potter's oven? And is not the lute that soothes your spirit, the very wood that was hollowed with knives?"

I love being able to alternate between writing fiction and memoir. There comes a point in memoir-writing when it gets too exhausting being the protagonist of the story, so I switch to novels to explore someone else's experience, someone else's pain.

What advice can you offer a writer who is struggling with whether to expose intimate details in their writing? Did you choose to keep some of your most precious memories for yourself?

That's a question we always struggle with when writing memoir. Obviously, we don't live alone on an island, so writing about yourself means writing about others, especially family and friends. You have to write about them, but how much you reveal about them requires careful consideration. In my quest to be honest and invite readers into my life, there are moments when I might have said too much. After I published my second memoir, *A Dream Called Home,* I had an interesting interaction with another memoirist. We were on a panel together, and every time he was asked personal questions, he would deflect and talk about society and politics instead. After the panel, I asked him, "Why didn't you want to answer the question about your mom?" And he looked at me and said, "I've given you as much as I am willing to give you." It startled me. I didn't realize you could set boundaries when you write memoir. I thought as a memoirist, if you are going to invite your reader into your home, you allow them access to every room. But here was this other memoirist telling me that it's okay if you only invite them into your living room!

To be honest, I'm not sure I agree. If I'm going to read about someone's life, I want to feel that I'm welcomed into that personal space and not held at arm's length. But I also understand the need to set boundaries, to keep a part of yourself to yourself. It's a conundrum.

What was the most surprising thing you discovered about yourself while you were writing *The Distance Between Us*?

I think the most surprising thing was understanding the cause-and-effect of all the events in my life. If A hadn't happened, then B wouldn't have happened. I realized that I wouldn't be the woman I am today if I hadn't gone through what I went through, if I'd made different choices, if the outcomes had been different. Understanding this helped me because I was constantly regretting things, wishing things had been different. Writing *The Distance Between Us* and *A Dream Called Home* helped me to see the value of each experience and appreciate the lessons I learned along the way. They've also taught me to be a better parent. It's a way of self-soothing when I hug my kids, when I buy them things, take them places, celebrate special moments with them, give them a loving, stable home with my husband—everything I didn't have as a child, I give it to them.

What's your relationship with your family like today? What happened after this book ended?

In many ways, my relationship with my family is better today than before. My father has been dead for over a decade, but I have a healthy relationship with him because I try to think about the positive things. I no longer have any anger or resentment, only love and gratitude. I think of him often, and I feel his presence wherever I go. My mother is still with us, but her health is failing, and I know that we might not have her much longer, so I try to maintain a good relationship with her. She and I will never be as close as I would like, but I am content with what we have. As for my siblings, we try to get along and be there for each other. Once in a while, we have our disagreements, but despite our sibling dramas, one of the things that unites us is our desire for our children to have a close bond. It is so beautiful to see the cousins together. To see them be there for one another. What a gift it is that our children are healthy, thriving, and pursuing their own dreams. And my siblings and I are there, making sure we help them reach their full potential.

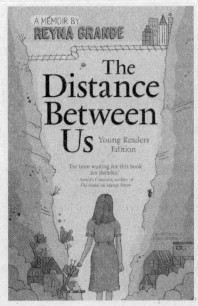
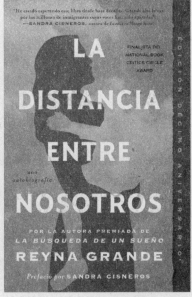